Losing Your Shirt

Losing Your Shirt

Recovery for Compulsive Gamblers and Their Families

MARY HEINEMAN

SECOND EDITION

■ HAZELDEN®

Hazelden
Center City, Minnesota 55012-0176

1-800-328-0094
1-651-213-4590 (Fax)
www.hazelden.org

Originally published by CompCare Publishers 1992
First published by Hazelden 1994
Second edition published by Hazelden 2001
Printed in the United States of America

Library of Congress Cataloging-in-Publication Data

Heineman, Mary.
    Losing your shirt : recovery for compulsive gamblers and their families / Mary
Heineman.—2nd ed.
        p.   cm.
    Includes bibliographical references (p.).
    ISBN 1-56838-733-4 (paperback)
      1. Compulsive gambling. 2. Compulsive gamblers—Family relationships.
    3. Codependency. 4. Twelve-step programs. I. Title.
    RC569.5.G35 H44 2001
    616.85'841—dc21
                                                                        2001024746

05 04 03 02 01   6 5 4 3 2 1

Editor's note
All the stories in this book are based on actual experiences. The names and details
have been changed to protect the privacy of the people involved. In some cases,
composites have been created.
    The Twelve Steps of Alcoholics Anonymous were adapted by Gamblers Anony-
mous (GA) and Gam-Anon with permission of Alcoholics Anonymous World
Services, Inc. (AAWS). Assuming GA's and Gam-Anon's permission to do so, AAWS
would have no objection to the GA and Gam-Anon Steps being reprinted here.
AAWS has not reviewed or approved the contents of this publication, and has no
opinion regarding the views expressed herein. Alcoholics Anonymous is a program of
recovery from alcoholism *only*—use or permissible adaptation of AA's Twelve Steps
in connection with programs and activities which are patterned after AA, but which
address other problems, or in any other non-AA context, does not imply otherwise.

Cover design by Theresa Gedig
Interior design by Elizabeth Cleveland
Typesetting by Stanton Publication Services, Inc.

To Ralph, whose love, support, and encouragement
helped turn my dream into a reality.

Contents

Appendixes

Preface to the Second Edition

ACCORDING TO A RECENT HARVARD STUDY, the United States has five million compulsive gamblers and fifteen million problem gamblers (people who are at risk for becoming addicted to gambling). If each compulsive gambler affects six other people in his or her life, then we have approximately thirty million people in this country who are affected by gambling.

In 1997, Americans spent $630 billion on legalized gambling. To put this into perspective, that same year, they spent only $450 billion on food. In 1999, gambling became more popular in the United States than baseball, the movies, and theme parks combined.

Gambling is the most expensive addiction known to humans. If we compare it to alcohol or drug addiction, we get an even clearer picture of what a gambling addict is up against in terms of financial cost. If an alcoholic spends four hours in a bar drinking, how much might that cost? Thirty or forty dollars? If a cocaine addict spends four hours in a crack house smoking crack, it might cost seven or eight hundred dollars. On the other hand, if a compulsive gambler spends four hours gambling on a baccarat table, how much might that cost?

When *Losing Your Shirt* was first published, it focused on the most common compulsive gamblers. For the most part, these were middle-aged males, married with families. The book did not reflect the increasing number of female compulsive gamblers, nor underage gamblers, senior citizen gamblers, and our latest "state of the art" gamblers—those who gamble solely over the Internet. This revised edition addresses populations who, until now, were rarely spoken of, nor were they being seen in treatment centers or in the fellowships of Gamblers Anonymous.

Until four years ago, Internet gambling did not exist. However, as the proliferation of recreational gambling continued, and as the word of new gambling options spread, an increasing number of nongamblers succumbed to the attraction of this enterprise.

We no longer have stereotypical gambling addicts. Today, if we take a look at who is gambling, we will undoubtedly see young adults, adolescents, and even children. Our youth are no longer restricted to pitching pennies or flipping cards. They have branched out to gambling in our middle and high schools and on our college campuses.

We will see women, some of whom are living under the poverty level, who state they gamble as their only hope of rising above this level. We will also see women whose income is well above the poverty level. These women are employed, independent, and have established their own credit. They are making their own decisions about when, where, and how much to gamble. Most of them claim they gamble because they are bored. These women are either single or married to men who are not there for them. Some of their husbands are suffering with an addiction of their own, and others are married to men with whom they have no communication.

As for the senior citizens who gamble, we will find them standing outside a bingo hall; in line at their neighborhood lottery agent; or climbing on the casino buses, bringing with them a voucher for a free lunch, a coupon worth fifteen dollars in chips, and their most recent Social Security check.

Then, there are our newest compulsive gamblers, whom we will not see. They are the Internet gamblers who gamble in complete privacy. These gamblers, for the most part, are divided into two categories: sports gamblers and stock market day traders.

Sport gamblers are able to place their bets on events happening all over the world. Thanks to the Internet, these sports enthusiasts can gamble twenty-four hours a day, seven days a week, without ever leaving their homes. The only ones who know how often and how much they gamble are themselves and their credit card companies. Their gambling is done in the silence of their rooms, their homes, or their businesses.

Then, there are the other "new-age gamblers," or day traders. Day traders are investors who try to time the fluctuations of stock prices from hour to hour or sometimes minute to minute. Upon entering this venture, most day traders do not know that this is an extremely high-risk type of investing. Nor do they have any idea that sixty-seven out of every sixty-eight day traders are losers and that 72 percent of all those who do day trading lose everything.

To understand the gambling addiction, it is most helpful to know exactly what was happening in the gambler's life before his or her gambling became compulsive. If prevention is the only means of stopping the spread of this devastating illness, then we need to become more aware of the signs and signals that indicate one's gambling is becoming a problem.

Preface to the First Edition

THE FACT THAT YOU are holding this book in your hands tells me that, on some level, you have an interest in compulsive gambling.

Perhaps you picked up this book because someone you love loves to gamble, and you are now concerned that the gambling is getting out of control. If that is so, this book has much to offer you. If you read every page, you will learn just how you could have been kept in the dark for so long and not know what was going on in your own home; why you are always feeling so confused; or why you continually blame yourself for much of the madness. You will learn how your partner can cover up so many debts and how he is so good at keeping you in the dark. You will learn how he is getting the money he needs to gamble when you can't even pay for the bare necessities or put food on your table.

If you are being affected by the gambling of someone you love, you need to read this book. You can find out what you are doing that might be contributing to the illness and where you can go for help.

Perhaps you are a gambler and are interested in this book because lately you have become concerned about your gambling. Perhaps your debts are so high and your illegal money lenders are so impatient that you can see no way out. Or perhaps your spirits are so low that you fear you may act on your thoughts of self-destruction. If you read this book, you will find out that there is a sure way out of all your troubles, no matter how deep, and that you don't have to deal with them alone. You will learn that many thousands of others who have been in your shoes have recovered from their debts, their depression, and their illness.

Perhaps you are a professional, and in the course of your work you meet people who are greatly affected by their own or someone else's gambling. Or perhaps you are a professional who believes you have never had a compulsive gambler in your office. If so, you are mistaken. If you are a medical doctor, you have treated compulsive gamblers for hypertension, ulcers, headaches, and heart problems. If you are a psychotherapist, you have treated compulsive gamblers for anxiety, stress, marital/family problems, depression, and attempted suicide. If you are an accountant, you have tried to help compulsive gamblers with their financial problems. And if you are an attorney, you have represented compulsive gamblers in court and defended them against charges of theft, forgery, and embezzlement. However, none of you were aware that the things you were doing to help would, in the end, be futile. Your patients and clients never revealed that at the core of their problems was a gambling addiction. Not only did their troubles remain, they continued to worsen.

Perhaps you have even tried to help the spouses or partners of compulsive gamblers. However, again, if these people did not know that their partners were gambling, you would not only be unable to help them, you might even have added to their pain.

One wife of a compulsive gambler went to see a psychiatrist because she thought she was losing her mind. She had become extremely forgetful. Many times, her husband told her she never informed him of an upcoming family event; therefore he was unable to attend because he had a prior commitment. She was sure she had told him.

This wife continually received past-due notices from utility companies, although she knew she had written out checks to them and her husband had mailed them. She could not solve this mystery. She often lost or misplaced money in her home. Her memory told her she had put it in a safe place, but when she returned to retrieve it, it was gone. In addition, this wife told the doctor she often hears voices at night when she is lying in bed. These voices talk about quarters and dimes. They are so disturbing, she cannot fall asleep.

The doctor could easily see that this woman was suffering from hallucinations, delusions, anxiety, insomnia, and depression, so he dismissed her from his office with prescriptions, sequentially, for Valium, Thorazine, Elavil, and Seconal. The woman left "knowing" she was losing her mind.

The reason this woman was so confused was because she was living with a compulsive gambler who was an expert in controlling her psyche. He had her exactly where he wanted her—puzzled and questioning her own sanity. He never mailed the checks she made out because he needed the money to gamble. Her checking account never balanced because he was removing checks from the back of the checkbook to get money to gamble. The reason she heard voices at night was because he had a transistor radio under his pillow and was listening to the West Coast football games that he had bet on. And when she thought she was hearing someone talking about quarters and dimes, she was actually hearing someone talking about quarters and downs.

Perhaps this book was given to you by someone who cares about you and is concerned about your gambling. You may feel you don't need it because your gambling is not a problem; you can stop anytime you want. Don't bet on it!

Acknowledgments

WHILE WRITING THIS BOOK I was fortunate to be surrounded by special people. For their help, support, and encouragement, I would like to thank first and foremost my editors Karen Chernyaev, Betty Christiansen, and Kathryn Kjorlien, whose editorial skills contributed greatly to the final version of this book. It has been a learning experience and a pleasure working with you.

I would also like to thank Henry Lesieur, Ph.D., professor of sociology and anthropology at St. John's University, Jamaica, New York, who swayed me, after years of being a clinician, to write.

Also, my colleagues who shared my desire for such a book so that others could begin to understand that compulsive gambling is a serious emotional illness.

My good friends, especially Jane Murphy, Franca Mills, Evelyn Di Capua, Gina L'Hommedieu, Jean Toy, Maryjoan Dunne, Penny Sussman, Marilyn Zetner, and M. J. Albiston. Their love, support, and ongoing interest made this endeavor a family affair.

Claire Heineman, whom I have long admired for her spirit, her independence, and her determination to succeed.

My parents, from whom I am blessed with memories of warmth and love. Mom, I wish you were here.

My children, Rolf, Jill, and Jennifer, each of whom occupies a special place in my heart, shared by none.

Tom Damato and Mari Heineman, who never forgot I had a dream.

Four little people, Tiffany, Aaron, Brett, and Kalani, whose angelic voices and endearing smiles continually remind me how precious are the years of childhood.

All the recovering compulsive gamblers and their family members who have allowed me to touch their lives. I thank you for touching mine.

My Higher Power, who set me free after I decided to let go and let Him.

Introduction

APPROXIMATELY EIGHT OUT OF every ten adults in this country gamble.

For the vast majority, gambling is a pleasant way to spend an afternoon or evening with friends or family. Such recreational gamblers decide exactly how much money they will gamble before they leave home. If the allotted money is lost, they spend the rest of the time enjoying themselves—without gambling. Recreational gamblers do not let the excitement of betting control them. They do not borrow from others or use their credit cards to continue gambling when the money they had put aside for gambling is gone. They gamble purely for fun. Recreational gamblers have no problem controlling this leisure activity. Their gambling fits nicely into their lives and is not costly to them. Most agree that purchasing something they want with their gambling money was a happy memory.

At the other extreme are those whose gambling gets completely out of control. It becomes expensive, causing financial burdens and emotional devastation for themselves and those they love. These are compulsive gamblers.

WHAT IS COMPULSIVE GAMBLING?

Until recently, compulsive gambling was seen as an activity indulged in by society's losers. Many were criminals who stole or embezzled money to feed their habit. When caught, they were incarcerated for their crimes. Nobody wondered why they did what they did. Their behaviors were viewed as freely chosen—certainly not the result of an uncontrolled compulsion.

Today, we know that most compulsive gamblers are anything but criminals. Rather, they are hardworking people who cannot control when, where, or how much they gamble. And it is estimated that as many as one in three compulsive gamblers is female. Yet very few females are in treatment. Only 10 percent of Gamblers Anonymous members are female, and only 4 percent of compulsive gamblers in treatment are female.

Because most of the people active in gambling recovery programs are males who are married, this book will focus primarily on these couples, although other situations, including those involving underage and senior gambling, will be presented.

In 1980, the American Psychiatric Association recognized compulsive gambling, also known as pathological gambling, as a mental illness. It is listed under Impulsive Control Disorder (312.31) in the *Diagnostic and Statistical Manual of Mental Disorders*. The manual offers the following diagnostic criteria:

1. frequent preoccupation with gambling or with obtaining money to gamble
2. frequent gambling of larger amounts of money or over a longer period of time than intended
3. a need to increase the size or frequency of bets to achieve the desired excitement
4. restlessness or irritability if unable to gamble
5. repeated loss of money by gambling and returning another day to win back losses ("chasing")
6. repeated efforts to reduce or stop gambling
7. frequent gambling when expected to meet social or occupational obligations
8. sacrifice of some important social, occupational, or recreational activity in order to gamble
9. continuation of gambling despite other significant social, occupational, or legal problems that the person knows to be exacerbated by gambling

In summary, this means that individuals may be classified as compulsive gamblers if they find they are chronically and progressively unable to resist impulses to gamble. They find that their gambling behavior compromises, disrupts, or damages their personal, marital, family, or vocational pursuits.

WHO ARE COMPULSIVE GAMBLERS?

Are compulsive gamblers all those stereotypical macho men sitting around a table playing poker, cigars hanging out of their mouths and gold chains dangling around their necks? Are they the lone gamblers standing off by themselves at the racetrack looking anxious and tense? Are they the men who sit in the bleachers, yelling angry words at those around them because their team is losing? Are they the men who look disheveled, "down and out"? Don't most compulsive gamblers fit one of these pictures?

These common images of compulsive gamblers are misconceptions. No one can pick out compulsive gamblers simply by looking at them. This addiction is so easily hidden, so invisible. The compulsive gambler can be a well-dressed stockbroker, a blue-collar worker, a minister, a businessperson, or a senior citizen. And, of course, the compulsive gambler can be female.

However, some common characteristics are present among compulsive gamblers. Male gamblers tend to be competitive, athletic, intelligent, and energetic. They learned at an early age to avoid adult responsibilities, frustration, and conflict in their daily lives. Most of them say they cannot tolerate boredom and continually crave excitement. Some experts believe that this craving for excitement is an inborn biological need that may contribute to the development of the illness.

Female compulsive gamblers are typically single, separated, or divorced. Many women reluctantly begin to gamble when invited by well-meaning friends or family for a trip to a gambling venue. Unlike male gamblers, who often get their first high with a big win, many compulsive gambling women never experience the big win. They instead enjoy the escape—the dissociative state gambling puts them in. In this trancelike state, women are able to forget about overwhelming problems, including grief, abusive relationships, loneliness, and boredom.

According to Dr. Robert Custer, a pioneer in the treatment of compulsive gambling, the compulsive gambler who hits bottom is typically male, white, married, Catholic or Jewish, and in his early forties. He began gambling as an adolescent, but is a high school graduate and may have some college education. He comes from a lower- or middle-class home and was brought up with traditional values. He is in debt for approximately one year's salary. Most likely, he never had any legal problems until his gambling progressed. There is a 20 percent chance that the compulsive gambler is suffering from alcoholism or drug addiction. In addition, when he hits bottom, he is fifteen times more likely to commit suicide than the general population.

The Council on Compulsive Gambling of New Jersey conducted a study of compulsive gamblers entering treatment in its state. The council's findings confirm and expand Dr. Custer's assessment.

- The average amount of money owed when the individual sought help was $43,150.
- The average age was thirty-nine years.
- All finished elementary school.
- 83 percent finished high school.
- 5 percent completed college.
- The average age when they placed their first bet was thirteen years.
- 50 percent made their own call for help and 33 percent of their spouses made the call.
- 75 percent of those seeking help were married.
- 85 percent said their game of choice was horses; 79 percent, sports; 74 percent, cards; 40 percent, casinos; 32 percent, numbers; and 5 percent, bingo.
- Almost 75 percent of those studied admitted they had thoughts of suicide, and 17 percent had attempted it.
- 78 percent said they had committed a felony because of their gambling—22 percent had cashed bad checks, and 18 percent had embezzled money.

Compulsive gamblers often come from homes where there was inconsistent parenting. Many had poor male role models for fathers and describe their fathers as being emotionally distant and cold. The father was also absent from the home, through divorce, desertion, or workaholic habits. Many compulsive gamblers describe their mothers as being controlling, overinvolved in their lives, and overly emotional. The probability is high that most compulsive gamblers were raised by at least one addicted parent, most often an alcoholic. There was always a strong emphasis on money. Conversations involving money were daily events.

Words used to describe compulsive gamblers include *narcissistic, procrastinating, dependent,* and *impulsive.* Some believe they are entitled to all the good things in life; others believe they are completely unworthy.

HOW MANY COMPULSIVE GAMBLERS ARE THERE?

Until recently, the only national prevalence study was conducted in 1975 by the Institute of Survey Research at the University of Michigan. It concluded that the national prevalence rate for pathological gambling in the adult population in the United States was .77 percent. The figure was double that in Nevada, then already a total gambling state. The rate is greater today because the availability and acceptance of gambling throughout this country have become more widespread since 1975. And the more available gambling is, the greater will be the number of problems related to it.

According to a 1998–1999 study by the National Gambling Impact Study Commission, more than five million Americans are pathological gamblers, and another fifteen million are at risk of becoming one.

WHY IS COMPULSIVE GAMBLING SO PREVALENT TODAY?

From colonial times, gambling has been available to those who desired it. However, with the 1978 opening of "Las Vegas of the East" (Atlantic City, New Jersey), gambling became available to people who previously could not afford to fly west to indulge in this pastime.

During this same time period, many states began sanctioning legalized gambling through lotteries and off-track betting. In the 1990s, casinos opened up on Indian reservations across the country. These gambling choices began to attract individuals who had never gambled in their lives except to play an occasional game of bingo or purchase a raffle ticket. Today, the ripple effects of available gambling can be seen everywhere: long lines at counters that sell lottery tickets, even when the prize isn't in the millions; young women with baby strollers in off-track betting parlors. And each year, the casinos cash thousands of Social Security checks for senior citizens.

WHY DO PEOPLE GAMBLE?

Most people gamble for fun, relaxation, and escape from the pressures of their daily lives. Others gamble as a form of risk taking. Our country was founded and developed by risk takers. To this day, those who came here from foreign shores, those who went west, and those who walked on the moon are admired for their courage.

Today, our youth do not have traditional rites of passage. There are no tigers to hunt and few new frontiers to conquer. There are no clear-cut challenges that would allow them to prove their adulthood—except, perhaps, risking their money on a game of chance.

During their school years, many students seek challenges by participating in team sports. Some compete because they enjoy it. Others compete because one or both of their parents insist on it. Whatever the reason, the goal is to win. In later years, when the athlete is no longer competing, he can still be a part of the game if he places a wager on it. This vicarious form of participation is satisfactory to most fans for all of their adult lives. But some will feel as if they are part of the game only if the wager is high enough to get their adrenaline flowing—the way it did when they themselves were out there trying to win.

However, it is not necessary for a gambler to be a former athlete. Many gamblers never competed in a sporting event, yet they can feel the excitement of gambling whenever they too are in *action*. *Action* is a word you'll encounter frequently in this book, and it's what gambling is all about—the thrill of a big risk. What would there be to admire if our astronauts had taken a proven, fail-safe route to the moon, if they took a short walk in a guaranteed danger-free environment? Taking a risk is greatly admired by most Americans. Yet many people would never volunteer for anything that involves high risk. When money is the only risk, however, they will step forward and accept the challenge, willing to pay the price for being viewed as a risk taker, a person of courage.

People gamble because it is fun, because they never have to gamble more than they are willing to, because they are often admired by others when their bets are sizable, and because it is a form of risk taking that cannot harm them—unless their gambling becomes an addiction.

WHY DO COMPULSIVE GAMBLERS CONTINUE TO GAMBLE?

This question has been answered by many professionals over the years. In the early twenties and thirties, Freudian analysts viewed compulsive gambling as a form of play indulged in by men who didn't want to grow up. They believed that compulsive gamblers were deprived of attention and love in childhood. The result was a strong desire for pleasure and immediate gratification in adulthood. Early analysts believed that compulsive gamblers found the pleasure they sought in gambling.

Sigmund Freud believed that the individual's drive to gamble was really a transformation of the child's drive to masturbate. Other early analysts believed that the compulsive gambler is a masochist who wants subconsciously to lose because he enjoys being punished. Such punishment is said to alleviate feelings of guilt.

Later, some behavioristic psychologists viewed gambling as a reinforcing activity because it produces excitement, arousal, and tension. They believed that the desire to alleviate feelings of guilt about gambling compulsively caused the gambler to return and gamble again. Behaviorists claim that gambling is a learned behavior and that it can be unlearned.

Some theorists believe that compulsive gamblers have a personality that lends itself to this type of activity. According to this view, most compulsive gamblers were raised in a home where they felt neither loved nor appreciated; therefore, they entered adulthood with very low self-esteem. As a result, whenever these gamblers faced a problem in life, they looked for relief and escape. In their early youth, they found relief by escaping into fantasy; later, they found it whenever they were in action.

Still other theorists believe there may be a biophysical basis for compulsive gambling. Compulsive gamblers are said to have low endorphin levels in their brains. Endorphins, chemicals that are manufactured naturally in our bodies, produce a kind of natural "high." People with low endorphin levels may turn to an activity that produces arousal, such as gambling, to give them this high. This view would explain why some compulsive gamblers become addicted from their first gambling experience.

The father of the treatment of compulsive gambling, Dr. Robert Custer, had his own theory about why people gamble compulsively. He believed that every human being has four basic emotional needs: affection, approval, recognition, and self-confidence. When these needs are not met, a person feels inadequate, rejected, helpless, and overwhelmed by life. Dr. Custer is supported in this theory by compulsive gamblers themselves. Most report that they grew up feeling all of those negative reactions and that when they gambled and won, they were able to "buy" friends, love, and self-esteem. In addition, the wins made them feel powerful, omnipotent.

Perhaps the best answer to the question of why compulsive gamblers continue to gamble is offered by Gamblers Anonymous in what they call their "Blue Book"—*Sharing Recovery through Gamblers Anonymous*. The Blue Book says: "We don't know and we cannot afford to care. Those who come to us need help immediately. There is not time for the intellectual luxury to explore each compulsive gambler's history and to interpret the results. There is no place in our fellowship Program for debate on the merits of different theories of recovery, on the conflicts between varying schools of psychological thought. The benefits of introspection and speculation are paltry when compared to the rewards of helping others regain their lives."

IS THERE HOPE FOR COMPULSIVE GAMBLERS?

The Blue Book says: "How can Gamblers Anonymous help compulsive gamblers recover from their disorder when its causes are not fully understood? The fellowship's Program relies not only on the benefits of understanding, but on the power of faith. Belief in the effectiveness of Gamblers Anonymous is based on the solid evidence that thousands of compulsive gamblers have recovered by following the Program. No other course of therapy has been successful without including regular attendance at Gamblers Anonymous meetings."

No theorist, no philosophy, no professional can challenge this statement. What the Blue Book says is true: No recovery appears possible unless the afflicted works the Twelve Steps of recovery in Gamblers Anonymous. In chapters 9 and 10, we'll explore these Steps in detail.

Facts on File

Compulsive gambling is not a bad habit. It is an emotional illness recognized as such by the American Psychiatric Association.

Anyone who gambles compulsively will find they are chronically and progressively unable to resist their impulses to gamble. This is true despite the fact that gambling damages their personal, family, marital, or vocational pursuits.

No addiction is more deniable or easier to hide than compulsive gambling.

Part 1

THE MALE GAMBLER

Regardless of whether you are male, female, heterosexual, homosexual, bisexual, married, single, separated, divorced, or widowed, the stories in this section will give you a deep understanding of what happens to individuals and relationships when someone is a compulsive gambler. Because statistics show that most gamblers are male and married, most of the stories in the section on male gamblers refer to married couples. As you read, keep in mind that these same dynamics apply in unmarried couples of either sex. It is not my intention as an author to offer sexual stereotypes or to cast men and women in rigid sex roles.

1

The Degeneration of the Compulsive Gambler's Relationships

IF YOU ARE A COMPULSIVE GAMBLER in recovery, this book is for you. If you are in a relationship with a compulsive gambler in recovery and you are not happy, this book is also for you.

More likely than not, the gambling started before the two of you met—or at least it has gone on for a very long time. Perhaps, in the beginning, it was part of how the two of you spent some of your leisure time. It gave a spark to your relationship. It gave you a common interest. You both looked forward to it. Your memories of those early years are probably pleasant. Perhaps you can still recall some of the things you bought or did with the winnings.

What results is a cycle of ups and downs, often reaching extremes. If we were to distill the essence of these cycles, we would come up with something like the analysis that follows.

To the Gambler: One thing you recall is how excited you always felt when you were gambling or about to gamble. Before gambling came into your life, you might never have gotten excited about much of anything. Chances are you were passive, quiet, and somewhat detached. Others might have described you as unhappy and bored.

To the Gambler's Partner: At first, the gambling was occasional, and it caused no problem. If anything, it gave you pleasure to see how much your partner enjoyed himself with his hobby. You might not have gambled yourself, but you might have gone along sometimes, just for fun.

To the Gambler: Gradually, you began to give more time to gambling.

When you weren't gambling, you were either thinking about it or reading gambling-related material to get better at your hobby.

Remember when you developed a "system" for winning? Because it turned out to be quite dependable, you became possessive of it and resisted sharing it with others. Why should you give away a good thing? You were proud of what you had accomplished.

To the Gambler's Partner: As the gambler's partner, you were most likely proud, too. You could see he was ahead of the game with his winnings. As a matter of fact, if anyone criticized or teased him about his gambling, or if they devalued his system, you were his greatest spokesperson.

To the Gambler: The first phase of your gambling career was a definite plus in your life. The excitement you received from your newfound joy was more than you had ever imagined. That joy led you to wager more often and to increase the size of your bets. Larger bets resulted in greater rewards. You not only bragged about your winnings, you used some of the money to buy beautiful and expensive items for yourself and your partner. Your friends and neighbors began to envy you.

During those years, you probably developed a reputation as a great guy who was extremely generous. Perhaps you were the first one to pick up the tab when dining with friends, or perhaps you were known to overtip.

On some level, gambling bonded the two of you as a couple. It was a common interest, and it was anything but a negative in your relationship.

Those years were the best, and it never occurred to you that things would change. You were on top of the mountain, and everyone knew it. You actually believed that luck was not only on your side, but also at your command. You were convinced you had found the answer to the good life without working for it. In your mind, you could only see life improving. You had it made!

One day, after a number of years of being a successful gambler, you placed a very large bet and won. That experience turned out to be the event that changed you, your relationship, and your life. From that one bet, you realized more money than you had ever dreamed possible. Remember how that felt? Nothing you had ever experienced before equaled it. You felt special, loved, successful, powerful, and your sense of self-esteem shot sky-high.

Although you couldn't see it then, that "big win" began to change you as a person, starting with your thoughts and beliefs. Prior to that time, you believed you were just lucky, but somehow that big win convinced you that it was more than just luck. You began to believe you were truly special, very special. And when you analyzed it, it all began to make sense. All your life you had felt short-changed. Perhaps you lost a parent at an early age; perhaps your parents were divorced; perhaps your mother was an alcoholic or you never felt accepted in the eyes of your father. Whatever the reason, it didn't matter. That big win led you to believe you deserved it. With that conviction you were raring to go on for even greater rewards.

For the first time, you began to fantasize about how you could gamble for a living, especially if your regular earnings were limited.

After all, why should you work so hard for your money when you had such a talent for gambling? You honestly believed you could not lose. So you began gambling more often, placing much larger bets in order to accumulate the money you needed to be able to give up your job. Gambling would be your new profession. You *knew* you would get rich by gambling, and you could hardly wait.

To the Gambler's Partner: You too were excited, pleased, and happy. Along with feeling hopeful, you fantasized about the many good things you believed were about to come your way.

To the Gambler: In reality, there was another reason you wanted to increase the size of your bets. It wasn't only to reap greater rewards; now you could no longer get the "kick" you once did with a twenty- or fifty-dollar wager. You now had to lay several hundred dollars on the line in order to feel a sufficient flow of adrenaline. You wanted to feel something. That something was action. Action! Wasn't that what it was all about? And wasn't it worth any price? After all, you deserved it. You truly believed you were entitled, and now it was payback time.

With hindsight, can you see how your "big win" influenced your future gambling? Until then, the gambling was an interest, a joy, and a pleasure. The excitement of your big win pushed you into the middle phase of your gambling career, where your gambling truly started to become compulsive, and its joy was gone forever.

Looking back, can you see how increasing the frequency of your gambling and the size of your bets began to bring serious problems into your life? You may have started to work overtime to earn the extra money you needed to gamble big. Then when you lost, you lost big, more than you could afford—a lot more. The losses not only hurt you financially, they hurt you socially, too. You no longer wanted to gamble with your friends or with your partner at your side; you didn't want them to know how much you were losing. You wanted desperately to protect your reputation as a successful gambler.

The losses continued. Your self-esteem started to decline. The extra money you were earning wasn't enough. In what seemed like a short period, you started to consider additional ways to gain access to money. The one thing you knew for sure was that you didn't want to stop gambling. Soon you'd have another big win, and all your problems would be solved.

It was in this middle phase of your gambling that definite changes in your personality started to take place. They came about as a result of your altered thinking, feelings, and behavior. You started to develop tunnel vision. You changed your priorities in life. And you stepped deep into the common defense called denial: *I have a great deal of financial troubles, but my gambling is not a problem.* Your thinking, which was becoming diseased, told you: *I'll be out of this hole just as soon as my luck turns around and shines on me again.*

Just about that time, your relationship with your partner and children began to change. For the first time, gambling was your number-one priority, and your family moved to second place.

You started backing away from family occasions that interfered with a chance to gamble. You started to hide some of the gambling because you didn't want your partner or children to know the truth: You'd rather gamble than be with them. You rationalized your desire to gamble. When you hit it big again, they would understand. They would be rewarded.

To the Gambler's Partner: You began reacting to your partner's attitude changes; you strongly sensed that something in your relationship was different. When you questioned him, he may have shared how difficult a time he was having making ends meet; even though he was working overtime, there was never enough money. Perhaps he blamed you, claiming you were always asking for money. You blamed him because he had become so tight with money. At any rate, he may have decided at this point that he would take over paying the household bills, writing out the checks, and balancing the checkbook. If you agreed to let him do it, you did so because you wanted him to find out firsthand what a careful budgeter you had been. But then, you had no idea his gambling had worsened.

To the Gambler: As your gambling increased, you started to manipulate the budget you were now managing. The months went by, and more and more you found that you had to "borrow from Peter to pay Paul." You abandoned your gambling system, which had rewarded you so well in the first phase of your gambling, because you had lost control and could no longer follow it. Your gambling now became compulsive, and your losses mounted.

Soon the overtime pay and the financial manipulations were not enough to keep you in action or keep you out of debt. Then you began to focus each day on recouping the losses of the previous day. You no longer gambled to win, you gambled to chase your losses and to stay in action because action eradicated reality, and your reality had become such that you could no longer deal with it.

To the Gambler's Partner: Meanwhile, you remained in the dark. All this time, you knew only that there was food on the table and that there were no eviction notices from the landlord or the bank. You had no idea what your partner was going through to prevent you from finding out the depths of his gambling.

However, you were aware that he was much less involved with you and the children. By now, the children had stopped asking whether Dad would be accompanying them on a family outing. They took it for granted that he wouldn't. They were the first to feel the lack of his presence and his distancing.

They were starting to experience more unhappiness at home, more arguments between the two of you. They were even aware that some of your anger was misdirected at them.

To the Gambler: Your experiences broadened when you had to think of additional ways of raising money without anyone finding out. You started to borrow on your credit cards and from your credit union.

You borrowed from family and friends, all of whom were happy to help you. These people liked and respected you. They believed that if *they* were in need, you would be the first to step forward. None of them knew why you needed money. Soon their help wasn't enough, so you applied for additional credit cards without your partner's knowledge. You probably had your mail sent to your place of business or a post office box to make sure she wouldn't find out.

This deceitful behavior, and the lying that went along with it, was the catalyst that started to make your love for gambling more painful than pleasurable. At this point, you could never again return to the days of old and experience gambling as something recreational, occasional, or joyful.

You had become somebody you weren't. Your values were changing. You were secretive, you lied, you neglected your responsibilities, and you continually put your need to gamble before anyone or anything.

Other areas of your life were affected during this middle phase. You shunned social gatherings because you were uncomfortable in the presence of others. You had no use for small talk, or so you said. Actually, you always knew people would be there to whom you owed money, and you didn't want to face them. Besides, you needed to spend most of your waking hours scheming to find additional ways to raise money to gamble or to repay the money you had borrowed (or stolen) the day before.

Now the pressures truly began to mount. It was getting harder to keep your partner from finding out about the overdue bills. You worried every day that your creditors would begin to call your home. You tried to stay on top of which one was most likely to make such a call so you could call them first. These pressures made you irritable, short-tempered, and distant with those most important to you. You no longer talked openly with your partner. Your lying had become so habitual, she stopped asking you questions because she knew she couldn't believe your responses. Your communication with her had worsened. Emotional intimacy was, by then, nonexistent, and physical intimacies between the two of you were rare.

Your children had also started to change. The oldest abandoned extracurricular activities in order to work after school and give the money to your partner. Your middle child began acting out—cutting school and talking back to you and your partner. Your youngest started to wet the bed and have nightmares.

You, however, rationalized all your children's behaviors as reactions to your partner's negative attitudes and constant nagging of both you and them. Certainly, *she* was the cause of most of the family's problems.

To the Gambler's Partner: You were always quick to blame yourself.

You started to buy the guilt your partner laid upon you. You were so confused, frightened, and worn out by the changes that had taken place in your family that you actually started to believe him when he said the gambling was all your fault. After all, you had become a nag, you got on his case about money all the time, and you had long since withdrawn from him sexually. Feeling exhausted and having had your self-esteem beaten down, you finally bought the guilt. You too blamed yourself for his gambling.

To the Gambler: After being in this stressful middle phase of gambling for some time, perhaps years, it finally caught up to you. Your unpaid bills were insurmountable. Your wife started interrogating you more often on money matters. She was no longer satisfied with your standard response: "Don't worry about it." She wanted answers, but you had none. About that time, she began to get calls from your creditors, the banks, and department stores. She saw that the checking account often didn't balance, and she began to refuse to believe you when you continued to blame the computer at the bank. She got wise to you and began rejecting all your excuses. She looked to your gambling, and she blamed it for the problems. Your relationship worsened so much that you could no longer stand it. The stress was killing you, and you knew that, without help, you couldn't get out of the deep financial hole you had dug.

To the Gambler's Partner: You had had it. It wasn't just the outstanding debts, it was everyday living. There might have been days when you didn't have a single dollar to your name. Perhaps you went to the supermarket one day and stood inside the door, trying to decide whether to buy peanut butter or toilet tissue; you couldn't afford both. You were the one who always had to answer to the children. They believed it was your job, as a parent, to make their father stop gambling. They were becoming more and more resentful that they had to do without essentials because you weren't doing what they believed you had the power to do. You were under as much, and perhaps more, pressure than your compulsively gambling partner.

To the Gambler: And what did you finally do? You went to your partner and told her all (well, almost all). You cried and begged for help (you didn't mean it, you only wanted money). Despite all her anger and fear, she was relieved. She believed you when you promised that if she helped you, you would never gamble again.

How did your partner help you? She went to her family to raise money, or she agreed to sign a consolidation loan, or she signed the bank papers for a second mortgage. She did what you asked because she wanted the debts, the financial troubles, and the gambling to end.

What your partner gave you was a "bailout." A bailout is just like a big win. It took all the pressure off you. It made you feel good again. You told yourself that your luck had returned and that, once again, you had a chance to see all your fantasies come true. It also told you that, should you fall to the same misfortune again, you could arrange another bailout.

To the Gambler's Partner: What the bailout taught you was this: Keep up your guard. Don't get lax. Watch him. Don't let him gamble again, or if he does gamble, see to it that it stays under control. As the partner of a compulsive gambler, you wanted to do the impossible. You couldn't. No one could.

To the Gambler: You continued to gamble. The financial pressure was alleviated for the moment, but the emotional pressure continued to worsen. You found you were living with a partner who wouldn't give up. Each and every day your gambling was her topic of conversation. There was nothing else in your relationship now—just gambling. Remember how she tried to control it? She made appointments with friends to keep you from gambling. She feigned illnesses to keep you from gambling. She withheld sex to keep you from gambling. She became seductive to keep you from gambling. And one time she ran up all the charge cards, thinking that if there were no more credit available, you couldn't afford to gamble. She had no way of knowing that your gambling had nothing to do with money. By then, your gambling had only to do with action, because action was what you craved. Every cell in your body cried out for it whenever it wasn't at hand. It was your "drug of choice"—your stimulator, your tranquilizer, and your faithful painkiller. It removed you from a reality you could not face and took you to nirvana. You had reached the final phase of your gambling career.

Feelings of anxiety, stress, fear, and helplessness plagued you. Gambling had affected your reputation and perhaps jeopardized your job; your relationship was severely troubled. Despite all this, you had only one thought each day, and that was to gamble. It no longer brought you joy or pleasure, but you had to do it to alleviate the pain.

By now, most of your resources were used up. You had no more friends or family members to turn to for another loan. They no longer bought your "poor me" stories and had stopped believing that you would repay the loan with your next paycheck. Since you could not stop gambling, you had no choice but to turn to illegal sources for support. For the first time in your life, you started to rely on loan sharks to support your habit. Because this was an extremely expensive way to borrow money, you soon found your debts piling up much more quickly than before. In no time, you were in greater debt than when you first cried out for help.

And that's exactly what you did again. But perhaps this time your partner agreed to help only if you would go to Gamblers Anonymous. You agreed, of course. You were willing to do anything to get relief from the pressures you could no longer overcome alone.

You may have even gone to Gamblers Anonymous meetings and stayed clean for a time. But you probably were in pain every day. You may have resented having to attend the GA meetings. You craved action—nothing else mattered to you. You finally concluded that action was worth any price. So once again, you returned to gambling.

To the Gambler's Partner: You could not shake the black cloud that had become your constant companion. It followed you everywhere. You could no longer tolerate his optimism about the future once he "hit it big." You had long since let go of his dream that the next win would solve everything.

By this time, you felt totally isolated and alone—you had no knowledge that compulsive gambling is a mental illness, so you told no one what you were going through. You felt too ashamed to let anyone else know. Besides, you thought nobody else had this problem. In addition, you continued to blame yourself for his behavior. The worse his gambling became, the more guilt you bought.

You became more and more depressed. By then, you were sure he didn't love you, because, if he did, he wouldn't be doing so many terrible things that devastated you and the children. During this last phase of his compulsive gambling, you lived every day with guilt, inadequacy, and helplessness. Because your attempts to get your partner to stop gambling were unsuccessful, you may have seriously considered suicide.

To the Gambler: You were starting to realize that your gambling was affording you more pain and less pleasure. Win or lose, you were unhappy. Your behavior was totally out of control, and you somehow knew it. Remember how superstitious you had become? For months you had worn the same piece of clothing because one time, when you had it on, you had won big. You actually believed that if you were going to win big again, you had to be wearing that article. Or maybe you recall other superstitious behaviors that you knew made no sense intellectually, but emotionally, you could not ignore or put aside.

Your final phase of gambling wore you out. You didn't exist anymore; nor did anyone else in your life. Your self-esteem fell below ground level. You could see only darkness. The light at the end of the tunnel had gone out. Only then did you know for the first time that you were going to die or surrender. You chose to surrender. You admitted that you were powerless over your gambling and that your life had become totally unmanageable. At last, you turned in sincerity and desperation to Gamblers Anonymous.

Facts on File

Before treatment, most compulsive gamblers believe that lack of money is their problem and that continued gambling is the solution.

Many believe they cannot be a compulsive gambler because they are too young, too old, too successful—or professional, female, or religious.

Action and/or escape is what compulsive gambling is all about. Gambling is like taking a stimulator, a tranquilizer, or a sleeping pill to put the gambler in a desired mood.

Questions

Gambler:

- Do you find yourself gambling on days when you promised yourself you wouldn't?
- Have you obtained credit cards without your partner's knowledge to obtain money to gamble or to pay gambling debts?
- Does gambling bring a special pleasure into your life—a pleasure like no other?

Partner:

- Is your partner secretive and defensive about how he spends money?
- Do you have severe financial debts that you cannot comprehend?

2

Dynamics in the Compulsive Gambler's Relationships

THE DYNAMICS IN A COMPULSIVE GAMBLER'S marriage or primary relationship are particularly complex. There is probably no addiction more deniable, more hidden than gambling. On the outside, the compulsive gambler looks like he has it all together. It is impossible, just by looking at him, to tell whether or not he has just placed a bet. You can't smell it on his breath, see it in his eyes, or detect it by listening to his heartbeat.

Even the partner of the compulsive gambler doesn't easily recognize that gambling is at the heart of the problems they have. She will tell you she fell in love with a man she viewed as intelligent, ambitious, motivated, full of energy, hardworking, and full of magnificent plans for their future. She committed to a man she believed in. And she continues, with faithful devotion, to believe in him, rescue him, and cover up for him. She continues, even amid his mounting excuses, hollow reassurances, and ultimately futile promises once gambling takes over as his highest "love."

From the outside, this pair may look like the perfect couple. Yet compulsive gambling, like most chronic, progressive, and fatal addictions, will tear away at every aspect of the couple's well-being. Without a doubt, the illness of compulsive gambling will render its victim financially devastated, physically deteriorated, mentally deficient, emotionally drained, and spiritually dead. The consequences for the victim's partner are equally monumental.

FINANCIAL RUIN

Financial devastation is inevitable. Almost invariably, the members of Gamblers Anonymous report that, by the time they finally asked for help, they were in debt so deep that they could see no way out. In fact, most new members of GA enter this program believing that money is their problem. Soon they learn by attending meetings that their problem is not money, but rather their addiction to gambling.

Once the gambler becomes honest, he will let others know that both his legal debts (to credit card companies, department stores, and credit unions, as well as his personal loans) and his illegal debts (to bookies and loan sharks) are not causing him as much pain as the consequences of these debts. His home may be in foreclosure; his furniture and car may have been repossessed; he may no longer have money to buy clothes for his family; and he may even be unable to put food on the table. This situation often brings the compulsive gambler to the realization that his love of gambling has brought his family to poverty.

Ironically, and despite his recognition of the dismal financial condition he is in, if one more person bails him out, he will gamble again. His diseased mind will tell him: *Just one more win and you'll be home free.*

PHYSICAL PROBLEMS

Physical deterioration surely accompanies this illness. Because the compulsive gambler's mind is continually focused on action, he has no interest in his physical state. Compulsive gamblers live a life of never-ending stress, and stress contributes to many illnesses. The afflicted find themselves facing such problems as high blood pressure, ulcers, headaches, backaches, intestinal problems, and serious heart problems. Unfortunately, gambling not only gives the compulsive gambler a high, it also kills his pain. When experiencing physical problems, the gambler knows that all he has to do is buy some action and the pain will leave. Compulsive gambling contributes to the demise of too many, simply because they ignore all signs of physical problems. When a compulsive gambler is, or is planning to be, in action, there is no room in his mind for anything else, even medical problems. Besides, the money a doctor would charge for services, he needs for gambling.

MENTAL LOSSES

Mental deficiency can be expected when you spend most of each day concentrating on nothing but gambling. Because there is no limit to the amount of money this psychological addiction will demand, the victim must devote most of his mental capacity to satisfying this need. As a result, the compulsive gambler will find his memory becoming faulty. If he is a student, he will be unable to study, concentrate, or remember. If he has a job, he will be unable to perform as expected. His mind will be distracted, and his performance will deteriorate as the illness progresses. He can only expect that whatever mental capabilities he once possessed will be unreachable as long as he remains in action.

EMOTIONAL COST

Emotional devastation is an expected outcome of this addiction. The illness brings with it nothing but negative and painful feelings. Any positive feelings the compulsive gambler once had are long since smothered by the emotions that accompany the consequences of many of his behaviors. Even gamblers who were once somewhat contented individuals eventually turn into isolated, lonely, guilt-ridden, depressed people who are unable to conjure up so much as an acceptable feeling. Many become totally numb. As the gambler sees it, once his luck has abandoned him, he walks under a dark cloud and senses there is no way out from under it. Despite the pain, his addiction lies to him, indicating that just one more big win will make everything all right. In reality, any win will lead to more gambling, which will lead to further emotional devastation, which all leads to more gambling. This is why the suicide attempt rate for compulsive gamblers is six times the national average and is highest among those with mental disorders.

A Feeling of Entitlement

Knowing what a big win does for a compulsive gambler makes it easy to understand why his gambling increases following one. He will gamble more frequently and wager greater amounts of money in order to purchase the feeling he desires. Intermittent big wins feed his low self-esteem. He will become demanding and selfish, developing a deep sense of entitlement that any other man or woman would question. The compulsive gambler truly believes he deserves exceptions to every rule. This is more than just defying authority figures. It is the sense that *I deserve what I want, when I want it.* This attitude persists well into the illness.

Lying

The afflicted will go to any means to get what he wants. One way is through compulsive lying. In order not to have to deal with what others want, he will lie to anyone about anything. His goal is twofold: to put his needs first and to avoid any conflict, no matter how small. Compulsive gamblers need to avoid conflicts because they distract them from their love of gambling. The partner of a compulsive gambler will often claim that he looks for conflicts so he can walk out and be free to do as he pleases. True! However, that is the one and only reason he will risk discord. If a confrontation requires something of a gambler, such as a decision to resolve a dilemma, the compulsive gambler will not get involved. He will say whatever someone wants to hear to keep that person quiet and allow the gambler to meet his goal— to gamble.

Childishness

The truest statement ever made about this addiction is that it is an emotional illness. Any spouse of a compulsive gambler will tell you that she is married to a child. This illness causes the compulsive gambler to become increasingly immature, impulsive, and irresponsible.

Immaturity

The immaturity comes from the fact that the gambler never learned how to grow up. Instead, he spent his adolescent years dreaming. The dreams were focused on how he could be successful and popular without having to put effort into his education or work up the ladder of success. His goal was to make it big with a roll of the dice or the turn of the wheel.

The magical thinking that goes along with this addiction is blatant. The afflicted proudly displays his dependence on special objects, people, or actions to get luck on his side. He will carry a good-luck charm with him when he is headed for action. He will continue to wear a particular article of clothing because it once brought him a big win. He will talk to his cards or blow on the dice, begging them to be good to him and bring him what he rightly deserves or desperately needs. He seems to believe that if he concentrates very hard, he will influence the turn of his cards or the roll of the dice. He will even exclude certain individuals when he goes gambling, because he believes that their presence will jinx him when he's in action.

The compulsive gambler's conviction that he will win big is so strong that he will completely devote himself to it. He will not allow anyone to sway him from it. He truly believes that, if he keeps gambling, he will eventually win enough money so that he will never have to work again; he will have all the luxuries he desires. He wants to accomplish this so that he will be accepted by others and, more important, prove to his partner that he deserves her love. He feels his winning will bind her to him in love and admiration forever, thereby accomplishing his goal of filling his internal void.

Because most compulsive gamblers begin gambling during their teens, they miss the stages of adolescent development that would have allowed them to enter adulthood feeling confident, responsible, and relatively mature. Gambling prevents them from learning how to interact and socialize with their peers, learning to interact with the opposite sex maturely, and developing coping mechanisms to help them survive in the adult world. It also blocks them from looking at options beyond their teen years for their life's work. The gambling and the amount of time they devote to it keeps them emotionally in prepubescent development; it keeps them children. They will continue to escape into fantasy to avoid any responsibility or stress in their lives. Unlike mature adults, who confront situations in their lives as they arise, immature adults do little or nothing. For those afflicted with this illness, emotional situations are dealt with by placing a bet.

Impulsivity

The impulsive nature of the compulsive gambler comes from an inability to delay gratification. His illness has always insisted that he have what he wants when he wants it. This is most noticeable when the gambler has money in his pocket. He cannot make a purchase at the store and come home with the change. His impulsive nature invites him to buy anything he sees, just to spend money. A compulsive gambler with money in his pocket will always find a way to spend it. To him, money has absolutely no meaning. He believes he can always get more.

A compulsive gambler's impulsive nature also results in his doing whatever he feels like whenever he feels like doing it. It doesn't matter if he has a prior commitment. A compulsive gambler always wants to be free to do as he pleases.

Irresponsibility

In addition to being impulsive, a compulsive gambler is also irresponsible. How can anyone so devoted to an activity be anything but irresponsible? As a victim, he never learned to be responsible in the first place. Looking back will most likely reveal that the compulsive gambler always had some kind of an enabler or overresponsible person in his life. Certainly, one of the most attractive features about his partner was her caretaking qualities. This trait can work in reverse in a relationship with a compulsive gambler, because the caretaker's behaviors—covering up, bailing out, giving money— only contribute to the addiction.

The compulsive gambler will eventually live with only one responsibility: to get the money to gamble. And the overresponsible person—his partner— handles everything else. All falls on her shoulders. Ironically, that burden never appears to be too heavy. Maybe that's because she was preparing for this role long before she met her gambling partner. Unless the overresponsible one takes a stand and begins to reverse her role, this illness may travel far beyond the bounds that either one of them can survive.

Spiritual Death

"Spiritually dead" accurately describes the compulsive gambler. Can you imagine anyone who lives for action bothering to stop to enjoy a sunset, a beautiful melody, or a child playing with a puppy? It doesn't happen. Not sunshine, nor beauty, nor the love of another human being has much place in the life of a compulsive gambler. His illness renders him deaf and blind to the many free gifts that are there for him to behold. In time, this life without spirituality will leave him with a huge void within, and he'll have no idea what the void is about.

For the afflicted, the demands of this addiction leave the gambler living a life filled with strife—a life in which he is most often irritable and restless, a life of uncontrollable mood swings, a life that will surely include many days without food and nights without sleep. Ironically, the one thing that always comforted him or even protected him from pain will turn against him. In time, gambling will offer no solace. Rather, it will leave him with heavy losses, perhaps career problems. At this point, he will have no place to turn to find a way out.

In the end, the compulsive gambler will have sacrificed his most precious values. He will find himself living daily with unbearable guilt and an uncontrollable urge to gamble. Eventually he will have hurt everyone in his life to whom he'd looked to fill his "love cavity." He will live with the belief that he is the scum of the earth. And, saddest of all, he may have no idea that he is suffering from a treatable illness that he can, with help, arrest.

THE GAMBLER'S PARTNER

Like the gambler, the gambler's partner experiences financial, mental, physical, emotional, and spiritual distress. Before examining these consequences, let's first look at what kind of woman chooses a compulsive gambler.

Craving Security

What are the partners of compulsive gamblers like? More than half knew on their wedding day that their life partner loved to gamble. Almost none knew that he had an illness that would render him totally unable to resist the impulse to gamble.

It is common to hear a gambler's partner say how much she was attracted to the gambler when they first met. She perceived him as outgoing, motivated, intelligent, exciting, a big spender, a risk taker, and a man filled with luxurious dreams. She may have thought he was very masculine, and that made her feel secure. Her need for security made her accept his aggressiveness and his domination over her.

Many gamblers' partners were raised in homes where one parent was an alcoholic or a compulsive gambler, or was abusive, emotionally ill, or absent. Many adopted the role of caretaker at an early age to fill the gap left by an emotionally distant or absent parent. Many of these women would describe their early childhoods as very unhappy. Perhaps this explains why so many married their childhood sweethearts. Being raised in a home with emotionally absent parents made these women passive and dependent on the first males who showed any promise of a prosperous future. These women entered adulthood with low self-esteem and almost no self-confidence. Many will admit that they married early because they could see no other way out of their unhappy home life.

Equating Material Goods with Love

One similarity that the partner of a compulsive gambler sees in her partner and in one or both of her parents is that they express love with material things. As this was the only expression of affection she ever knew, she is quite comfortable when her partner expresses love by buying presents with his gambling winnings. A problem arises, however, when the compulsive gambler starts losing and can't continue the gift giving. No more gifts means only one thing to this woman: *He no longer loves me.* In reality, when the partner of a compulsive gambler accepts a share of his winnings, she gives him a double message. She wants him to stop gambling, but she doesn't want him to stop buying her nice things with the winnings.

As the illness progresses and the debts mount, the gambler's partner will go to great lengths to keep their household financially stable. She will become an excellent money manager. She has no choice, because whenever she goes to him to talk about their debts, he will tell her not to worry. If a compulsive gambler were to wear a T-shirt that best described him to his partner, it would read: DON'T WORRY ABOUT IT.

The gambler's partner will do whatever she can to keep others from finding out what is going on in her marriage. If necessary, she will get a job to ease their financial burdens. She is especially likely to do so if the gambler keeps yelling at her, complaining that he is working hard but just can't make ends meet. Compulsive gamblers are good at transferring their guilt to their partners, and their partners are good at accepting it. They learned it in their own troubled childhoods.

Filling the Caretaker Role

A compulsive gambler chooses his mate carefully. He is unlikely to marry an independent, assertive woman whose self-esteem is intact. Rather, he will marry a caretaker, because he desperately needs an overresponsible caretaker—a mother. The caretaker carries all the family's burdens, thereby lightening the load for the gambler, making it possible for him to continue his irresponsible behavior.

The caretaker's T-shirt would read: MARTYR. That means she will work overtime, get a second job, cosign loans, cover bad checks, lie for the gambler, and deprive herself so that all his needs can be met. She will do anything to keep him out of jail or to keep him from being hurt. She demands nothing for herself. In time, she will find her self-esteem so low that she'll doubt she has any value as a human being. Living her life for her compulsively gambling husband and trying to adjust to his behavior eventually makes her totally dysfunctional and depressed.

Succumbing to Fear, Stress, and Ill Health

As the problems mount, the gambler's partner will go to her family to borrow money to pay debts and keep their problems from worsening. She lives with unbelievable fear because her partner keeps telling her he is in great physical danger from moneylenders who are neither patient nor understanding. Her fear increases if she receives a phone call from a stranger who confirms what her partner has said or who threatens her safety.

When the creditors and bill collectors start to haunt the couple, the gambler's partner is the one most likely to argue with a department store, the utility company, or the bank. Eventually, she is the one who will face each day worrying about what will happen next if her partner continues to gamble. She knows if she cannot get him to stop gambling, they will eventually lose everything—their home, their furniture, their car, his job, perhaps his freedom, and certainly her sanity. In time, the financial strain will lead her to dread the arrival of the mail, a stranger at the door, or the ring of the telephone.

Eventually her partner's gambling and all the accompanying anxiety will wear her out. The fact that this mental illness is so invisible, so deniable, makes her feel insane from its effects. She will succumb to emotional stress and physical problems sooner than he. She is the first to go to a doctor because she cannot sleep or eat. She is the first to start taking tranquilizers and sleeping pills.

Doubting Self

A compulsive gambler is a master at playing with his partner's psyche. He is a gem at convincing her she never told him something when she knows she did. He is a genius who always comes out the winner in these conflicts. The thing that makes her question her memory and convinces her that he is right is the degree of his anger. At times it frightens her so much that she will apologize for something she knows she did not do. His only goal is to blame her for anything that might get him off the hook so he can continue to gamble. The result is that she feels so guilty that she cannot make any changes in her behavior; nor can she walk away. Added to that is the fear that her husband might leave her, and she would find herself alone and unable to cope with the world.

Further Effects

As the illness progresses and the gambling continues, the gambler's partner becomes a bitter, nagging, miserable woman. Eventually she will blame everything on his gambling, because everything seems affected by it—including her own value system. She knows she was never a woman to lie, take her anger out on others, hate her partner, or resent others for not helping her out "one more time." In the end, she will blame herself.

Sexual Deprivation

The gambler's wife is devastated not only financially and emotionally, but sexually as well. The physical, sexual closeness she and her partner may have shared no longer exists. The reason is not limited to the tension between them; it includes the fact that when the compulsive gambler is winning, he is so elated that he doesn't need sex. And when he's losing, he's too depressed to want it.

Living with Lies

It is not uncommon for the partner of a compulsive gambler to focus more on the second and most obvious problem she is living with: his compulsive lying. She eventually believes nothing he says. Once she realizes he is gambling heavily, she becomes suspicious of his every move. Should she ever accuse him of coming home late from work because he was gambling, he responds with anger and accusations. She will then fear that he will go out and gamble just to get even.

Eventually, she never wants to give him the freedom to leave the house without her. To prevent him from gambling, she will make every excuse to go with him, regardless of where he is going. And she will avoid any occasion that would require her going alone, leaving him to his own devices.

Social Isolation

Because of his gambling, the gambler's partner avoids friends and family, either because he has lied to them or owes them money, or because she borrowed money from them and has been unable to repay it. Even in situations that do not involve money, she will stay away. It is too painful for her to be with couples who do not have her problem or who appear happy.

Increasing Distance

For the gambler's partner, the saddest part of the addiction is this: She has no knowledge that her partner is suffering from an emotional illness. From her perspective, he is unreachable. He is never there for her, no matter how much she needs him and expresses that need. She talks to him, and he doesn't seem to be listening; she doesn't know that, inside his head, he is obsessed with action. In time, she learns that she cannot depend on him. The communication between them is completely lost. His gambling addiction makes him completely uninterested in anything she has to say. And her desire to communicate is destroyed because she knows he is a compulsive liar.

When she puts her pieces of the puzzle together, she comes to only one conclusion: *He doesn't care about me.*

Because the partner of a compulsive gambler is unaware that she is dealing with an emotional illness, and because of the excruciating pain it causes her, she cannot see what lies beneath the tough exterior of the gambling partner. She sees him as fearless. But he is anything but fearless. Underneath his facade lies a sensitive, wounded human being; a man who has felt inadequate, unloved, unimportant, and impotent all his life; a man who has yearned to hear that he matters and that he doesn't have to measure up to another to be accepted.

Since a compulsive gambler is not fearless, what exactly does he fear? Having lived all his life feeling inadequate, he fears criticism. Having low self-esteem, he fears rejection. Having no self-confidence, he fears making wrong decisions. Having lived with impotence, he fears conflict. But his greatest fear of all is fear of intimacy—a totally foreign state to the compulsive gambler. More than likely, he has never experienced intimacy; he has no idea what it is. And when he senses he is getting too close to another, he pulls away. Pulling away is something that the compulsive gambler is used to, and isolating is something he has done all his life. That feels comfortable; that he can deal with.

The couple, then, live in painful isolation from each other. Both feel ashamed, guilty, fearful, and overwhelmed—hardly the dream they had envisioned when they fell in love.

Facts on File

As long as the compulsive gambler remains active, the disease will continue to whisper in his ear: *One more big win and you're home free.*

Many believe they can't be compulsive gamblers because their only indulgence is playing bingo or buying lottery tickets.

The rate of suicide attempts among compulsive gamblers is six times the national average—the highest among all those with mental illnesses.

Partners of compulsive gamblers will soon find that their arguments center on money, the gambling, and behaviors related to the gambling.

Most partners of compulsive gamblers describe their partners as compulsive liars.

Questions

Gambler:

- Do you lie to avoid family gatherings so that you can be free to gamble?
- Have you ever missed a significant event in your life or the life of a loved one because you were "on a roll" or chasing your losses and could not leave?

Partner:

- Do you avoid discussing financial problems with your partner to avoid his reactions?
- Have you cosigned loans to relieve your debts?
- Have you signed blank income tax forms enabling him to keep you in the dark about your family's financial situation?

3

The Afflicted

MOST COMPULSIVE GAMBLERS began gambling during adolescence. Many, but not all, were raised in families that lacked closeness and failed to nurture them adequately. Some claim they had fathers who were never there for them. Others state that their mothers were overprotective and never allowed them to do things their friends could do. Still others never knew why they felt so alone and unaccepted. But why did they turn to gambling? What did gambling—a leisure activity—have to do with these unmet childhood needs? And what about the compulsive gamblers who did not experience unsatisfactory early years? Why did *they* begin gambling compulsively?

Compulsive gambling is devastating. By the time the afflicted hits bottom, he is most likely in great financial debt and in poor physical health, feeling mentally incompetent and emotionally wiped out. Although his love of gambling has done a lot *for* him over the years, what matters in the end is what it has done *to* him.

Perhaps a better understanding will come about by sharing the experiences of some recovering compulsive gamblers.

SEARCHING FOR ACCEPTANCE

Eric's Story—In the Beginning

"Before I began gambling in my teens, I was very unhappy. My mother was extremely controlling, and my father did nothing but put me down. In my family, I never felt I mattered. My feelings were negated so often, I finally questioned every emotion I had until I became so confused, I just stopped feeling altogether.

"My mother's nagging made me feel so inadequate. I had absolutely no self-confidence. I was afraid to try out for any sports for fear I wouldn't be chosen, and I just couldn't stand the pain. My father was very disappointed that I didn't get involved in sports. He took every opportunity to let me know how worthless I was as a son. He was forever telling me how well some of my cousins were doing in their sports and how proud their fathers were of them. The longer this went on, the more my self-esteem plummeted. I was so hurt and angry at him, I was determined never to get involved in anything that would make him happy. Everything he said to me made me feel more and more like a worthless human being, and I hated him for it.

"I was a shy kid, but no one would have ever guessed it. I covered up my shyness by acting like a leader. But inside I knew I could never lead anyone. I couldn't even lead myself.

"When I was thirteen, I was introduced to poker by four older boys who wanted a fifth player to join their game. I loved it from the beginning. Every time I sat down to play with them, I felt accepted.

"A little more than a year after I started to play, I had my first big win. That big win netted me almost two hundred dollars. I felt great when I returned to school the next day and my poker buddies were telling everyone how I had wiped them out. I got more attention from my schoolmates than you can imagine. After school I invited several of them to the pizza parlor and bought them pizza and Cokes.

"Maybe nobody can understand this, but that was the first truly happy day of my life. The only joyless part of it was I couldn't tell my parents, because if I did, they would have taken the money away from me, and with it would have gone my self-esteem and my newfound friends. I knew I would never let anyone or anything come between me and my gambling. Gambling made me happy."

Eric's Story—In the End

"What did my gambling do *for* me? In the beginning, it certainly made me happy. Why wouldn't it? My father had hammered my self-esteem into the ground. Perhaps his goal had been to make me a mature, independent, responsible human being. If so, I never attained it.

"The only relief I ever got from my deficient feelings was at the poker table. In the beginning years, I won often, so I came to feel special. I had big dreams of becoming rich by gambling. I would use my winnings to make others happy. Whenever I was out with friends, I would insist on picking up the bill. Anyone who knew me during those years would have only positive things to say about me.

"As a child, I was always starved for love, and I learned to fill the emptiness by living more in dreamland than reality. I imagined myself in situations where I felt loved and appreciated. But as I got older, particularly in my teens, my childhood dreams no longer satisfied my needs. As a young adult, I needed the love and acceptance of my family, but I also needed the love and acceptance of my friends. When I started to gamble and became good at it, I found what would fill my new needs. Gambling and winning made it possible for me to buy the friends I needed. That's what gambling did for me, and I thrived on it.

"For me, a more important question is: What did gambling do *to* me?

"As the years passed and my gambling increased, I lost my ability to concentrate, to remember, and to make intelligent decisions. Gambling destroyed my mental capabilities.

"It also destroyed me physically. My blood pressure has been high for over ten years. My cholesterol is beyond borderline, and my stomach ulcers have brought me under the surgeon's knife three times in the last seven years.

"Gambling has cost me six good jobs and has landed me in my present position, which is well below my capabilities, education, and intelligence.

"Gambling not only caused me to behave unethically but also to betray my highest personal values. I have become a thief and a pathological liar.

"Gambling brought me to stand before a state supreme court judge, where I was charged with embezzling eighty-seven thousand dollars from my last employer.

"Gambling caused me to reject, ignore, and quit caring about my wife and my children.

"Gambling cost me any kind of peace of mind.

"What did gambling do *to* me? It made me just like my father. And it enabled me to attain my goal of never doing anything that would make the father I despised happy."

LIVING OUT THE PATTERN

Addictions are repeated in families. If a parent suffers from an addiction, the probability that the children will acquire the same addiction is much greater than if neither parent were afflicted. Whether the reason for this is nature or nurture, or a combination of the two, is uncertain.

Stuart's Story—In the Beginning

"I was born a gambler. My father was a compulsive gambler, and he taught me to gamble long before I started kindergarten. The only games we played were games of chance. I became my father's most devoted fan. I looked up to him the first ten years of my life. He was fun, exciting, active, and always doing something new and daring. I felt privileged when he would allow me to accompany him to the track or to off-track betting parlors. He taught me to read a scratch sheet. He used to have me call him at work after I got home from school to give him the results of the P.M. races. I knew Dad looked forward to my calls, and I would be especially excited if I was calling to tell him he had won. Often he gave me extra money when he had it, and boy, did I love that!

"My first gambling experience with others was pitching pennies after school with two kids in the fourth grade. I had already been pitching pennies for over three years, so I was pretty good at it. I couldn't wait for my father to get home from work so I could share my good luck with him. He always listened to me when the conversation was about gambling.

"To me, gambling meant having a father who would talk to me, care about me, and be interested in what I had to say. I could always get his attention if I had a gambling experience to share.

"By the time I was in junior high school, my father's gambling had gotten way out of hand. He and my mother were fighting all the time. We never had any money, she couldn't pay the bills, and we were getting endless phone calls from banks, department stores, and loan companies. It got so bad at times that we had to walk more than two miles to my grandparents' house to get food. Those visits were never pleasant. We would have to listen to Grandpa pressure Mom to leave Dad because of his gambling. That always scared me.

"Shortly after my sixteenth birthday, I realized just how angry I was with my father. He had become so consumed by his gambling that we hardly ever talked. Our common interest and the fun we used to have sharing it had long since gone. It's ironic, because at that time, my gambling was going just great. I was winning much more than I was losing, I had a great reputation with my friends, and I felt great.

"At that point in my life, the one thing I knew for sure was that I would never let my gambling control me like it controlled my father. I was too smart to let that happen."

Stuart's Story—In the End

"What did gambling do *for* me? It brought me closer to my father, because it was a common interest. In addition, I got a great deal of excitement from gambling. I was always the kind of kid who could not stand boredom. I wanted to live 'on the edge,' and gambling let me do that. I could never feel bored while sitting on a bet that was made with money badly needed for living expenses, or, better yet, with money that belonged to someone else.

"When I gambled during my teens, I found out that I could ignore things that others were concerned about—taking tests, getting a job, having money to buy a car, or getting a date for high school dances. My main concern during that time was simply where to raise the money I needed to be in action the following day. Action was my only interest. I could get a date anytime—that wasn't a problem. But I didn't want a date, because no girl ever made me feel the way I did when I won big.

"Winning big made me feel important, strong, powerful, and potent. I was raised by a macho father, and I guess I adopted his attitudes. My first twelve years of gambling kept my self-esteem high. Everyone knew I had a great deal of self-confidence. They could see it in my face and hear it in my voice. I feared no one. Gambling, with its occasional big wins, made me feel like a man.

"That's what gambling did *for* me, and it would have been nice if that would have continued; however, I was much more affected by what gambling did *to* me.

"Gambling prevented me from learning how to socialize. When my friends were beginning to interact with the opposite sex, I was at the track. While my friends were dating, I was out trying to raise the money I needed to be in action. My nineteenth birthday came and went, and I had never even had a single date. By the time I was twenty-one, I couldn't get up the nerve to ask a girl for a date. I just kept gambling and put the whole idea of dating out of my mind. The few friends I had started pairing off, marrying, and moving away. I pretended not to care. As long as I could be with the horses, I cared about little else.

"Gambling prevented me from getting interested in any hobby or craft. I had no special talents. I couldn't play tennis or golf, and I could barely swim. During my teen years, I devoted all my time and energy to my one love.

"Eventually, as my gambling progressed, it took hold of me completely. No matter what was going on in my life, I had to gamble. I became the world's greatest liar. I had to lie to so many people to get the money I needed to pay debts or to gamble. I ignored my family and the people I cared about. No one could count on me ever showing up for an important occasion, because I would only go if it didn't interfere with my going to the track. Whenever I was invited anywhere, I would always answer yes, because I never cared about what I said. My only concern was that my answer make the other person happy. That prevented me from being pressured.

"I was whatever anyone wanted me to be. I would promise anyone the world if it would get them off my back. My daily goal was to avoid conflict so I could be free to put my energy elsewhere.

"I let everybody down. No one could trust me. No one would confide in me. In the end, no one needed me.

"What did gambling do *to* me? It controlled me just like it had controlled my father, even though I had been so sure I was too smart to let that happen."

BIDDING FOR ACCEPTANCE

Not every gambler devotes his life to gambling because he wants to punish a parent who didn't meet his needs or who squelched his self-esteem, or because it was the main activity in his family of origin. In some cases, gaining acceptance and status among peers may be the motivation.

Dan's Story—In the Beginning

"I was a spoiled brat. My dad was a very successful businessman and well-respected in the community. Despite his busy schedule, he always attended my school activities. He encouraged me to do the things that interested me.

He tried to motivate me in anything he saw as a plus in my life, and he often praised me in front of others. I was an only child, and I truly felt he was proud of me.

"My mother wrote children's stories (one was made into a movie). Since she wrote at home, she was always there for me. Sometimes I felt she was too focused on me and overprotective, but even at an early age, I knew that she always had my best interests at heart.

"If compulsive gamblers need parents to blame for their addiction, I am out in the cold. I loved and respected my parents more than any kid I knew. They did everything they could possibly do to show me their love.

"Gambling was part of my family's lifestyle, and it was never a problem. Both my parents loved to visit the casinos a couple of times a year, and they'd have dinner at the racetrack every few months. It was one of their leisure activities, among many others: opera, theater, tennis, golf, traveling, and socializing at the country club.

"My dad thought of gambling as a manly activity, so he didn't discourage me from an occasional wager on my favorite games, even at a young age. As a matter of fact, he often wagered with me. I enjoyed that because it gave us a common interest.

"I started to gamble without my parents' knowledge when I was in the ninth grade. I was fifteen years old and the smallest kid in the class. Although I loved sports, I never tried out because of my size. I did the only thing I could think of to get involved with sports: I became the high school bookie. I ran the pools for the weekend games. While I was managing the money and keeping books, I started to wager heavily myself. I didn't wager because I needed money (my parents were always generous with me). I wagered heavily to show off in front of my school friends. I wanted them to see me as a risk taker, not a wimp. I felt that some of my classmates looked down on me because I was short and slight. They never really said anything derogatory, but they were somewhat sarcastic, and I felt hurt. I needed their acceptance. I did not want to feel different.

"At any rate, I found out very quickly that gambling was one way I could get what I needed. My reputation as a successful sports bettor spread fast and stuck with me throughout high school.

"Gambling afforded me something my parents could not buy: the acceptance and respect of my schoolmates. I loved it."

Dan's Story—In the End

"Gambling made me believe that all the things my parents said about me were true—that I was bright, creative, and intelligent. Before gambling, I never believed in myself because I never felt accepted by my classmates. I always felt like an outsider.

"My first big win proved to me I could be popular. I fooled myself into thinking the kids liked me, when I now know they liked my money and my generosity. Before I started winning, I was never invited to join the others at school activities. Because of my size, I couldn't get a date. I stopped asking girls to go out with me by the time I was a junior in high school. However, in my senior year, I had a number of girlfriends because I could afford to take them wherever they wanted to go.

"Gambling and winning allowed me to grow approximately six inches in the eyes of others. It made me feel six feet tall.

"Today I know it is more important for me to remember what gambling did *to* me and not *for* me.

"By the time I had graduated from college, I had few coping skills. I was irresponsible, very immature, and totally consumed by my gambling. The amounts I was betting and the frequency of my gambling caused many problems. The more problems I had, the more I gambled; and the more I gambled, the more problems I had.

"My parents bailed me out over and over again to the tune of over thirty thousand dollars. Each time they came to my rescue, I promised them, often with my tears, that if they helped me I would never gamble again. I would have promised them anything, as long as it got me whatever I needed to remain in action.

"Gambling made me so incredibly selfish, I felt resentful on the night our American prisoners of war were returning from Vietnam because I had to miss the football games that the news coverage preempted.

"Gambling made me hate any family occasion when it was necessary to give a gift, because I wanted to spend my money on nothing but gambling.

"Gambling made me make a new friend only if I thought he would be good for a touch when I was in need of money.

"Gambling made it so that the only time I ever felt emotionally comfortable was when I was in action.

"Gambling convinced me that my problem was money and that one more big win would solve everything.

"What did gambling do *to* me? It removed all the positive characteristics my parents worked so hard to foster within me, and it destroyed them emotionally. I knew that when they first realized my gambling was a serious problem, they blamed themselves. I used my knowledge of their guilt to manipulate them. They raised me in hopes I would adopt their most precious values, but I ignored every one of them. I didn't care about their values; I didn't care about their feelings; I didn't care about anything but being in action. I cursed them, blamed them, stole from them, and, in the end, I attacked them physically because they refused to give me the money I needed to pay gambling debts in order to keep my credit with my loan shark.

"What did gambling do *to* me? It resulted in losing the people most dear to me, my parents—the two people who would have died for me, the two people who gave me their hearts. I took those hearts and broke them."

WINNING OVER DAD

Because many compulsive gamblers describe their fathers as cold and distant, and because many of those fathers are workaholics who have been successful in their careers, some compulsive gamblers seem to set out to prove they can be just as successful in a shorter period of time by the turn of a card or the roll of the dice.

Matt's Story—In the Beginning

"My father was hardly ever home, and when he was there physically, he was absent emotionally. His whole life was his business. He lived, breathed, and ate the business. It was a constant topic of conversation around the dinner table. Because my mother did his books, she too was devoted to his business. I don't think they ever had a husband-wife relationship. I know I never had a parent-child one.

"I hated the long hours my father worked. I wanted him to be like my friends' fathers, to come to my games, talk to me, care about me, and guide me in matters I felt were important. I never knew what his expectations of me were because I couldn't tell what he was thinking.

"Dad's income afforded many comforts, but he never had the time to share them with us. What bothered me most was that it never bothered him. He never seemed to need me. Never! My greatest resentment in my young years was Dad's business. It was his mistress and his child. While I could never compete with it, I thought I could find a way to prove to him how wrong he was to devote his whole life to obtaining material things that he had no time to enjoy.

"For many years, I believed gambling was the answer I was looking for. I had my first big win during my second year in college. School was less than a mile from a racetrack, and I went there almost daily. One day, when I walked away with a purse of over three thousand on an eighty-dollar wager, I knew I had found the answer.

"I had several big wins during that year, each of which made me feel I was going to be able to accomplish what I had set out to do—prove to Dad I could make more money than he and not have to spend my whole life working for it. I had a very real need to prove him wrong, and I came to believe gambling was the means to satisfy that need."

Matt's Story—In the End

"What did gambling do *for* me? It made me feel like a man. All my life my father led me to believe there was only one way to prove you are a man, and that was work, work, work. I felt I had only one parent.

"But the sense of abandonment I felt because of my workaholic father's absence during my childhood resulted in my looking for a way to be as successful as he without devoting all my time and energy to a job. When I started gambling and winning, I believed I had found the answer.

"I had so much resentment for his business—I hated it—and the one thing I never wanted to do was to work in it. However, when I graduated from college, I realized the only job that would afford me the money I needed to continue to gamble the way I wanted to was with my father. He always wanted me to get involved with his business, but until that time I was very resistant. When I approached him for a job, he agreed to the salary I requested on the condition that I promise to stop gambling. Of course, I promised.

"Naturally, I lied, and in time his business and my gambling became terribly enmeshed. I was stealing time and money from work in order to gamble. My father was completely unaware. The few employees who knew what I was doing kept quiet because I was the boss's son.

"After working for my father for three years and successfully keeping him in the dark about my 'love,' I approached him and urged him to put me in sales. I needed this position badly because it would afford me the two things I needed most: free time and large commissions. I knew that as long as I produced, my father would not question my absences from the office. Those absences gave me more time to gamble.

"Shortly after I entered sales, my father had a severe heart attack and had to cut back the number of hours he could devote to his work. Because he believed I was clean from gambling, he allowed me to become more involved in the decision-making end of his business. This pleased me very much for only one reason: I could make even more money available for my passion.

"My gambling got completely out of control. I manipulated my father's employees, his customers, and his books to get the money I needed to chase my losses. I took risks I never would have taken if my decisions weren't controlled by my need to be in action. At that point, action was my only concern. Mentally I was nonfunctional, physically I was a mess, emotionally I was numb, financially I was in great debt, and spiritually I was dead. I had the gambling fever, and at the time, I knew of no antidote.

"Eventually I stole so much money from the business, cheated so many of his customers, and restructured so many of his accounts that his business failed. He went bankrupt. He had a stroke and died. I haven't seen my mother or spoken to her in more than a decade. I know I'll never have her back in my life.

"What did my gambling do *to* me? It killed the one person I longed for in my life. I competed for his attention, acted out to obtain his notice, and gambled to obtain enough money for his acceptance. I gambled for my father. But my gambling stole from me the love I most desired."

Facts on File

Many believe they can't be a compulsive gambler because their only involvement is playing bingo or purchasing lottery tickets.

The one thing that most separates compulsive gamblers from recreational gamblers is that compulsive gamblers chase their losses.

As the illness progresses, the compulsive gambler will steal from others and eventually turn to illegal money lenders to obtain money to gamble or to pay gambling debts.

In the end, most compulsive gamblers will violate most of their previous life values in order to stay in action.

Questions

Gambler:

- Have you arranged to have your mail sent to your place of business or a P.O. box in order to prevent your spouse from finding out the extent of your debts?
- Have you ever considered suicide as a way out from all your gambling problems?

Partner:

- Have you started to nag your partner because, even though his income has increased, you have less and less money to feed and clothe your family?
- Have you begun searching your husband's pockets or wallet in order to find out if he has gambled or if he is hiding money from you?

4

The Affected

FOR THE PARTNER OF A COMPULSIVE GAMBLER, the battle over money is endless. When paying household bills, the partner is continually trying to convince the compulsive gambler to see that each creditor gets paid, at least a little. But the gambler rarely cooperates. Despite all the partner's efforts, they are always behind. She has already allowed her self-confidence to become eroded by the gambler's frequent cutting, demeaning comments. She doesn't know that she is fighting an addiction and that she can do nothing to control it. No matter how good she is at managing money, there will never be enough to feed his habit.

THE DOWNWARD SPIRAL

What makes it difficult for the partner of a compulsive gambler is that things were different in the beginning. His gambling was acceptable. In fact, she may have joined in or encouraged it.

However, what was once a pleasure and even a source of optimism eventually leads to disillusionment and devastation. Her self-esteem is deeply scarred, the family finances are out of control, and she is exhausted. Yet she tries over and over to confront, to coax, to compromise with the gambler—desperately wanting to make things turn out all right. But she always loses.

Alice's Story—In the Beginning

"My dad was a couch potato, spending every spare moment staring at the TV screen. I know he loved me and would give me anything I asked for, but

I could never get him to pay attention to any of my interests. All through high school, he never came to one of my tennis matches. He knew how much I loved the game and how hard I practiced, but no matter how many times I asked him to come, he always had an excuse.

"I believed Father was lazy because he never wanted to do anything outside the house. Mom often complained because he wouldn't go shopping with her, not for household needs, his own clothing, or family gifts. All he ever wanted to do was stay at home and watch TV or read. He used to say he liked being home. He didn't have any friends; maybe they got tired of trying to get him to join them in things they liked to do. But I needed him and wanted him in my life. He always refused.

"By contrast, my husband was full of energy, active in sports, and very competitive—at least when I first met him. Sports were Peter's life. We were a perfect match, because there was nothing under the sun I enjoyed more than being active.

"Peter played baseball all through high school and college. In his senior year, he was offered a position on one of the American League's farm teams, but he turned it down because I was pregnant, and we were getting married.

"Fortunately, he got a job with a very good starting salary just before the baby arrived. We were young, but we were very much in love and happy. He continued to be involved in baseball, playing with a local bar team, and I was always there to watch him.

"Betting on the games was something he never used to do. I can't even remember how it started, but I do know I never objected. I had no reason to. If anything, it added excitement to the game. I learned to love baseball as much as he did. When our first son was born, I remember thinking how wonderful it was going to be that Peter would still be able to enjoy the sport through his son's involvement with it, even when he himself would be too old to play.

"For a long time, Peter was the captain of his softball team. He was the one who took all the bets and made the payoff at the end of each game. No one was more respected, trusted, or liked.

"For at least the first ten years we were together, gambling was very much a part of our lives. It never caused a single problem, and I never breathed a word of opposition. It was just something we did on a regular basis along with most of the other players on the team. In the beginning, gambling was synonymous with fun."

Alice's Story—In the End

"The fun of gambling came to an end about the time our son entered junior high school. My husband's drinking increased with his gambling. It soon seemed to me that Peter was spending more of his free time in the bar, where he would place bets and then watch the games on which he'd wagered.

"Many times he would come home drunk and abusive. If he was drunk and had lost money, he would often become violent. At first he took out his anger on our belongings, then he got rough with me. As crazy as it may seem, I defended him to the children when they got angry at him for abusing me. Our children were very bright; they could see their father's anger was coming from the alcohol in him and from the fact that he lost money gambling.

"The friends we had during the early years together were no longer around. When they saw Peter's pursuit of gambling moving beyond their degree of interest, they backed away. He was very angry when they did that. He called them wimps.

"One time I threatened to leave Peter if he didn't stop gambling, because we couldn't pay our bills and our children were lacking necessities; I lacked everything. But I never left; instead, I got a part-time job. I wanted to pay off some of the bills, but the money I made wasn't enough, so in less than four months, I was working full time. It didn't take me long to realize my working did only one thing—it gave him an opportunity to gamble more because I began taking on the responsibility of paying most of our family's expenses. I hardly even noticed it happening. Peter was so manipulative and controlling; he got me to do that in no time at all. He even got me to feel that his gambling was my fault. I knew that was not true, but somehow I believed him.

"A little more than a year after I began working, we were overdrawn on our credit cards, two months behind in our rent, and haunted by creditors. When I sat my husband down and seriously threatened to leave, he broke down and cried. He begged me to stay. When I told him I saw no way out, he asked me to go to my parents and ask them to take out a home-equity loan so we could get ourselves debt-free and begin all over again. He seemed so scared; I was convinced he meant what he was saying. I also felt so sorry for him. I'd never seen him cry before, and despite all our troubles, I still loved him.

"When my parents agreed to help us, I was greatly relieved. Peter agreed to let me handle the family budget, and we began repaying my parents immediately. For the next four months, things improved greatly. I was beginning to feel like we were starting anew. The children were happy to have their father back in their lives. The only disappointment was that Peter did not stop drinking. The difference was that now he drank at home instead of at the bar. As crazy as it may sound, I even accepted that because I believed that if he stopped gambling, everything would get better. In my mind, gambling—not drinking—was destroying our lives.

"How wrong I was. As the months passed, Peter's drinking worsened. He was drunk almost every night. When he was like that, all he would talk about was how I made him give up his only pleasure—gambling—how I exaggerated the consequences of his gambling, and how I was to blame for all our debts because I was always buying things for our home and our family. His anger often frightened me, but I continued to believe it was easier to live with his anger than his gambling.

"Sometime during those months Peter returned to gambling. Unbeknownst to me, he had taken out another loan from his credit union. And he began to borrow money from two loan sharks as well. I found out about both loans on the same day. An unknown man on the phone told me that, if he didn't receive twenty-seven hundred dollars within twenty-four hours, he would have my husband's legs broken. I was petrified. And then the thought of him having returned to gambling enraged me. He had begged me to convince my parents to go into debt to help him, and then he turned around and gambled again.

"How could he borrow more money when we were so in debt? How could I ever face my parents? How could I stay with my husband? On the other hand, what choices did I have? I wasn't earning enough money to support myself and my children. I could see no options.

"I decided I would not go to my parents and tell them Peter was gambling again. I couldn't do that to them. I began to think seriously about his gambling being my fault. The more I thought about it, the more I believed it. His gambling was not a problem when he lived at home with his parents, nor when he had his own apartment and lived alone. It worsened after we married and especially after I left my job to stay home with our children. At the time, he had agreed to that, but I could see how that put more of the financial burden on his shoulders.

"In some ways, Peter's only relaxation was to wager on some of his favorite football and baseball teams. I decided that maybe we could work it out so that he would limit his gambling, and we could still afford the necessities. That way he could have his relaxation. To make this feasible, I would get a part-time job in addition to my full-time one. Our children could fend for themselves while I was at work.

"Peter bought this plan. He promised to stick to it and everything would be back to normal. He was right. Everything did get back to normal, considering that 'normal' in our home was chaos, tension, and financial problems. My well-meaning plan changed nothing except that now I was working two jobs and our son was beginning to get into trouble in school. That started when he cut gym because he didn't have the proper sneakers to play basketball. He was angry at me for not fixing our family's problems. He thought that it was my responsibility as a mother to make his father stop gambling.

"Our family relationships continued to deteriorate. My son was suspended from school for a week for coming to school drunk one morning. He was fifteen years old, a sophomore. My daughter never had money to go out with friends, so she spent more of her free hours in front of the television. Her friends stopped calling her because her response to their invitations was always no.

"Today, Peter's gambling is synonymous with pain and loneliness for me."

LIVING ON THE EDGE

Some people view compulsive gamblers as men who rule their wives and their families with an iron hand. They see compulsive gamblers as strong, assertive risk takers who fear no one. Others see them as energetic, competitive, immature, irresponsible, and emotionally stunted. But compulsive gamblers do not fit any one profile. One thing is certain: Gambling eventually changes them into isolated, desperate men. At first, though, the changes they experience are positive, and their partners are usually happy for them.

In time, however, these partners who live with the gamblers' repeated lying and secretiveness are constantly on edge—wondering, guessing, and scared. Sometimes compulsive gamblers are so skillful at deception that their wives never suspect the truth: Their love for gambling has gone from a hobby to a costly obsession.

Sadie's Story—In the Beginning

"Do you have any idea what it is like to be married to a man for forty-five years and then, after the two of you retire, find you are living with a stranger? That's what happened to me.

"When Harold retired, he left behind a life of corporate meetings, instant decisions, luxurious business trips, and dinners with the jet set. In a period of one day, he went from a highly respected chief executive officer of a large corporation to a retiree without an identity or a purpose in life.

"The first few months weren't so bad. He seemed to enjoy relaxing and catching up on his reading.

"But less than six months after he retired, he had regained the energy he'd lost to the long transition period, and he didn't know what to do with it. It became apparent that we had planned well for our retirement years in all areas but one—how to fill his empty hours. In no time at all, I found him underfoot and didn't know what to do. He started to criticize how I did my housework. At first I tried to listen and pretend I was interested. But then I got fed up. I began to resent the fact that he thought he could manage our home better than I. When he tried to change my daily routine, I got angry and let him know it. I suggested he develop a new interest, but no matter what I suggested—from learning to fish to working with the committee that managed our condominium—he said no.

"Before retirement, I had no idea what a tough transition it would be for Harold to go from CEO to retiree. It took us many months to agree on who should be responsible for what in our home. Because he had always been a fussy eater and because he was accustomed to eating in expensive restaurants, he chose to do the food shopping. This seemed to work out well. He would take the time to shop in specialty stores for certain foods. That got him out from under my feet and let me do my housework and spend some time alone. Time alone was something I always treasured, and with his retirement, I was losing it.

"About a year into retirement, a new shopping mall opened a mile from where we lived. In the mall was an off-track betting (OTB) parlor. One day, a neighbor invited my husband to join him. Harold found it fascinating. He was very impressed with how much our neighbor knew about the horses and jockeys, and he began reading up on the sport himself. He studied the history of the sport and how the horses are trained. It was a great distraction. He loved it. I loved it.

"Once he started going to OTB, his mood picked up, and he seemed happy and involved. We argued less, I had more alone time, and peace seemed to return to my life. In the beginning, my husband's gambling solved my problem and made me happy."

Sadie's Story—In the End

"If my husband were an alcoholic, I wouldn't have seen more drastic personality changes than the gambling caused. Harold was a self-confident, intelligent, and pleasant person, but he became a self-centered, high-strung, distant, moody old man.

"Our early retirement years were painful because of his gambling. He became 'schizophrenic' about money. On the one hand, he was tight with every penny and on my back about every purchase I made. On the other hand, money meant nothing to him when we were out with friends. He always insisted on picking up the dinner bill and leaving a large tip. In the presence of others, he was most generous.

"What at first seemed like a solution to our problem of adjusting to retirement turned out to be a curse. My husband's love of off-track betting almost destroyed his life and mine. His brief stops at the OTB parlor each day grew into long visits. I used to ask him why he had to spend so much time there if he was only gambling ten dollars daily. He would say that he'd made friends at the place, and that they'd just hang out and talk over the races scheduled for the following day. That all made sense to me, yet a small part of me felt anxious, and I didn't know why.

"As time passed, Harold began objecting to our socializing and to any occasion that required the giving of a gift. One year, in early December, he started to nag me about how much money I planned to spend on our four grandchildren for Christmas. But when I got on his case about his gambling, he backed off.

"The thing that made me suspicious was his behavior one spring when our son, the father of our only granddaughter, came to visit. Harold was extremely fond of this five-year-old. She was our youngest grandchild. During that particular visit, he was irritable, so much so that our son cut short his visit by two days. When my son returned home, he called me to express concern about his father's health. He believed his father had to be ill to act so negatively during their visit. The tip-off was when he put off his granddaughter's plea to take her to the pool and play with her. He answered her in such a way that she ran to her mother in tears. That was definitely not my husband. He would never do anything to hurt his favorite grandchild.

"Because I was in denial about the fact that the changes taking place in Harold meant he had a serious problem, I defended him to my son. That irritated my son, and he hung up.

"One morning soon after that event, Harold was still at home at noon. He seemed a little strange, yet I tried to ignore the fact that he was breaking his normal pattern, which was to be at the OTB parlor when it opened. Just after lunch, he suddenly ran out of the house. I looked out the window and saw him approach the mailman. They spoke a few words, then my husband took something from him, got in his car, and drove away. When the mailman came to the house, he handed me the mail minus a Social Security check. I said nothing, but my heart started to pound. I was overwhelmed with fear.

"When Harold returned home, I confronted him about what had happened. He started to lie, and I knew it immediately. He had never lied to me before. I confronted him further and he began yelling, became defensive, and blamed me for any problems we were having. He told me his gambling certainly was not a problem and that if I wanted to know what was wrong with our lives, I should begin to look at myself. He stormed out of the house.

"I was devastated. Confusion, hurt, frustration, and anger began to consume me. I could not understand how he could blame me. I could think of nothing I had done that would warrant him gambling our money away. I had to search for answers.

"My snooping revealed that a little more than half our life savings of $1,340,000 was missing from our investment accounts. My phone calls confirmed that my husband had been withdrawing about four thousand dollars a week from several accounts. I didn't know what to do. I felt heart palpitations and pressure in my chest. I feared a heart attack. For some crazy reason, I truly believed at that moment that I was to blame for his gambling.

"I began to look at myself and to what I could do to make things right before we lost everything. When I asked my husband what it was I was doing that was causing him to gamble so much, he said, 'Everything.' His anger was ever present, and I knew that was the result of my confronting him in the first place. I started to change my behavior. I tried to be especially nice to him. I tried to work harder around the house. I tried being more loving to him. But nothing worked. He became more accusatory and I more resentful. In addition to feeling hurt and guilty, I began to feel completely inadequate.

"Despite all this, I told my sons nothing. I was too ashamed to let them know I was causing their father to gamble so heavily that we would soon lose everything.

"My relationship with Harold is worse than it has ever been in over forty years. We do not communicate at all anymore. His gambling continues, and my pain grows day by day.

"I can foresee that we will soon be penniless, and I am powerless to prevent it. His gambling makes me feel angry, hurt, lonely, and hopeless. I wish I knew what I could do to stop him from gambling."

KEEPING SECRETS AND HIDING SHAME

In some cultures, gambling is as much a family function as going on a picnic. For some couples, gambling is something the men do after every family get-together, while the women clean up and do the dishes. It's automatic. Sitting down and playing cards just naturally follows dessert.

A young man raised in this culture not only learns to play cards at an early age; he views this activity as a means of getting together with other men to talk, relax, and share camaraderie. He comes to realize that being good at cards earns him respect and acceptance from other men in his family. It also may win him a welcome into his partner's family. This pleases her greatly as well.

However, if the gambler's gambling becomes obsessive, his partner will experience a great deal of shame. She too will become secretive in order to hide what is happening from her family, who she knows would never understand. By choosing this option, she may stave off their criticism and judgment, but she also loses her all-important emotional support system.

Stella's Story—In the Beginning

"One of the most comfortable things about my marriage was that we were both raised in the same culture. Many of the foods I already knew how to cook were exactly the foods Ivan liked best. We celebrated the same holidays and shared the same religion. Our parents shared our commonalities.

"There is a great deal to be said for people marrying within their culture. Life is so comfortable. We all understand each other and boundaries between generations are clear. The elders are respected and esteemed.

"My grandfather was raised in Europe by strict parents. They instilled in him a work ethic that they believed would bring him happiness and admiration. He in turn passed that value down to my father, and my father to my brothers. To be accepted in my family, you had to meet my grandfather's expectations. Although he was quiet and terse, everyone respected him and wanted his approval.

"When I married, there was nothing I wanted more than for my husband to be accepted by my family, especially my grandfather.

"One of the things my grandfather, father, and brothers loved to do was play cards after family dinners. Because Ivan did likewise in his family, and because he too loved cards, he was a good match for my family. I was so proud that my husband fit in so well with the other men in my life.

"My grandfather took his card games seriously. Perhaps he related a man's talents at cards to how a man lives. On many occasions, Grandpa would hug my husband and kiss him on both cheeks after my husband beat him at his own game. Without a doubt, Ivan's skill earned him much respect from my family.

"I always enjoyed these frequent after-dinner card games. It was important to me that the man I married fit in with my family, and nowhere did I feel this more deeply than when all sat around the card table talking, laughing, and, on occasion, playfully slapping each other on the cheek. In the beginning Ivan's gambling bonded him to my family, and that made me very happy!"

Stella's Story—In the End

"From my perspective, traditions are sacred; they ought not be broken. They bind families together, and to abuse them is equivalent to rejecting your family. The large gatherings my husband and I had with my family were held often. There was nothing going on in any of our families that each of us didn't know about. There were no family secrets; secrets were never part of our tradition. Even though the elders had been in this country for many years, they still encouraged and supported the idea of the extended family. If one of our children had a problem and the parent wasn't nearby, the child would share the situation with an aunt, an uncle, or a grandparent. In many cases, the child would share it with an older cousin. Closeness was the mainstay of our lives.

"That was true until Ivan began playing cards with his friends and raised the amount of money he wagered each week. His friends took card playing much more seriously than my family. They saw it as more of a challenge than fun. For me, it had become something to be leery about. I was afraid that Ivan's gambling was getting out of hand, so I approached him and expressed that fear. He was supportive and reassured me that he would never let that happen. He said he knew two guys on his job who lost everything because of gambling. He calmed me down and told me not to worry about it.

"I didn't share my concern with my family because I didn't want to involve them. It was the first time I had deliberately kept something from them. That fact alone made me uncomfortable in their presence.

"My family didn't seem to notice the change in Ivan's attitude when they played cards together, but I couldn't help noticing. He would be irritated if they dealt the cards too slowly, or if they talked while playing (something they always did), or if they even left the table during a hand.

"I began to dread going to family dinners, because I knew it was only a matter of time until someone would notice and comment on what was happening. I didn't want to have to deal with that. Of course, if my father or brothers saw some discontent in my husband, it would automatically be my fault. That's the way the men in my family are.

"As much as I tried to discourage our joining the family gatherings, my family wouldn't hear of it. Actually, Ivan wanted to avoid them, too; he felt their gambling didn't offer enough challenge for him. He wanted only to gamble with 'the boys,' because they didn't shy away from 'man-sized' wagering. Ivan never tried to keep his gambling from me, but he wouldn't dare allow me to criticize his 'hobby.' He said he had the right to spend his money any way he saw fit, and he saw fit to gamble it away.

"As the years passed, I felt trapped in a vise that grew tighter each passing day.

"The first time Ivan was confronted about the amount of time he was devoting to card playing was when our daughter was in her first school play. Her father never showed up, because he was on a 'roll' and wouldn't leave his game. My daughter was terribly hurt. She went to him and said she hated his card playing because it took him away from her. I don't know how he *felt* when she said that, but then I never knew how he felt about anything. He seemed to be void of human feelings. However, I know how he *reacted* to our daughter's plea: He went out and bought her a telephone for her room. That delighted her so much, she backed down and didn't mention his gambling again. It was so typical of Ivan—a gift to take the pressure off.

"Our family had become so abnormal that we had no choice but to grow apart. When we went to my parents' home, I could sense the difference between my family and my brothers' families. It was obvious we didn't communicate as openly and honestly as we once had.

"In time, as I knew would happen, my mother suggested that something wasn't right in my marriage. I lied and told her she couldn't be further from the truth. I blamed the strain she saw on the fact that Ivan was working two jobs to give us all that we needed and wanted. That reassured her, just as I was reassured when I confronted Ivan for the first time on his excessive card playing.

"As the children grew, my fears worsened and the gambling continued. The longer Ivan gambled, the worse his personality became. His conversations all centered on what a financial burden the children and I had become. His attitude was so bad that sometimes we were glad he didn't come home. It was so much more peaceful when he wasn't there. As much as I tried to hide our problem from my family, it was impossible.

"My brothers and I had always been close. One night when Ivan wasn't home, my oldest brother came over to talk to me about why it was that I seemed so sad all the time and why I was making more and more excuses not to come to family dinners. He caught me at a very vulnerable moment. I fell into his arms and told him everything. I showed him thousands of dollars of back bills that I couldn't pay because most of our income went to gambling. My brother was shocked. He could not believe Ivan would continue to gamble so heavily when his family was doing without so many necessities. He grew angry and wanted to wait for Ivan to return home. I knew I had to get my brother out of there, because if Ivan had suffered losses at the tables, he would come home in a most unpleasant mood.

"I should have known that as soon as I told my brother the truth, he would tell the rest of the family. He did. The following Sunday, my father and brothers came to my house and confronted Ivan. It was a painful scene. My husband threw them out. They wanted me and the children to go with them. When I refused, they left in anger.

"Immediately my husband turned to me and blamed me for the horrendous display that had taken place. He told me I was lucky he wasn't packing his bags and moving out. And you know something, I felt the same way. For some reason, he was always able to convince me that I was the cause of everything.

"My son left home at age eighteen. I see him occasionally away from the house because he won't take the chance of seeing his father. He claims he has no father because his dad was never there for him when he was growing up. My daughter, nineteen, lives with her boyfriend, who I think is an alcoholic. He is abusive to her. She tries to reassure me that many times he is good to her, better than her father ever was.

"I still live with my gambling husband. What can I do? I have tried everything to get him to stop gambling, but he says he has a right to gamble, and I guess that's true. He has supported me all these years, whenever he had the money. And besides, he never left me, even though I did cause him to gamble so heavily. Without a doubt, I feel I am as much to blame as he is."

BASING LIFE ON ILLUSION

Some addiction professionals say that compulsive gamblers pick partners who will fill their emotional need for someone who will take care of them, who will go to great lengths to make them happy. By the same token, isn't it possible that some partners of compulsive gamblers may also pick partners who will serve some deep personal need?

Mary Beth's Story—In the Beginning

"As the oldest of seven children, I never felt like I was a child. By the time my youngest brother was born, eight years after me, I felt I had been a parent for at least three years. Just about the time I started school, I was my mother's right-hand helper. By the time I was in second grade, there was nothing I couldn't do. I don't ever remember complaining, though. I just accepted things as they were.

"The only time I felt cheated was when I felt I was missing out on things that my friends did. As a junior in high school, I didn't want to miss dating. I especially didn't want to miss out on parties and dances. These I had to fight for, because when I turned fifteen, my mother developed kidney problems, and she wanted me to help her even more with my brothers and sisters.

"By working harder than ever, I got what I wanted. I didn't miss a single high school dance, nor did I miss a post-football-game party. For two years, I worked hard and I played hard. Two months after graduation, I married the first boy I had dated.

"My husband was popular, respected, athletic, and an all-around fun person to be with. Being an only child, he was also spoiled rotten.

"Growing up in my family, I learned how to take care of other people. My husband was very used to being taken care of. We fit like a hand in a glove.

"Because I was used to a large family and enjoyed being part of one, and because my husband never liked being an only child, we decided to have at least five children.

"By the time we'd been married eight years, we had our five children. By that time, my husband was working long hours and spending most of his spare time watching sports on TV. I found I was doing more and more of his chores. I took care of the household bills, I took care of our car, I took care of our lawn, and I maintained our home. If the children needed anything, they came to me first. I never resented doing more than my share.

Actually, in time, I came to view my husband as another child, because he seemed to be unable to handle any adult responsibilities.

"When gambling first became part of the fun things we did together, I enjoyed it. My husband bet only on football and basketball games. As time went by, he would bet on other sporting events, too. He especially liked the fact that a man he worked with would place his bets for him, allowing him to buy some action without having to be present to enjoy the events. He always told me which games he bet on and how much he bet, so I could enjoy it with him.

"The one thing we enjoyed doing together was attending sporting events. I think what I enjoyed most about those games was watching my husband enjoying himself. He would get so excited whenever the team he bet on won. I just loved seeing him that happy.

"In the beginning, gambling was a great pleasure for me, and it added to the happiness we shared together."

Mary Beth's Story—In the End

"As the years passed, our financial problems worsened; however, I always agreed with my husband that the reason we never had any money was because we had six kids, two dogs, and two cats. I had become so hooked into the small rewards of his meager winnings that I never wanted to encourage him to give up gambling. I was completely unaware that he was gambling a great deal more than I ever imagined. When I look back, I can see how naive I was. I never questioned the fact that he never won more than a couple of dollars on a game. My daily life was so hectic and overwhelming that I rarely looked closely at my reality.

"By the time our youngest child entered junior high, we had a nine-year-old, four teenagers, and one unemployed twenty-year-old drug addict living at home. Every day was hell. Never a day passed that I wasn't screaming at my husband about money. He always blamed our poverty on the fact that I wouldn't get a job and bring home a salary. By then I was wise enough to know that much of our scarcity was the result of his compulsion to gamble. My sister had six children and her family income was less than ours, but she and her family lived within their means and they went on a short vacation every summer.

"In the end, when we signed the separation papers, I was not only penniless and without a home, I had lost three of my children to my husband. They blamed me for all our marital problems. They had no direct knowledge of the depths of his gambling, and because I appeared to be such a witch, they decided their father was faultless and I was the one to blame. No matter what I said, not one of them would support me in my time of need.

"What did the gambling do *to* me? It cost me my marriage and three of my children, and I believe it was a contributing factor in our firstborn's turning to drugs."

LIVING IN AN EMOTIONAL VACUUM

When most people think about compulsive gambling, the first thing that comes to mind is financial problems. However, some people who gamble compulsively do not have financial problems, and their partners experience no threat of financial hardship. These partners live without emotional support from their families and friends, who do not understand why they are complaining if the gambling isn't hurting them financially. For these partners, their greatest pain comes from the fact that the husband's attention is always focused on his other love.

Christine's Story—In the Beginning

"My parents sent me to an Ivy League college, hoping that I would fall in love with an intelligent, ambitious young man from a wealthy family. And that's exactly what happened. My husband majored in business because his father was a commercial real estate tycoon in New York City. It was a given that he would follow in his father's footsteps and one day take over his father's business.

"From the day we married, I had every luxury imaginable. By the time we celebrated our silver wedding anniversary, our son was in pre-med and our daughter owned and operated a boutique on Madison Avenue.

"My husband never gambled to obtain money. He did it to enjoy himself. He got a great kick out of risking money when he could not control the outcome. In his business, he was responsible for the aftermath of every major or costly decision. He lived with tension daily. Gambling removed these pressures and helped him to relax. The fact that the outcome of his gambling was not determined by a decision of his was pure pleasure.

"It never mattered to either of us how much he won or lost when he indulged in his pleasure. Money was to be used to purchase relaxation and happy memories. In the beginning, gambling was a complete pleasure for my husband and for me."

Christine's Story—In the End

"For me to speak of what my husband's gambling did to me makes me feel so ungrateful. I have recently been spending time with some new friends, all of whom are married to compulsive gamblers. When I hear how they have suffered as a result of this addiction, I shudder.

"My husband has given me a life of luxury. Since I married him, I have been able to get whatever I needed or wanted. Actually, that's not true. The truth is that since my wedding day, I have longed for him.

"I'm sure many people who have struggled financially believe they wouldn't complain if they could only pay their bills and live in peace. What they don't realize is that you can't live in peace when you are very much in love with your husband and he is in love with another—action.

"I could never get my husband to put me before his only true love— gambling. I've never known anyone to devote an entire life to gambling the way he has for the past seventeen years. Some of my friends refer to themselves as "golf widows" because their husbands play golf one full day each week or for several days when away on vacation. But they do not play golf at night, nor for two consecutive days and nights, nor when their wives are giving birth, nor when their mothers are dying, nor when their children are crying out to them for attention. But that's what happens when you are married to a man who only answers to the driving call within him for action.

"Nobody could possibly understand this. I know because I have tried to explain it to several friends, and they thought I was an ungrateful wife who doesn't appreciate a husband who works hard and never questions how much money I spend, nor how much I give to my family when they are in need. They are right. All those things are true. But I don't believe they understand the hurt and pain I hold inside, because all I ever ask for is some indication that my husband truly cares about me, some indication that I matter in his life, some indication that he still needs me the way he did when we first came together. I neither see nor feel any of those things. My husband continues to gamble compulsively, and I continue to long for him in my life.

"What did my husband's gambling do *to* me? It made me a very lonely, isolated person who feels unsupported even by those who I know care about me. It has made me continually question my feelings and my self-worth."

LIVING TO RESCUE

Perhaps a pain that was once a pleasure is in some way more endurable than a pain that had no initial payoff. In truth, some partners of compulsive gamblers never received even the smallest pleasure from their partners' gambling. These women knew their partners had a problem with gambling. What's more, they rescued the gamblers many times, even before they had wedding rings on their fingers.

Frances's Story

"I was fifteen years old the first time I ever gave my husband money to cover a gambling debt. I had earned the money baby-sitting. My husband-to-be was sixteen, and we had been dating for about four months. He didn't ask me for the money. I insisted he take it because I felt sorry for him. He told me how he played cards with money his mother had given him to pay for his school baseball uniform, and that he would be grounded for weeks if she found out what he had done. I reacted to how sad and scared he seemed. I was planning to buy new jeans with the money, but I wanted to help him. Of course, I also didn't want him to be grounded for weeks; then I wouldn't be able to see him.

"I remember how much more interested in me he seemed to be from that day on. I thought that was because he saw me as a caring person and found that attractive.

"We dated four more years before marrying. During that time, I gave him hundreds of dollars to get him out of trouble because of his gambling. I can't say I didn't know that his gambling was a problem, because he was suspended from high school twice because of it, and before he turned eighteen his gambling cost him two part-time jobs.

"What bothered me most about his gambling during those years was that it was the only thing we ever fought about. I spent many nights crying because he didn't show up for a date, because I couldn't give him the money he wanted, or because he'd rather gamble than spend time with other friends. Even then, he never wanted to socialize. He wouldn't even come to my home for dinner. More than once I begged him to come. I never could figure out why he wouldn't. I finally attributed it to the fact that he was basically shy and uncomfortable talking to people. His father was an alcoholic, and I knew he was very unhappy at home. From what he told me, his family stayed very much to themselves because they never knew when his father would come home drunk and embarrass them. To avoid any embarrassment, they just isolated themselves from everybody.

"If I could look beyond the fact that the gambling made it impossible for us to ever go anywhere that cost money, the worst part of the gambling was that he always seemed distant to me, even from the first time I dated him. His attention span was short, his concentration was poor, and his interest in anything I had to say seemed nonexistent. Most painful was that he was never there for me when I needed his emotional support. When my sister was killed in an auto accident, he didn't come to the wake. When I broke my leg ice-skating, he called only once in two weeks. When I failed my driving test, he never offered to help me for the second attempt. Regardless of the money he lost gambling, not having him there for me when I needed him was my greatest pain.

"I never questioned my desire to marry him. Despite all the negatives in our relationship, I loved him. I used to tell myself that he would change after we became husband and wife. I believed I could change him once we lived together and had to be responsible for ourselves. And of course I truly believed that, once we had a family, he would *have* to change and become responsible.

"How wrong I was. Not that he didn't change; he did, but for the worse. His gambling continued. Our debts grew, and we continually moved further and further away from each other. Although we had five children, he wasn't there for any of their births, nor was he there for them as they grew up. Our youngest was born mentally retarded. He never could accept that and seemed to feel responsible for it. After that birth, his gambling sharply accelerated.

"Although we were married for seventeen years, I always felt like a single parent. Actually, it would have been better if I had been a single parent. At least then I could have avoided all the arguments, violence, pressure, and pain I experienced by staying with him.

"My husband's gambling was out of control when we met. In the beginning there was pain, and in the end only more pain. For me, there were never any rewards or happy memories as a result of my husband's gambling."

COPING WITH THE REVELATION

As incredible as it may sound, not all partners of compulsive gamblers live the experience of "in the beginning" and "in the end."

Because compulsive gambling is so easily concealed, it is called the "hidden illness." It is quite possible for someone to gamble compulsively for many years without his partner's knowledge. For the partner, the revelation of gambling is most devastating. This is a woman who placed total trust in her partner. She never questioned his integrity. When she finds out about the gambling, she suddenly feels she is married to a stranger. She also has a tendency to turn on herself for being blind. *He was gambling and I never suspected a thing!* The anger and rage she expresses is far beyond the feelings expressed by someone who knew about her partner's gambling.

Dorothy's Story

"For me, there was no beginning. I was trusting, I was giving, I was naive, I was stupid. I think back, trying to understand how it could have happened. I can't find the answer.

"I am part of the baby boom—a college-educated, career-minded, hardworking woman who didn't want to even think about marriage and family until I established myself firmly in my profession. I am a psychologist.

"Human behaviors are my specialty. I get paid well for evaluating, diagnosing, and treating people with behavior problems. Becoming aware of my husband's compulsive gambling not only devastated me emotionally, mentally, and financially, but also professionally. I had spent years developing expertise in my field. I have had many papers published in scientific journals and have been consulted by several of the finest criminal attorneys in my state. When I found out about my husband's gambling, my self-esteem plummeted.

"Because I had made a decision not to marry early, I had an opportunity to prepare well for my financial future. When I was thirty-four and fell in love with my future spouse, I already had over $100,000 to my name. Following our marriage, our money became 'joint.' I suggested my husband manage all our finances, because his area of specialty was accounting, and I knew he was good at it.

"Our plan was for me to work for two years and then start having a family. We knew by that time we would have enough money to buy a home of our own. I would give up my full-time job at the hospital but continue working as a court consultant.

"A few months before our second wedding anniversary, I brought up the topic of looking for a home. My husband put me off several times under the pretense that he was too exhausted to discuss it. Because he worked harder than anyone I knew, I didn't doubt for a moment what he said. He took many out-of-town trips to his clients' places of business to do their books. I confronted him more than once about the long hours he put into his business. I was concerned about his health. Although he was rarely ill, I believed he was emotionally, if not physically, burned out and was too tired to enjoy anything.

"My own diagnosis of my spouse was that he was a workaholic. I couldn't get him to take a day off, never mind an escape weekend in the country. His drive kept growing stronger. When he was home, he was only there physically. His attention was elsewhere and he had memory lapses about things I would tell him. I often had to tell him something several times, because he would tell me I had never told him before. Actually, because of his reactions, there were times I started to question my own memory and sanity.

"I have always seen myself as a patient woman, so when my husband put off talking about buying a house, I let it go. However, a year later, when he was still resistant to discussing it, I got angry. My anger was new in our relationship. His reaction to it surprised me. He became defensive and verbally attacked me. This behavior shocked me. I tried to explain to him that I was worried about putting off having a family, since I was approaching thirty-seven years. His response was one I could not understand:

He didn't want to discuss it. I later came to the conclusion that the only reason he was behaving so erratically was because he was ill and didn't want me to know.

"As the months went by, I became more convinced I was right. He had wide mood swings, although mostly he was depressed. Our communication was deteriorating, and I felt his distance from me grow each week. Whenever I looked for the right moment to bring up my concern about his health, he would walk away. I delved deeper into my work and started to consider separation because we had grown so far apart and because he refused to go to a doctor or to a marriage counselor.

"Fortunately, over the years, I had made some very good friends in my profession, and I turned to them for guidance. Most of them supported my position. We all knew there is nothing anyone can do if another person does not want to change. And as far as I could see, such was my husband's position.

"After talking about my situation at length, I was satisfied I had no choice but to seek legal counsel. I turned to an attorney I had worked with over the years and for whom I had a great deal of respect. His specialty was marital law, and he had many years' experience. He suggested I gather together as much information as possible about our financial situation. I decided to start with our savings and CD accounts at our local bank, where I knew we had more than one deposit.

"My visit there brought our financial situation to light. I was shocked. Our bank manager made me aware of the thousands of dollars my husband had withdrawn from these accounts over the last two years, especially over the previous ten months. I got so weak he offered me a glass of water and helped me into his private office. He was able to see by my reaction that I had no idea what had been going on. I was sick, enraged! I wanted to kill my husband. Then I got control of myself and said that I was sure there was some explanation. After all, my husband was an accountant and he had to know what he was doing. I convinced myself—and the manager—that this was the explanation.

"That short period of comfort lasted only until my husband returned home from work that evening. I confronted him with my new knowledge, and he admitted he had started gambling heavily a little over a year ago. He told me he did it because he was very lucky a couple of times and he believed his luck would continue. At the time, he decided not to tell me because he wanted to wait until he won big and surprise me with the news that we could fulfill our dream sooner than planned.

"I lost control of my emotions. I started to hit him and curse him; I didn't know what I was doing. All I could think of was that the person I trusted most in the world had used me, stolen from me, deceived me, and lied to me. I was never so enraged in all my life. He tried to calm me down, but he never once said he was sorry. All he could say was that I didn't understand. He began trying to convince me that he had a foolproof system of card counting that had realized him thousands of dollars at the casinos. He told me he had a recent run of bad luck but, with a little help from friends, he could recoup all his losses on his next try.

"*Card counting* and *casinos* were words I had never heard out of his mouth before. Gambling was one thing that was never on our lists of interests. As a matter of fact, when two friends of ours suggested we go to Las Vegas with them on a four-day gambling trip, both of us said we had no interest in gambling. How could he be such a phony? I thought I knew him so well. How could he have deceived me so?

"I grew confused and depressed. My work was affected, and I could not look at my husband without unbearable pain. Within one month, we separated and I filed for divorce. It wasn't that I didn't want to work through what had happened. My decision to divorce was based on his attitude once I learned about his gambling. He tried hard to convince me that he could win every penny back if I would help him raise the money he needed. He couldn't see that gambling was controlling him; in addition, he was not interested in giving it up. As a matter of fact, he became very angry when I asked him to. He actually said I must be sick if I thought he would ever give up his plan and his goal of winning enough money to afford every luxury he desired. Besides, he told me, no one ever gave him the excitement or thrills he feels when he is gambling.

"For me, there was no beginning. There was only an end—an end to a marriage, to a plan, and to a dream."

Facts on File

Every compulsive gambler has a good enabler behind him.

In time most partners of compulsive gamblers dread it when the phone rings, the mail arrives, or a stranger knocks at the door.

Too many partners buy the guilt the compulsive gamblers pile on them. They blame themselves for the addiction.

Regardless of what the compulsive gambler tells you, his gambling is *never* your fault.

Most partners of compulsive gamblers see themselves as over-responsible caretakers and feel like martyrs.

Most partners of compulsive gamblers describe them as being emotionally unavailable.

Questions

Partner:

- Does your partner continually promise to stop gambling, but doesn't?
- Have you noticed that your partner never lets you see his pay stub, so you never know how much money he actually takes home?

Part 2

THE NEW GAMBLERS

The advent of casinos across the country in the 1990s coincided with the introduction of Internet gambling. The two phenomena account for an influx of women, youth, and seniors who now have easy access to more socially acceptable games of chance. Slot machines, sports betting, and day trading are a relaxing bus ride away or can be accessed by an anonymous click of the mouse.

Part 2 includes chapters on women, underage, senior, and Internet gamblers. Regardless of whether you are a male or female gambler or have loved one, you'll enhance your understanding of the chapters in this section by first reading Part 1, which fully explains the dynamics behind compulsive gamblers and their relationships.

5

Female gamblers

APPROXIMATELY ONE-THIRD of all compulsive gamblers are women. Most are single, separated, divorced, or widowed. What starts out as recreational activity becomes an escape from problems ranging from boredom to poverty to grief over the loss of a loved one. The course of the woman gambler will roughly follow that of a man—she will win, lose, and become desperate, yet the problems presented by these women are unique to the female gender. Most of them find themselves in the role of nurturing parent while working full-time outside the home. In a bingo hall or casino, where it is acceptable for women to be unaccompanied by a male, it is safe for them to be away from their families for short periods of time or to socialize with other women.

Compulsive gamblers who are mothers will often resort to using household funds for gambling, thus depriving their children of basic needs, and may also neglect their children by not being there physically or emotionally. It is not uncommon for a compulsively gambling mother to become so absorbed in her addiction that she will leave her young children unsupervised for hours or days at a time.

The most common reason women give for gambling is to escape. Most female gamblers know that when they want their world to go away, all they need to do is place a bet. For these women, gambling is a guaranteed way of shutting off their thoughts and anesthetizing their feelings. Many female gamblers claim they have no other effective outlet, so they continue to gamble regardless of the risks or consequences.

GAMBLING ON WELFARE

When a woman is single, unemployed, the mother of fatherless children, and living on government subsidies, she may live with ongoing feelings of fear and hopelessness: fear because she knows that everything she does that affects her children will be scrutinized by her caseworker; hopelessness because she sees no "light at the end of the tunnel"—she believes her children will live in poverty for the rest of their lives.

Shakila's Story

"I've never been married, but I do have two children. My daughter Sasha was fathered by my first boyfriend when we were both in high school. Before Sasha was born, my boyfriend left town and never returned. Later, I found out his parents had sent him to live with friends out West so he could graduate from high school and go on to college. Although his parents continued living in town, they never made an attempt to see their grandchild. After they moved away, I never heard anything more about them.

"Both my parents suffered with emphysema and lived on government assistance most of their lives. They both died before the age of forty-five. Being alone and with no one to turn to, I too applied for government assistance.

"For a year following my parents' deaths, I did nothing but take care of my daughter. I was determined to raise her myself even if it meant we would have to do without, and that's exactly what we did. Then one day my life took a turn. I was at the Laundromat when a man I had never seen before came in to do his wash. We began talking. His name was Sal, and he told me he was newly divorced and had just rented an apartment nearby. We must have sat there for two hours in conversation. We just hit it off right away. He seemed lonely and happy to have someone listen to him.

"A few days later Sasha met Sal, and she took to him immediately. Sal had a daughter a little older than Sasha, whom he hadn't seen since his wife took her back to her hometown to live.

"Within one month of meeting Sal, Sasha and I moved into his apartment. At first things were much better for Sasha and me. Sal's job as an auto mechanic offered us many things that were not available to us before Sal came along.

"Sal always blamed his former wife for the breakup of their marriage, stating she was never satisfied—not with him, not with their modest home, and not with her life. He said she always wanted a better life, so she left him. Within six months of moving in with Sal, I came to realize the real reason his wife left him. Sal was an alcoholic and extremely abusive. I wanted to leave him, too, but by then I was four months pregnant. So I stayed hoping things would get better. They didn't.

"Sal never put a hand on Sasha, but he beat me regularly even when I was pregnant. Sal wanted a son so badly that when I gave birth to Tamika he was furious. He blamed me for not giving him a son.

"Sal's abuse continued until one day when he came home, packed his stuff, and left. Sasha was five and Tamika was seven months. I could not afford to keep the apartment, so I went back to social services for help. As much as I hated to do that, I was determined to raise my daughters alone. I also made a decision not to get involved in another relationship, but rather to focus on being a good mother. My greatest fear was that my daughters, too, might find themselves repeating my mistakes and having to live the life I was living. I wanted better for them even if it meant I would have to sacrifice myself.

"The day I returned to social services, I was remembering how supportive the caseworker was the last time I reached out, so I did not feel uncomfortable about returning; that is, until I met my new caseworker. Her attitude made me feel like dirt. She talked down to me, and she had no interest in hearing why I needed help again. In her opinion, the fact that I had two children by two different men automatically made me an unfit mother. Her attitude scared me. I just wanted to get out of there before she reported me to some higher authority and my kids would be taken away.

"Once I left that office, I never went back. I accepted my monthly checks, as meager as they were, and I did the best I could. I was careful with how I spent the money they gave me because I did not want to have to see that caseworker again. I never told anyone what a hard time I was having. There was never enough money to feed and clothe my daughters. There was no end to the things Sasha and Tamika needed. Then one day, in order to be able to fill their needs, I began shoplifting. I never took more than we needed—no toys, no TV—nor did I take anything for myself. Mostly what I took was children's shoes, pajamas, coats, and underwear. I worked hard at being frugal and taking really good care of the things we had. My goal was to give my daughters a better life than the one I had and to raise them in a religion I believed would give them the strength to get through trying times. Because I was with them all the time, we three were very close.

"One day after walking Sasha and Tamika to school, I had a stroke of good luck. I was standing on the corner waiting for the light to turn when I looked down and found a twenty-dollar bill. You can't imagine what that was like. My first thought was to buy something for the girls. Twenty dollars may not seem like a lot, but it made me feel rich.

"I went into the candy store and, after walking around for a while, I decided to buy Sasha a doll and Tamika a small stuffed puppy. Then I went to the supermarket and bought some fruit, a gallon of vanilla ice cream, and three small chocolate bars. I didn't want to spend the whole twenty dollars right away. I wanted to take time and think about how I should spend the balance.

"As I was paying for the items I bought, I found myself facing a big sign advertising the lottery. Something came over me. I thought since I was lucky in finding the money, maybe the luck would continue and I would actually win if I bought a ticket. I can't explain it; I just felt very lucky, like I couldn't miss. I bought five one-dollar tickets.

"What a great evening we had. Sasha and Tamika loved their presents, the ice cream, and especially the chocolate. It was the most fun we had had in a long time.

"If I had to pick a happier day in my life it would be the following Saturday when the winning lottery numbers were posted at the candy store. One of my tickets was a winner. The prize was one thousand dollars. Because there was one other winner, the prize money was split between us.

"I couldn't help but think that I had truly become blessed and that my life was about to turn around. And it did. I began buying lottery tickets every day. Long after the money from my first win was gone, I continued to spend two dollars every day with the hope of buying a dream. I absolutely believed I would win again and win big. I had a strong need to recapture the feelings I had when I won the lottery the first time. That first big win made me feel not only lucky but special. I know I never before felt like that.

"I was gambling to win. I wanted things for my daughters and for myself. I was thirty-four years old and I felt like fifty.

"I don't know when it happened or why, but buying my lottery tickets became the focus of my daily routine. I was so distracted thinking about how I would spend my winnings, I had less time to give to ten-year-old Sasha and five-year-old Tamika. I had no patience with them. If they came to me to ask for something they needed, I would get very angry. Financially, we were hurting more than ever; I was spending sixty dollars a month for a chance to fill a dream.

"If gambling would have only hurt us financially, we could have survived. But for reasons I don't understand, my need to buy those tickets consumed me. I could not let a day go by without having those tickets in my hands. I think I was afraid my numbers would come up and I would miss my chance for a better life. That dream was what kept me going and kept me gambling.

"By the time Sasha was eleven, I was spending at least two hundred dollars a month on my passion for gambling. Because the local lottery salesman knew I was receiving government assistance, I could no longer buy all my tickets from him. I spent most of my day on buses traveling to different neighborhoods to buy my tickets. It was a full-time job.

"When Sasha had turned ten, I had told her I had gotten a night job that paid very well. She was so happy. So at her young age she became responsible for five-year-old Tamika. Sasha would give her sister dinner, give her a bath, and put her to bed. When Tamika was asleep, Sasha would sit alone and do her homework and put herself to bed by nine o'clock. While all this was going on, I was street-walking in a distant neighborhood.

"My new job enabled me to give up shoplifting, to dress my girls in new clothes, to buy a TV, and to move into a larger apartment. Despite all this, I was not prostituting to get a better life; I was doing it so I would have the money I needed to feed my gambling habit. I could not see how my obsession with gambling was affecting my life.

"For five years I worked the streets. I had some steady customers. My tips grew and things were a great deal better. By this time, I was spending hundreds of dollars each month on lottery tickets. Most of the agents selling me the tickets just assumed I had gotten a good job or a wealthy husband. I had neither.

"With all of the lottery tickets I bought over the years, I never once won big. Oh, I occasionally did win, but it was never more than a few hundred dollars. Still, even those wins would fuel my belief that the big win was on its way.

"One night when I was in the car with one of my steadies, two cops approached us and told us to step out of the car. When the john got out of the car, a Rolex watch fell on the ground. The cops considered this suspicious and so they searched the car and in the trunk they found a box filled with other expensive jewelry. We were both arrested.

"I never saved any money, so when my bail was set for eight thousand dollars, I could not come up with it. My trial didn't come on the calendar for four months. The jury found the john and me guilty of grand larceny. We were both sentenced to ten to fifteen years in prison.

"I sat and I thought and I thought, yet I could not explain how all this came about. I could only see that I was innocent of any crime. I didn't steal anything. I didn't deserve to be in prison. No one would listen to me. I was a victim and nobody cared. Now after three years, I still have twelve years to serve.

"My daughters? Tamika is thirteen now and living somewhere with foster parents. I haven't seen her since she was ten. And Sasha is eighteen and is a single mother of a two-year-old son. She is living in our old neighborhood. She has a caseworker that she likes. I have never seen her son; neither has his father."

CARETAKERS WHO GAMBLE

Because one of the reported benefits of gambling is escaping reality, it is an enticing activity for professional caretakers. Caretakers devote most of their waking hours meeting the needs of their charges. They have little time and even less energy to care for themselves. Being overwhelmed emotionally and physically exhausted at the end of each day, they tend to forego personal pleasures. However, when they are faced with an exciting activity such as gambling, their interest often spurs them into action and their pursuit of personal pleasure begins.

Ruth's Story

"For years I was employed as a nanny for children of wealthy couples. I loved my work and although it afforded me little time for myself, I never complained. When I first started working as a nanny, I was in my early thirties—that was twenty-six years ago. For the last couple of years, I have had less patience, and I tire much more easily. In my last job as a nanny, I had in my care a newborn baby girl and a two-and-a-half-year-old boy. In addition to being hyperactive, the boy was a very cranky child. No matter how hard I tried, I couldn't satisfy nor comfort him. I'm sure he was reacting to having a new baby in the home. I had dealt with that situation on many occasions, but previously I had been able to help the toddler adjust to the dramatic change in the family. I was so worn out at the end of each workday I could hardly move. I knew my age was a contributing factor. At fifty-seven, I did not have the physical strength nor the patience to care for little ones. All I seemed to do was work and sleep. I knew I had to give some serious thought to changing my career. I was torn because I really liked being a caretaker.

"When I returned to my agency for a new assignment, I told my placement counselor about my mixed feelings of continuing as a nanny. She suggested I consider caring instead for some of her elderly clients who were in need of assistance. She told me that they are so grateful for the help, they treat their caretakers wonderfully in order not to lose them. She assured me that experienced, well-qualified caretakers were not easy to come by. She made it sound very enticing. I agreed to take one placement for three months.

"Those three months flew by. I was so glad I had taken the counselor's suggestion. The couple I worked for were Edith and Sidney. They were both in their eighties. Edith was in much better health than her husband. He had Alzheimer's disease. He must have been in the late stages, because he at times didn't recognize his wife. Most of the time Sidney was quiet and pleasant. He had a health aide and a masseuse who visited him daily. The health aide was a young male who would bathe Sid, shampoo his hair, and make him comfortable. In the afternoon, the masseuse would come and give Sid a forty-minute massage. He loved that. He never had any problem recognizing the masseuse. I think the combination of these two visitors kept Sid happy.

"Edith was another story. She and Sid had been together for fifty-three years. She was a homemaker who loved to travel and entertain. She was continually irritated with Sid because he was extremely tight with his money. No matter what Edith needed or wanted, she had to fight to get Sid to give her money. Sid was a numismatist, one of the world's most knowl-edgeable coin collectors. There was seldom a question he couldn't answer if it concerned foreign or domestic coins.

"I was more than content working for Edith and Sid. I took them to visit friends and to their doctor appointments; I shopped for them and made sure they had everything on hand that they needed to run their home. Whenever either of them wanted something fixed in the house, I was the one who saw to it. This was so much easier for me than taking care of small children.

"Edith loved to shop, and now that Sid was no longer sharp enough to be aware of how much she was spending, she was making up for lost time. When Sid would take his afternoon nap following his massage, Edith and I would go out, and she shopped to her heart's content. She liked nice things, but truly she was not extravagant. Just having the freedom to do what she loved doing made her happy.

"Edith and I grew closer with each passing month. By the time I had worked for her one year I was already handling some of their financial busi-ness. Mostly I would make out their monthly bills and see to it that every-thing got paid.

"Because I was less tired at the end of each day than I was when caring for children, I found myself having more energy and being willing to go out a few evenings a week and enjoy myself. On those evenings, I would go out with my friend Gail. Gail enjoyed visiting the new riverboat casino that was docked near the apartment complex in which she lived. I didn't think I would like gambling because I've always been careful with my money, since I never made a substantial salary. I agreed to give it a try. I liked it! Without exaggeration I became totally addicted to my game of choice: video poker. When I began, I didn't even know how to play, but because I loved it so, I became a fast learner. Gail did not like the passion with which I approached the video machine. She said each time I sat in front of the machine to play, I seemed to go to another world, a world that could not be permeated by anyone else. Gail felt it didn't matter to me whether or not she was there. She was right.

"Somehow I came to believe that the video poker machine gave me everything I ever wanted. When it paid off, I interpreted that to mean that the machine thought I was special.

"My own most personal and intimate problem all my life has been my weight. Except in childhood, I have never weighed less than two hundred pounds, and in the last years I have not weighed less than two hundred and fifty. For the hours I sat and played video poker, not once did I feel pressure, not once did I feel I wasn't normal-looking, and not once did I long for things I did not have.

"Weight was the one thing Gail and I had in common. The thing that bonded us was food. Most of the time we spent together was spent eating out. Gail could not understand what the video poker machine did for me. She actually felt threatened by it. She thought it had replaced her in my life. I have to admit being with Gail never gave me the feelings that the machine gave me.

"Needless to say, my gambling rapidly increased. Believe it or not, within a few months I went through my entire savings. I had not a penny left. In order to keep gambling, I had no choice but to put my rent and utility money into the machine. Two months later, when I was three months behind in the rent, I found an eviction notice under my door. I had five days to vacate the apartment. It didn't take me too long to devise a game plan that would rescue me—Edith. I knew she was concerned I might leave her employ, because at times, when Sid was angry, he would put me down and say cruel things to me. I was confident Edith would do whatever was necessary to keep me with her.

"I made up a story that would melt Edith's heart. I told her I lost my apartment because my landlord needed it for his mother who was ailing. I told Edith I was considering moving back to my hometown, where the salaries and working conditions were better than they are in the Midwest. Edith shed genuine tears while listening to me. She practically begged me to stay. She offered me a nice salary increase in addition to a large room with a bath in her home. When I mentioned that Sid might not approve, she assured me that would not happen because his illness was worsening, and he was no longer showing interest in anything.

"My life got better than ever. I had no bills, I had more money with which to gamble, and Gail was no longer on my back. I wasn't seeing her anymore. She was just jealous of my good fortune. My gambling became all-consuming. I could no longer think of anything else.

"Since Edith was allowing me to live in her home for free, I was able to spend all of my income sitting at the video poker machine. I did not cheat Edith nor Sid out of the time they had coming to them. I was up and dressed every day at the appointed time, and I continued to do my job as expected. Edith was kind to me, and I treated her like my own mother. The new problem I had at that time was that my desire to gamble was growing. Some days I just couldn't wait for six o'clock to come so I could rush out and get to the riverboat. Edith had no idea I was gambling. She even asked me if I was seeing someone special. I was evasive with my answer because she assumed she was right.

"Gambling my week's pay was no longer enough to satisfy my need to feel special. I wanted to gamble longer hours and larger amounts. When I did win, I would regret that I didn't put more quarters in the machine so my winnings would be greater. Larger winnings meant I could continue to feed my habit and continue to escape my painful reality without dealing with my overeating. I knew it was the extra pounds I carried that kept me isolated and distant from others, putting me in a position of constantly having to deal with feelings of loneliness.

"An alcoholic can only spend so much on alcohol, and a drug addict is limited as to how much can be spent on drugs, but when it comes to gambling, there is no limit. I found that out the first time I stole money from Sid. In my mind, I didn't really steal money from him, I just took one of his precious coins. He had so many, he would never miss it. I took the coin to a dealer who gave me two hundred dollars for it. I told the dealer my father died and left me his coin collection, and that I might be interested in selling more of the coins. The dealer was definitely interested.

"I have no idea how many coins I sold, nor do I know the exact value of the coins. To me the coins were nothing more than trinkets. I did not think of them as being of great value. I received only a few hundred dollars for each coin I sold. Sid didn't need the money. He had plenty of money. And besides, his illness would prevent him from realizing some coins were missing.

"If I used any excuse to justify taking Sid's coins, it was the fact that I was doing more things with and for Edith. She loved to visit antique shops, something I had no interest in, but I took her without complaining. I told myself that whatever coins I took were payment in exchange for the additional things I was doing with Edith. I must add that I had gotten close to

Edith, and I know she considered me not only her companion, but also a friend. She was generous and kind. Those were not the things I wanted in my life at that time. I wanted to escape the pain of my feelings of loneliness and isolation.

"One day, several months later, when Sid was taking a nap, Edith went to his room to check on him. When she entered the room, she caught me stealing several coins from one of the trays. The sight of me doing that shocked her so I thought she was going to have a heart attack. She didn't yell; she didn't try to stop me; she just put her head in her hands and sobbed.

"I quickly ran out of the house. I wanted to be alone. I needed time to come up with a story that would satisfy Edith and explain my behavior. There was nothing I could think of that would justify stealing from people who trusted and befriended me. I decided to go back and tell Edith the truth. Her nature was such that I knew she would give me a second chance.

"I was wrong. When I rang her doorbell, Edith motioned for me to enter. She pointed to the den and for me to sit down. She didn't say a word. I immediately started to apologize when the doorbell rang. It was the police. She had me arrested. Since I had no money, I couldn't raise bail. I sat in jail and awaited my trial date.

"I was charged with grand larceny theft. After an appraisal of Sid's remaining coins was completed by another numismatist, it was determined that the value of the coins I had stolen was $128,000. I was shocked. Even though I had no idea how much I had received for the coins I stole, I do know it was nowhere near that amount.

"With less than a two-hour deliberation, the jury found me guilty. One month later, the judge sentenced me to eighteen months to five years. My sentence could have been much longer, but the judge gave consideration to the fact that it was my first offense.

"I've had a good deal of time to think about my gambling, and looking back, I can say the gambling was so consuming it caused me to abandon my values and hurt people who were kind to me. In the troughs of my gambling, the only thought I ever entertained was sitting in front of my VLT [video lottery terminal] machine and feeding it as many coins as necessary to transport me to Eden.

"It has been some time since I last gambled, and it is only since I have been incarcerated for the last two years that I can now see the reason I gambled was not to win, but to escape my reality, which was too painful for me to handle."

WHAT CAN YOU LOSE BY PLAYING BINGO?

How is it possible for a simple board game to fit the definition of gambling? One dictionary defines bingo as a game in which numbered balls are drawn at random and players cover the corresponding numbers. This hardly sounds like an activity that would get your adrenaline going. For most people, playing bingo is a pleasant way of passing time. And the amount of time spent playing can be determined by the player.

Bingo has been around since the Great Depression, when people had very little money. For a small fee, one could spend a couple of hours socializing and playing a game that might result in going home with a few dollars. The prize money was never large, but the time spent was worth the cost to play. Without a doubt, the vast majority of bingo players never ran into financial problems as a result of playing this game.

In the last few years, Super Bingo has been introduced in some of the Indian reservation casinos, and this has drawn large groups of bingo fanatics. At these bingo games, the cost to play is significant. Some of the games require the player to make a reservation for a seat weeks in advance. The fee can be as much as five hundred dollars to play a specified number of games, and the jackpot can be as much as one million dollars.

Patti's Story

"It's common today for couples to marry at a later age than their parents. When Tim and I married, we were in our early thirties; we had been dating since our senior year in college. We were without a doubt two of a kind. We thought alike, we had the same goals, we liked the same things, and we both wanted to plan our lives very carefully. The only two things we disagreed upon were our tastes in music—rock and roll vs. jazz—and our religious beliefs. Although we were both Christian, we belonged to different denominations. Tim's church was much more conservative than mine, and he was more active in his church than I. However, we did not see this as being a cause of any problems in the future.

"After graduating from college, we each found jobs; Tim as a journalist for a small-town newspaper, and I as a fashion designer in business for myself.

"Tim had a gift for writing, and while in college he continually registered for extracurricular workshops on creative writing. Before he graduated, he had a few of his writings published. One of his stories was published in a national magazine. This accomplishment did not bring us any income, but it did make for a great resume when Tim began looking to move up in his career.

"I'm the type of person who loves to work alone. I never wanted to work for a corporation, nor for anyone. I wanted to be self-employed and make a name for myself. My other goal was to choose a career that would allow me to stay home and work. Tim and I knew we wanted to have children and that I would be a stay-at-home mom. Neither of us wanted our children to be raised by a nanny.

"In less time than we expected, Tim had gotten a job as a journalist on a mid-sized newspaper, and I was getting referrals for my clothing designs. One thing that helped my reputation to grow was that I kept my prices below what others were charging. I knew this would result in my clients recommending me to their friends, and I felt confident this would all pay off in time.

"With hindsight, I can see what a wonderful life we had together. We were very much in love, we each considered the other a best friend, and yet we each had interests that did not include the other. Tim belonged to two writers clubs and devoted two evenings a week to them. He said the people he spent time with at the clubs were extremely supportive of his writing efforts, and their feedback helped him to continue to learn and grow.

"I would spend those two evenings a week playing bingo at a local bingo hall and at a nearby church. I loved bingo. I began playing when I was eleven. My mother would take me along with her and her sister.

"Whenever I was at bingo, I would be amazed to witness the number of women who had such good senses of humor. Despite the fact that some of these women were in the midst of a family crisis and others led lonely lives, when they sat in the bingo hall, they were fun-filled. There was more laughter heard at these tables than at a comedy café.

"After Tim and I had been married for six years, we began talking about starting a family. I was more than ready and so was he. Thus we set about on a journey of which we could never have predicted the outcome.

"I stopped taking the pill and began planning for a baby. I read four baby books, and I got Tim to start thinking about names for our child. I found myself looking at baby clothes and furniture. I wanted to be well-prepared so I wouldn't feel overwhelmed when the time came.

"Things were moving along slowly, but then I was glad, because during this time Tim got an offer to work as a journalist for a large New England daily. I was happy for him and even more happy when I realized we could live in a town that was not too far for my steady clients to travel. Things could not have been more perfect.

"After settling into our new home, Tim and I returned to our daily routines. My old clients kept coming, and because there was no other designer of women's clothes in the area, I began getting new clients.

"I found a new bingo hall on an Indian reservation. I couldn't believe how huge it was. It had to accommodate over a thousand players. They offered games twenty-four seven. I no longer had to be at the hall at a specific time since they never took a break between games. My first thought was how convenient this would be for me. My second thought was that if I won at one of these huge games, I would really feel special.

"Ten months after coming off the pill, I still was not pregnant. I chalked it up to the fact that we had just made a major change in our lives, and the adjustment was somewhat stressful; therefore, I just wasn't getting pregnant.

"By the following spring there was still no sign of becoming pregnant. My periods were like clockwork, so I had no doubt that our problem with infertility had to lie with Tim. I asked him to go with me to my gynecologist so we could ask for help. He agreed right away. I inferred there was something wrong with me so Tim wouldn't feel blamed when he found out that it was he who had the problem.

"I could not have been more wrong. After completing a series of tests ordered by the doctor, we were told that both of my ovaries were underdeveloped, and although I had regular periods, I was not producing any viable eggs. It was a total shock. After hearing that, I heard not another word she said. She wanted to talk about alternative means of becoming a parent. I knew this was not the right time to talk about that. We ended the visit and went home.

"Neither Tim nor I talked about what the doctor told us. We just went through our day as though it was like any other. Two days passed and nothing was said. On Saturday morning, I told Tim we needed to talk. To my surprise, Tim said there was nothing to talk about. He said he loved me and even if we couldn't have children, we could have a happy life. He spoke as if it were a done deal. I, on the other hand, didn't feel that way. I definitely wanted to consider what other options were open. I was determined to have a baby.

"I brought up the idea of adopting a baby. Tim was 100 percent against that, stating we wouldn't know anything about the baby's background, and even more important, this would not be his biological child.

"Without telling Tim, I made another appointment with the doctor to get more information about what we could do to have our own baby. She explained that we could try in vitro fertilization using Tim's sperm and an egg from another female. If that didn't work, we might then consider eliciting the aid of a surrogate mother. With this option, Tim's sperm would be placed into the uterus of the surrogate, and although the baby would have none of my genes, it would be Tim's biological child.

"All the way home I felt uplifted, because whichever method Tim would choose would be fine with me. I just wanted a baby. And now with this new information, I knew it was possible.

"While all this was going on, nothing else in our lives changed. Although we were in a kind of crisis, we each functioned as usual. My business was thriving, and I did not miss a single chance to play bingo. Tim didn't miss any of his writers club meetings. I didn't know how he could function at these meetings when he had so much on his mind. As for me, bingo was always a stress reliever. No matter how tired nor how much stress I was under, I would leave the bingo hall feeling better. I liked the bingo games on the reservation. They were more exciting than the smaller games, and there was so much more energy generated in the larger room. I was beginning to understand why my mother was such a devotee of bingo. She got more out of the few hours she spent in the bingo hall than she would have gotten if she'd spent the time in therapy.

"When I returned home after talking to my doctor, Tim could see my mood was lifted. I explained to him all that the doctor told me. Then I told Tim I would go along with whichever method he chose. I was just so elated I couldn't wait to get started.

"Tim just sat there and didn't say a word. That made me feel uncomfortable and a little scared. I knew Tim ruled out adoption, but surely he wouldn't rule out either of these choices since either one would produce his biological child.

"When Tim finally did speak, he said that he could not possibly choose either one of those options. Tim's conservative religious beliefs did not permit in vitro fertilization nor the use of a surrogate mother. He was dead serious. I was shattered. There was to be no discussion; end of story. For the next few days we hardly spoke.

"A few days later I asked Tim if he wanted a divorce. I knew he wanted children very badly, but if he stayed married to me, he would be childless. He reacted in a completely loving way. He definitely did not want a divorce. He said he wanted children as much as I, and he was willing to do just about anything to make that possible. I asked Tim why we couldn't just try in vitro fertilization. I said no one would have to know anything about how the baby was conceived, and no one would have to know the child was not biologically mine. As soon as I said this, I could see by the expression on Tim's face that he was thinking about it. I kept quiet; I didn't want to push him.

"In the middle of the next week, I suggested to Tim that we spend the following weekend driving up through New England and enjoying the fall foliage. I suggested this because we had both been under a great deal of stress, and I knew a few relaxed days away would do us both good. And of course, I hoped it would give Tim more time to consider my suggestion about trying in vitro.

"Just before we were about to return home, Tim told me he decided we should try my suggestion. His rationale was that he knew we would make good parents, we have a very good relationship, and a baby would fill both our dreams. I was in ecstasy!

"The first three tries at getting pregnant were not successful. In vitro is not a simple procedure; it is difficult, costly, time consuming, and very wearing on the emotions. There is a continuous feeling of hope and elation when each procedure is performed, and when it doesn't work out, the mind jumps right into projections and says this will never work. For some reason, Tim was more patient and more optimistic than I. He supported me and encouraged me to try and keep a positive attitude.

"My bingo playing picked up. I began going to afternoon games so Tim would not know how often I was playing. I was under a great deal of stress, and I needed the relief the game provided.

"Our fourth attempt at in vitro worked. When we got the phone call that I was pregnant, I was filled with joy, and if it was possible, Tim was even more elated than I. The first trimester passed quickly and uneventfully. I felt well with the exception of some morning sickness. Our families were so happy and excited for us. Even the women I played bingo with took an interest in my well-being and the progression of my pregnancy.

"In the beginning of my sixth month, a problem developed. I had some staining so my doctor recommended I stay on complete bed rest for the remainder of the pregnancy. I didn't like having to stay in bed every day, and I missed my bingo games terribly, but I just kept focusing on the day when I would hold the baby in my arms.

"That day finally came, and believe it or not, the birth went smoothly. Our son, Michael, was perfect. Once we got set in a new daily routine, things went back to normal for Tim, but I was not yet back to designing clothes for my clients. Instead I was dealing with an infant who had colic. I can't tell you how wearing this is for any mother. Although Michael was an excellent sleeper, when he was awake he did nothing but cry. No matter how I tried to soothe him, nothing worked. Each night when Tim came home from work, he would spend time with Michael and give me a break.

"The nights were the worst. I was exhausted all the time and needed sleep. Because Tim had to get up early for work, I couldn't ask him to tend to Michael in the middle of the night. I loved Michael with all my heart, and I just wanted him to stop crying.

"Two months went by and the colic continued. The only break I had was when Michael was sleeping. He was still taking two three-hour naps a day.

"Each day I grew more stressed out. I had no relief, but I couldn't complain. I wanted to return to my routine of going to bingo, but that was not possible. I almost felt desperate for the relief the games offered, so I asked Tim if he would mind if I went to bingo one evening. Tim asked that I wait just a little longer because he felt too anxious about taking care of Michael all by himself. He saw Michael as being very fragile, and he was not confident enough that he could interpret his cries and know what to do.

"That night Michael slept almost five hours without interruption. I felt a glimmer of hope that just maybe he was getting over the colic. That glimmer faded very quickly when he awoke from his morning nap crying at the top of his lungs. Although he drank two-thirds of his formula, he kept on crying. Two hours later, Michael was still crying. Not being able to comfort him was my greatest problem. I felt so inadequate. It was at times like these that I wondered if I was meant to be a mother. That particular day I was at a low point. I had to get relief. Since I couldn't get to a bingo game, I decided to take Michael for a long drive. Riding in the car often helped Michael fall asleep.

"We weren't in the car ten minutes when Michael fell asleep. I knew he wouldn't wake up for at least three hours. That was his regular routine: cry for two hours then sleep for three. I didn't know where I was going. I had no particular destination in mind, but I was enjoying the peace and quiet. Without forethought I found myself pulling into the bingo hall parking lot on the reservation. Just sitting there in the car parked in front of the bingo hall made me feel better. I almost felt like a drug addict about to get a fix.

"I knew the schedule of the games, so I knew the next game would begin at one o'clock. I had ten minutes to decide what to do. I knew if I picked up Michael, he would awaken and cry again. I also knew if I left him alone, he would sleep another two hours. I decided it made the most sense to let Michael sleep and let me play just three games. That would take less than an hour.

"I picked out a quiet spot to park my car. It was a beautiful spring day and not too warm. Just to be sure I placed my car in a shady spot under a tree so I could be sure Michael would be comfortable. After I placed a light baby blanket over him I opened the driver's window just a crack.

"By the time I finished the first game I was already feeling relief. It's funny how a simple game can bring such relief. I won one hundred dollars on the second game. I didn't care about the money, but I did care that I was feeling better than I had in several months. I needed more relief than I realized so I continued to play. Nobody can believe this, but I lost track of time. I didn't have a clue how long I was sitting at the table playing bingo. I was brought back to reality when a message came over the loudspeaker for the owner of a car in the parking lot to come forward. At first I ignored the message, but when they repeated it the second time I realized that it was my car.

"I quickly got up and headed for the exit. As I walked through the exit door, I found four policemen standing there. My first thought was that someone must have damaged my car and they wanted to help. It never entered my mind that their presence had anything to do with Michael. As unbelievable as it sounds, I forgot I had left Michael in the car.

"Then one of the policemen stepped forward and told me I was under arrest for endangering the welfare of a minor. Only then did it hit me what I had done. I became hysterical, demanding to go to Michael, fighting with the officers and screaming at the top of my lungs. They handcuffed me and took me to the police station.

"At the station, I called Tim on his cell phone. He did not return my call. I was frantic. No one would tell me anything. I cried for hours. Later that night a policewoman came and told me Michael was dead. He died of dehydration and heat prostration.

"Today, I can tell you this without feeling any emotion because I no longer allow myself to feel. If I were to allow my feelings to surface, I would certainly end my own life. But I don't deserve to die and escape the pain of what I did. I will be released from prison in eighteen years. I don't want to be released. Michael never had a chance to live because of me, and I don't deserve to have a life after what I did to him. I hate myself and I can never forgive myself for killing my son.

"I strongly resisted sharing my story with anybody because what I did is so unbelievable. How could anyone believe I totally forgot I had left my four-month-old baby alone in a car for over three hours? How could anyone believe I forgot the time? How could anyone believe that I could do such a hideous thing to my own child?

"Bingo? It's a simple game in which numbered balls are drawn at random, and players cover the corresponding numbers. It's not betting on sports, it's not frequenting a racetrack, and it's not gambling in a casino. It is a game played by many good God-fearing people, a small minority of whom find bingo eradicates stress and actually causes temporary amnesia. This small group of people play bingo not for fun but for what bingo does *for* them.

"Tim? I haven't seen or heard from him since the morning he left for work and I went on a leisurely drive in the country."

Facts on File

As the proliferation of gambling continues throughout this country, more females are becoming attracted to it. The average age of today's female compulsive gambler is forty-five. Most often their game of choice is the slot machine. Female gamblers tell us they can go into a casino alone, feel safe, and play the slots without interference from anyone. When asked to name one of the benefits of playing the slots, many females state that the slot machines make them feel appreciated. This is because, when they begin to play, the machine welcomes them by name and then intermittently rewards them with vouchers for free food, drinks, and games.

As this addiction progresses, the female gambler may very well find herself involved with our judicial system by being charged with a felony. The most common illegal acts perpetrated by female compulsive gamblers are writing bad checks, stealing, forgery, child neglect, and child abuse.

Many female compulsive gamblers claim they do not gamble to make a killing, rather they simply want to escape from pressures in their lives.

Questions

- Have you ever resorted to using household funds to gamble, thus depriving your family of basic needs?
- Has gambling ever caused you to neglect your children by not being there physically or emotionally?
- Do you feel having a big win is the only chance you have to improve your economic status?
- Is gambling the fastest and most effective way for you to turn off your thoughts and numb your feelings?

6

Underage gamblers

MOST ADULTS WHO GAMBLE are mature enough to make responsible decisions about gambling. Our youth, who have not yet matured, are not able to do the same.

If teens were to enter a casino to gamble, there's a good chance they would be stopped at the door or removed from the floor by security. The same scene would probably take place at a racetrack. But when teenagers gamble over the Internet, there is little or no chance a responsible adult will intervene. As long as they submit a valid credit card (even a parent's card), they can gamble until the card is maxed out. The Net does not ask for proof of age.

When adults get into trouble from gambling, they have available a number of options for raising money to repay debts. Younger gamblers do not have these same options. Many youth have no choice but to go to illegal moneylenders, who know that the monies they give out are really guaranteed loans. When parents find out their child is in debt from gambling and that an illegal moneylender is involved, they immediately make arrangements to satisfy the loan. Parents are very fearful that their child or another family member will be hurt if the money is not repaid immediately. When there is an opportunity for the moneylender to be prosecuted, parents very often refuse to allow their child to cooperate with the authorities for fear of reprisal.

The most commonly seen traits in underage compulsive gamblers are that they are highly intelligent, extroverted, and masters at verbal skills. It may be hard to believe, but some of these gamblers have learning disabilities such as dyslexia, attention deficit disorder, or hyperactivity. Because they have such difficulty reading and comprehending, they begin to develop other strengths. Many afflicted with a gambling addiction excel in math and have exceptional memories when it comes to figures, and this holds true for underage gamblers. Some bingo players are able to play many cards and never cover a single number. Yet they always know when to shout "bingo." Still other compulsive gamblers with a limited capacity to learn turn to playing cards and in time become card counters. Many casinos block proficient card counters from playing in their gambling establishments.

Americans are very competitive. With most sports, winning is more important than playing the game. When teenagers win, they receive a great deal of praise and admiration from their peers, friends, coaches, and parents. This results in teens' self-esteem surging. Self-esteem is one of two things most teenagers desire. The other thing they need and want is money. It doesn't take teens very long to figure out that if winning makes them feel good, winning money will make them feel better.

How is it possible for teens to view gambling as anything but an activity that is acceptable and enjoyable? They are surrounded by adults who gamble, and they see that not only their government, but also many of their churches approve of and support gambling.

A school's codes of conduct clearly state that no smoking or drinking of alcoholic beverages is allowed in school or on school property. It would be difficult to find schools that clearly state that gambling is equally outlawed. As a matter of fact, more and more high schools are instituting Las Vegas night in place of the senior prom with the goal of keeping the kids from drinking and driving.

It is difficult for parents to see how vulnerable teens are when it comes to recreational gambling. Because teens are still developing and maturing, they do not yet have the ability to reason as an adult reasons. They are impulsive and immature, and at times they possess a kind of pathological optimism whenever they place a bet. They will tell themselves they are on a roll or they can feel a big win in their bones.

A recent national gambling impact study found that 5 percent, or 1.1 million, of adolescents in the United States engage in pathological gambling each year. All of these youth are between the ages of twelve and seventeen.

LEARNING DISABILITIES AND GAMBLING

When children struggle all through elementary school with a learning disability, they will naturally look for ways to raise their self-esteem. About the time they enter middle school, they already know they cannot compete on an intellectual level, so they will look for some other means to excel.

Keith's Story

"From the day I entered first grade, I always felt like a dummy. For as long as I can remember, I struggled to learn. My teachers would work with me until they just threw up their hands and gave up. My parents also tried to help me until, one day, my father decided I wasn't doing my part. My teachers told Dad I had great potential, but I lacked motivation. Following that, I was continually being accused of not trying hard enough. Not one person in my life was ever satisfied with my effort except my grandmother. She is the only one who never accused me of not trying hard enough. She made excuses for me and defended me. I always felt she just loved me no matter what I was like. I never had to satisfy her. Just my presence seemed to be all she needed or desired.

"Each year I was moved from one grade to the next even though I could not read. I excelled in math and had good verbal skills. I continued to try hard to learn to read, but nothing helped. As the years went by, my parents became more and more frustrated. My father tried many things to motivate me, but nothing worked. When it came to being able to read and comprehend what I had read, I was a complete loser. I had my eyes checked, my ears checked—no sign of any problem. My parents once took me to a child psychologist for an IQ test. I scored above average. Those test results only made things worse for me. My parents were relentless in their pursuit to make me a better student. They would not accept the fact that I was unable to read or comprehend.

"My father's last attempt at motivating me was when he pulled me off the high school swim team. He accused me of giving my all to the things I liked and ignoring the things I needed. I pleaded with him to allow me to remain on the team. He knew how much I loved swimming and that I was one of the team's best competitors. My coach even spoke to Dad, but it was all to no avail. My father removed from my life the only thing that made me feel important. Needless to say, from that point on my grades worsened. I no longer wanted to try at all.

"The only other area of my life that I could excel at was math. I could do almost any kind of math in my head. All during school I never failed a math test. For fun I used to challenge my friends to solve a math problem with them using a calculator and me using only my head. So often they were amazed at what I was able to accomplish.

"When I was a sophomore in high school, I was introduced to card playing. One of the seniors approached me and told me I could make a fortune playing cards since I was so good with numbers.

"I loved it from the first time I sat at the table. I won most of the time. This went on for almost a year. Then I became a little reckless with my bets. No, I didn't become reckless, my gambling became compulsive. I was no longer careful. Playing and betting was all that mattered to me. My parents were fed up and saw me as a loser. That was how they labeled me, and I bought it. When I won big, my self-esteem soared. When I lost big, I always became depressed, and my self-esteem plummeted. The size of my bets kept growing, and needless to say, the same was happening with the size of my debts.

"For me to continue doing the only thing that gave me pleasure, I had to start selling some of my possessions. After a while I sold everything I could that I thought my parents wouldn't miss.

"When I ran out of things to sell, I didn't know what to do or where to turn. None of my friends had any money, and my parents weren't about to lend me any. Then one day, with empty pockets and a tremendous need to gamble, it came to me that there was one person who would never say no to me. I went over to Grandma's house.

"I knew I would have to sit and visit with Grandma for a little while, and I also knew she would slip me a ten- or twenty-dollar bill when I was leaving. I gambled that day and I won big. I was able to stay on top for quite a while. Of course, during those winning days, I didn't think once about Grandma.

"By the time my gambling had taken a serious turn for the worse, I found myself lying big time to Grandma. I had no choice. My debts were often very high. I had no way of coming up with the money, and besides,

Grandma used to tell me that it gave her great pleasure to give me money. I never once saw a change in Grandma's heart; she loved me unconditionally. She could never see me in a bad light.

"With hindsight, I can see how I was on a downward spiral that would only end in disaster. Gambling made me blind and deaf. I didn't notice that Grandma was in poor health. I only noticed that she had become even more generous with me. One time when I needed over seven hundred dollars to cover a debt, I told Grandma that I needed the money because I had gotten a girl pregnant, and she agreed an abortion was our best option. Grandma gave me the money immediately. She said because I was so young, fathering a child could ruin any chance I would ever have to have a happy and successful life.

"My trips to Grandma's house became more frequent. One day Grandma hesitated to give me money. I thought my parents had gotten to her. I thought they had told her about my gambling. I was furious. I left in anger. I didn't care if my behavior upset Grandma. The only thing I cared about was finding a way to get the money I needed to gamble.

"That night the answer came to me. I knew Grandma kept large sums of cash in her home. She always worried that something might come up that would require instant cash. So she saw to it that her liquid funds never ran dry.

"The thought of stealing from Grandma didn't bother me in the least. I rationalized it by remembering that Grandma told me she was going to leave her money to me anyway.

"I started visiting Grandma more often. I treated her kindly and helped her with little things she needed to have done. She was happier than she had ever been. So was I. I never left her home without feeding my gambling pockets with the money I needed to keep me in action.

"My last visit was seven years ago. I relive that visit every day and every night. When I arrived, she was lying on the couch. She didn't smile when I walked in. She looked wiped out. When she spoke she mumbled, and I couldn't understand a word she said. I paid her no attention. I was only there to get more money. I took a few hundred dollars and drove over to the card room.

"When I got home that night, my parents were sitting in the living room; it was after midnight. Dad stood up and said: 'Grandma had a stroke. She is in the hospital, unable to speak or move. Her condition is very serious.' He asked me when I last saw her. I told him it was several days ago. As soon as I got those words out I felt a large lump in my throat. All I could think about was that maybe the reason she was mumbling when I was in her home earlier was because she was having the stroke at that time. I went to my room and said nothing.

"Just before sunrise, the phone rang. Grandma had passed away. Now I could never, never tell my parents the truth. How could I? How could I ever reveal that I was with her when she needed me, and I just turned and walked away?

"For weeks I didn't gamble. I had no way of getting money to gamble, and besides, I blamed Grandma's death on my uncontrollable need to gamble. I swore to myself that I would never gamble again. I had no question in my mind that I would keep this promise. The next night, I returned to the card room with twenty dollars I stole from my mom's purse.

"My hatred of myself grew. I knew I had to get honest and reach out for help. When I got home, I woke up my parents and told them everything about my gambling. I told them I stole from Grandma and that I stole from Mom. I did not tell them I was in Grandma's house the day she died. I just couldn't let them know that. It would hurt them too much and they would probably hate me even more than I hate myself.

"At first my parents were very angry. But when I said I would do whatever they wanted me to, my father said I needed to go to Gamblers Anonymous immediately. I attended my first meeting the following night. I was surprised to see two other guys my age sitting at the meeting. When they spoke, I identified with them so strongly, I knew right away this was where I needed to be.

"The only ones who know the truth about why I stopped gambling are the men and women in my GA room. It took me three and a half years to remain totally abstinent from gambling. My relapses were the result of all the guilt I carried over Grandma's death. Without a doubt, I was directly responsible for her demise. Until I shared this pain, this guilt, with other members of my fellowship, I could not maintain abstinence from gambling.

"I haven't gambled in more than three years, and my life has completely turned around. I graduated from high school with a general diploma. Following that, Dad sent me to a technical school to become a draftsman.

Today I am an excellent draftsman, I have a good job, and I have many friends, none of whom gamble.

"I gambled to be accepted. I gambled to be admired. I gambled to obtain all the things in life that I thought would make me happy and feel loved. My addiction to gambling made it impossible for me to realize that I was already accepted, I was already admired, and I was already loved unconditionally by the one person who never criticized me, who never put me down. My gambling took from me everything in life that really matters—unconditional love."

ANYTHING FOR ACTION

Despite sincere efforts to keep our youth from gambling, many teens are able to bypass these roadblocks. As a result, numerous underage compulsive gamblers are mired in heavy debt, under pressure from illegal moneylenders, and overwhelmed by the thought that they have no means to raise the money they need to relieve themselves of pressure. For some young gamblers, even a few hundred dollars represents an amount they just cannot raise. The fear and guilt they live with too often leads the young gambler to consider thoughts of self-destruction.

Neal's Story

"When I was fourteen years old, my dad took me to a racetrack. He would go there a couple of times a month with some friends. Even on my first visit I knew I would be back. I was so excited watching the horses run, hearing the sound of their hoofs hitting the dirt, and especially listening to the screams and shouts of the players as they watched the horses come down the home stretch.

"Following that visit, I thought about it for days. I convinced my dad to take me back a couple of weeks later. I wanted to find out if my reaction would be the same as my first visit. It wasn't. It was much stronger. I knew instinctively that I had found something that would enrich my life. Just being at the racetrack made me feel so alive.

"For some reason, Dad sensed that I was a little too impressed with horse racing so he refused to bring me there again. I did the wrong thing. I haunted him to let me return, and that only irritated him and reinforced his stance that I did not belong there.

"For the rest of that year, I didn't bring it up again. But I never forgot the exhilaration I felt on my two visits to the track. I remember at the time wondering how any event could produce such feelings of excitement. My desire to return became so strong I developed a compulsion I could not ignore. For the next few months, I began to plan how I could go to the track without my parents' knowledge. Better still, because I was only sixteen years old, I wanted to find a way I could place my bets and not be ID'd by the pari-mutuel clerk. One thing in my favor was my size. I was already almost six feet tall and weighed just over two hundred pounds.

"As much as I wanted to make horse racing a part of my life, I never told anyone. None of my friends had ever gone to a racetrack, and so I believed I was the only one with this strong interest. It didn't matter. All I wanted was to once again experience the feelings I had standing at the track railing.

"For my sixteenth birthday my parents gave me a used car. I didn't care that it was used. I was thrilled because I knew with wheels I could get to wherever I wanted to be. And the only place I wanted to be was at the racetrack.

"At noon, I celebrated my birthday with my whole family. It was a happy day. They were happy, and I was happy, too. Everyone thought I was happy because of the car. In a way I was, but only because it would enable me to satisfy a dream I had nourished for over a year.

"My parents were liberal with me as far as going out after dinner. I was a good student and never got in any kind of trouble. And as long as my grades were decent, they stayed off my back. That night I went to the track.

"I was amazed that I got in without question. I guess that was because of my size. But that alone didn't give me the courage to try and place a bet. I watched every race, placed a mental bet, and 'recorded' every outcome. For a novice player I did very well.

"When I got home I could hardly sleep. All I could think of was returning the following night. The following night was what turned my life around. I repeated what I had done the previous night (placed mental bets), and I won big. I wanted to shout it to the world, but I couldn't. Who could

I tell? No one would be happy for me. No one would support my interest. I had to keep quiet.

"I just had to find a way to place my bets. On my next visit, I decided to just observe what went on when the players went up to the windows and placed their bets. What I saw I didn't like. As far as I could see, every clerk ID'd each player who looked underage. I returned home thinking I was going to have to sit on my dream for another five years.

"This was all I thought about the following day. Because I had already seen that I was capable of picking winners, I decided I would continue going to the track until I found a way to play. Within a week I found the answer.

"As the evening goes on, I noticed the lines for the seventh and eighth races are longer than the lines for the earlier races. Gamblers always want to win back their losses. So they play every race. Many of the gamblers on these lines are annoyed and irritable because they have not had a winning night. The clerks are very well aware that the players have no patience. The clerks need to be efficient and fast in taking their bets. This is especially true when the race is about to take off. I was sure if I got on that line I would not be ID'd because the players in line behind me would not stand for it.

"Following that night, I waited patiently for the seventh race to begin. Just as I had predicted, the line was long and the players were impatient. When I reached the window, the race was within two minutes of running and there were at least four players behind me. I made my wager without so much as a peep from the clerk. I was right. He couldn't take the time to ID me because the rest of the players would have been furious at him. All they wanted was to place their bets before the race began.

"From that night on, I had no problem ever gambling at the track. As a matter of fact, within a short time the clerks knew me and never once attempted to check my age.

"In the beginning I often won big. As a matter of fact, at one point my Dad noticed that I seemed to have an awful lot of money in my possession. I had become a quick-thinking liar, and without hesitation I told him I was helping my teacher after school with some of his personal projects, for which he paid me. Dad was so pleased he praised me for doing that.

"As bad as my gambling had become, I never let up on my studies. My freedom to get out at night and gamble was directly related to how good my grades were on my report card. Learning came easy to me, and both my parents knew that. If I were to begin failing, they would immediately know something was seriously wrong, and they would be relentless in their pursuit to find the answer.

"Within a few months my gambling got completely out of hand. When my winning streak ended, I began to steal from my parents. My debts kept swelling. I met a loan shark who did bail me out a few times by lending me money, and I repaid him within a week. I thought this was a pretty good business deal until my losses became far greater than my wins. It all happened so fast. My losses just continued to swell, and I kept borrowing more and more from the loan shark. The interest he was charging me kept growing, too. At first it was 45 percent, and it soon rose to over 75 percent. I was drowning in guilt and fear. I had nowhere to turn. There was no place from which I could borrow money. And it had been weeks since I'd had a winning night at the track.

"The only one I could talk to was the loan shark. He was, at this point, threatening to hurt me or my family. I was panicky. I knew he meant business. Then he made me an offer I could not refuse. He told me he had a friend who had been dealing in drugs but was arrested and sent away. He told me his friend's supplier was looking for someone to make one delivery, and he would reward that person accordingly. The shark said I would get enough money to more than pay off my debts.

"All I could think of was that I would get the pressure off me, and best of all, I could get back in action and continue to indulge in my one love. Without much thought, I agreed to make the delivery.

"I don't know how it happened or why, but I was pulled over by the police. When they looked at my driver's license and saw I was seventeen, they questioned what I was doing out on a school night at almost one o'clock in the morning. They took me out of my car. They searched my car, found the drugs (cocaine and heroin), and arrested me.

"My parents were devastated when they found out what had happened. I didn't get to see them until after my father obtained the services of an attorney. The attorney was able to get my bail lowered from ten thousand dollars to twenty-five hundred. The judge agreed to the lower bail because I had never been in prior trouble.

"My extracurricular activities in school really saved me. I joined the school newspaper and the debating club as an investment in my parents' trust of me, but also as an excuse I could use when I wanted to go out on a school night to gamble. All the school activities took place either right after school or before my first class, but my parents did not know that.

"When my case came before the judge, my attorney had put together enough information about my school activities to convince the judge not to send me away. I got five years of probation and two years of community service. I was so grateful.

"My attorney recommended I begin attending Gamblers Anonymous meetings. I did just that, but at first I hated them. I was the only guy there under the age of forty. I felt I didn't fit in. One night a young man about twenty-seven years old attended my meeting and told me of another meeting about twelve miles away that had three other teenage boys in attendance. I gave it a try, and I knew right away that that was where I belonged. I could identify with everything those guys shared.

"A year into abstinence, I graduated from high school with fairly decent grades. When my father offered to let me attend college out of town, I insisted on staying home so I could work part-time and begin repaying all the gambling debts I had accumulated. I also wanted to stay local so I could continue to attend my GA meetings. I did not feel strong enough to relocate and start in a new recovery room. This was suggested by the guys in my GA, and I've learned not to question them but rather to follow them.

"My gambling career was short-lived. The consequences of my gambling will be very long-lived. My parents were devastated, embarrassed, and ashamed. We have a large extended family, and some of them blamed my parents for my behavior. I don't know if things can ever be the same again.

"With hindsight, I can't believe my need to gamble was so strong, so uncontrollable that I would risk all I did just to be able to place a bet. It was only with the help of other compulsive gamblers that I realized I have an addiction, an addiction that controlled me. There was no way I could ever have been able to stop gambling on my own. The pull for the feelings I got when I was in action (sitting on a bet) was stronger than any other feeling I had ever had in my life.

"Presently, I am working in my uncle's garage to earn the money I need to repay my gambling debts to my family.

"My parents are attending Gam-Anon. From what they have learned there, most of their anger has subsided. Now when we sit down for dinner together, we can talk calmly, and sometimes we even laugh together. I am gaining back their trust and as much as I previously wanted to gamble, I now want nothing more than to have them believe in me. For the first time in years, I feel good about myself and I feel loved by my parents. No big win could have ever bought me that."

ATHLETES AND GAMBLING

One of the first things parents do when a serious problem arises with one of their children is to find out why it is happening and what caused it to come about. Adolescents are not known for having effective communication skills. Parents sometimes spend a great deal of time trying to find out what is going on, and it is often to no avail. Since gambling is an activity that is easy to hide, it can be almost impossible to find out that it is at the core of a child's problem. This is especially true if the child is female and the problem is gambling.

Page's Story

"My father is a high school physical education teacher and a tough coach to his school's lacrosse team. My mother is a registered nurse who also works in a school system.

"From the time I was very young, my parents exposed me to many activities that they thought would be good for me and that I might like. I went to dancing school, took gymnastics, had swimming and skiing lessons, and when I was in sixth grade, I joined the school's field hockey team. Within a year of playing field hockey, my parents believed I had the potential for being a great athlete. I loved competing.

"My parents encouraged me to get involved with other sports. The sport I chose to focus on was tennis. Right from the start, I loved it. What I liked most was that I wasn't part of a team. Tennis is an individual sport. I do the work; I get the credit. Within a few months, my coach suggested I begin practicing with the boys because that would improve my stamina and my strength. I was pleased and excited about this idea.

"My game did improve and the coach suggested to my parents that I get involved in more competition than the school was able to supply. I started competing in games offered by private tennis clubs and the National Tennis Association.

"By the beginning of my junior year, I was almost unbeatable in my age group. However a serious problem started to develop with my father. When I first played tennis, Dad was pleased because I played well and I was happy. When I began entering heavy competition, Dad got more involved and attended every event. I always knew Dad was a tough lacrosse coach, but his team ranked second in the county and that was all that mattered.

"I knew Dad loved me and wanted to support me, but as my competition got tough he also got tough. He would scream at me as I was playing whenever I made an error or didn't play the shot as he thought I should. Dad never played tennis in his life, but all of a sudden he was an expert in his own mind. His criticisms and put-downs were unbearable. I was embarrassed and humiliated every time I played. Even when I won he would find some fault with my game. My coach saw how upset I was with Dad's behavior so he spoke to him and tried to get him to back off. Dad refused to listen stating the reason his lacrosse team was so successful was because he never let a single player slack off. He pushed them, embarrassed them, and put them down so they would be so angry they would play harder.

"Although Mom saw what a difficult time I was having, she said little. After a while she stopped attending my matches. She never said why, but I think she too was embarrassed with Dad's behavior.

"My situation only worsened. I hated every day I had to compete. I lost my love of the sport. My hands were tied and I was powerless. At the beginning of my senior year I looked for outside relief. I knew if I started drinking my parents would notice. I couldn't do drugs because they were expensive and also illegal. But in time I did find my relief. I began to play lotto. It was safe. No one would find out. I enjoyed it. Whenever I went to buy my lotto tickets, I was happy.

"At this point in my tennis career the only relief I was ever able to feel was when I won a tournament without making a single mistake. It got so that winning, to me, had only one meaning—relief. Relief from my dad's put-downs and criticisms and relief from my feelings of embarrassment and humiliation.

"Just a few months after getting involved in buying lotto tickets, I made my first trip to a casino. I played the slots for four hours with the money my grandparents sent me for my birthday. That was the longest period of relief I had in more than a year. I knew I had to come back again.

"Soon I wanted to play the slots more than once a week, but I didn't have the money. I manipulated some money from Mom a couple of times saying I needed something for school. My devotion to tennis lessened. I didn't want to practice, but Dad wouldn't let me give it up. He felt sure if I continued I would be offered a college scholarship. At one time I would have been elated over that, but at this point the only thing I wanted to do was gamble.

"In the last half of my senior year in high school, Dad got a position coaching a local college lacrosse team. I was so happy because this team competed on weekends and practiced at night. That kept Dad out of the house three nights a week until at least eleven o'clock.

"Mom always trusted me and would believe whatever I told her. When I said I was studying with a friend, she believed me. When I said I was getting extra coaching time, she believed me. The truth was, I was rushing back and forth to the casino to buy relief.

"At that time my gambling really picked up. I moved to the quarter slots because the thrill I got was stronger at those machines and because when I won, I won big. Still there were days when I lost everything. At this point, I knew that no matter what, I wanted to continue gambling. I was hooked, but I didn't care. Gambling had become my tranquilizer, my pain-killer, and my escape venue. I was able to handle all the pressures in my life as long as I gambled.

"Soon I was introduced to a moneylender who specialized in helping out young gamblers who had limited ways of obtaining funds. I couldn't understand why 'Ed' was so trusting and generous, but he was, and that was all that mattered to me.

"My gambling continued throughout the summer. The relief it gave me made it possible to deal with the continued pressure from Dad whenever I competed. He continued to attend every match and, of course, remained relentless in his criticisms.

"That September I began my senior year in high school and at the time I had no idea how much debt I had accumulated. Ed never haunted me for money, and I never kept any record. My first day at the casino in early September, I found myself face-to-face with Ed. He said I had overextended my credit and he wanted his money—all eight thousand dollars. I was shocked at the amount. I had no idea that it had gone so high. No matter what I said, he wouldn't listen. He just wanted his money, and he wanted it now. I was panicky. I had nowhere to turn. He told me if I didn't pay him immediately, he would see to it that I could never play tennis again. I was scared to death.

"The only person I trusted to tell my situation to was my coach. I knew he would listen. When I finished he drove me directly home and made me tell everything to my parents. As much as I protested, he said I could not avoid facing them, and it had to be done now because I could be in immediate danger if I didn't do it right away.

"My mother became hysterical and my dad was furious. My coach warned them that this Ed could be a very dangerous man and that my life could be in jeopardy. I had Ed's cellular phone number so Dad called him. Together they made arrangements to meet, and Dad would pay him the money I owed.

"My family was destroyed by my gambling. I kept it secret for so long the revelation made it even worse for my parents. My parents and my coach insisted I join Gamblers Anonymous so I could stop gambling and get my life back on track. I did that, and during my early months in abstinence I began to realize the reason Ed lent me so much money and didn't bug me to get it back was because he knew all along that he actually was lending the money to my parents. He knew they would pay any amount to protect me and to keep me from being hurt.

"There are many 'Eds' out there who have an innocent co-signer for every dollar they lend to an underage gambler. These co-signers are called parents. What price wouldn't any parent pay to protect their child from harm? Ed could have asked my parents for double the amount and gotten it."

SECOND GENERATION AND GAMBLING

As devastating as compulsive gambling is for teens, it can be even more so for the parents. No matter what situation teenagers get into, most parents are there to support them and to do whatever they can to help. Few parents would turn their backs on a child in trouble. When the situation is one involving gambling, heavy debts, and the threat of physical harm, parents will open their wallets and their hearts to rescue their child.

Koto's Story

"My parents arrived in San Francisco from Vietnam in 1982. They were part of what was once referred to as the 'boat people.' During the Vietnam War, my father was a reporter for a South Vietnam newspaper and my mother was a teacher.

"For the first three years in the United States my parents lived in a two-bedroom apartment with two other families, both of whom were cousins of my mother. Within a week of their arrival, both of them were working. Because my father spoke so little English, he could not get any kind of a well-paying job. He became a dishwasher in a Chinese restaurant close to where they lived. My mother began working at home as a seamstress. Within two years my parents were able to get a place of their own. By then they were each working two jobs to get the money they needed to live independently. About fifteen months after that I was born, on my father's fortieth birthday.

"My memory of growing up was that my life was ruled by consistency, rigidity, and great expectations. My father saw America as a land where you could be whatever you wanted as long as you continually worked toward that end. His personal goal was to work hard and make his parents, who were still living in Vietnam, proud. That meant I had to turn out 'right,' or he didn't do a good job.

"My parents tried very hard to raise me within the Vietnamese culture, but I was not living in Vietnam. Although I spoke Vietnamese at home, I spoke English everywhere else. In my heart and mind I was not Vietnamese, I was American. Being in this situation made life difficult for me and my parents. My parents (especially my father) had only two goals in life for me, to get a good education and to make them proud. I did not want to disappoint them. But my goal all through high school was to do well with my studies, be accepted by my peers, and have fun. On the few occasions when I did cut school or fail a test, I never let them know. In order to keep this from them, I would often lie.

"Leaving home to go to college was one very happy day for my parents.

I was given a full scholarship to a major Eastern university. They gave it to me because my grade average was 3.6 and because I was the child of 'boat people.'

"Because I had a good head for science and because I enjoyed science, I decided to major in pre-med. I never wanted to work as hard as my parents, but I did want to one day live in luxury, so I chose medicine as my major.

"Surprisingly I got through my first three years at the university with only moderate effort. In my final year, my world fell apart. I didn't need to work since my father sent me a generous allowance each month, and because I often had time on my hands, I developed a new hobby. I began gambling on sports over the Internet. I must have become addicted within the first month. It was so easy. I didn't have to go to the games. I didn't have to use a bookie. I didn't have to let anyone know.

"My grades actually went up the first few months after I began gambling on sports. The reason for that was because I viewed my gambling as a reward for doing well in my studies. I convinced myself that I deserved an outlet because I worked so hard. At first I bet only on basketball because I was a fan and familiar with the players and the teams. Soon I found myself betting on any sport. Almost immediately I was spending every penny my father sent me on sports betting.

"When I could no longer support my gambling with my allowance, I started tutoring other students who were having a hard time with some of their science courses. Eventually this was too time-consuming, so I started a new business. I offered to take tests for students who were on the brink of failing. The classes at my university were so large that there was no way the professor would know the name and face of each student. This worked out great because I charged a hundred dollars for each test. Most of my clients were from wealthy families, so money was no problem. A couple of kids I sat for got the money from their fathers, who would pay anything to get their sons into med school.

"I thought my 'business' would be enough to support my gambling, but it wasn't. My need to be in action had become so strong I could not satisfy it. I began lying to my father, saying I wanted to join several clubs at the university but I would need additional money to do so. He didn't care. He was so proud of me, he sent me whatever I requested.

"Right after the holidays in my senior year, I began receiving free credit cards in the mail. Some of the cards had credit limits of five thousand dollars. These cards were the answer to my dreams. I decided to use the cards to get money to gamble. I planned to pay off the credit cards before the following semester with the grant money that was coming to me to attend medical school.

"By the end of January, I had begun my downward spiral into the pits of pathological gambling. Out of guilt, and because I no longer needed money from my father, I told him to stop sending me the extra money because my studies were so grueling I had no time for extracurricular activities.

"Gambling turned me into someone even I wouldn't recognize. I was capable of anything. I became a proficient liar and manipulator. One thing I still wanted to do was keep my grades up, but it was impossible. I could not pull myself away from the computer. I was gambling on the Internet day and night. By the time I maxed out my fifth credit card, the other four card companies were haunting me for money. I fell into a deep depression. I had nowhere to turn. I began writing bad checks to satisfy some of the card companies and to buy time until I could get a summer job and start paying my debts. Even there I wasn't thinking straight. My debts were over twenty-three thousand dollars. A summer job would pay no more than seven dollars an hour. I was totally overwhelmed.

"In early May, my parents began asking me for my date of graduation. They were looking forward to this as a milestone in our family. My father was so proud. I knew I wasn't graduating—I had failed three science courses. I was adamant about keeping my state of affairs from my parents. I could never face my father with what I had done. Even as I sat drowning in guilt and feeling totally depressed, I was thinking of new ways to get money to gamble. I told myself that no one would ever understand what this feels like. To me, nothing mattered, nobody mattered, only satisfying the urge to be in action mattered. And I was willing to pay any price to be able to place my bets.

"On the second day of finals my parents showed up at my dorm room. I was gambling on the computer when they arrived. They didn't pay attention to what was on the screen. They asked my roommate to leave us alone, then they closed the door. Only my father spoke. He told me the previous night two policemen came to their apartment looking for me. They wanted to arrest me for writing bad checks. My mother was sobbing quietly. My father spoke with disbelief. He was asking only for an explanation. He said he knew there had to be some error, and he wanted me to explain it to him.

"I was so depressed and overwhelmed with guilt I fell to my knees. I didn't move. I didn't say a word. When I looked up and into the eyes of my father, I realized for the first time the extent of the damage my gambling had caused. I have never seen such pain on the face of another human being. This time I couldn't lie. I told them everything. My father said nothing. Instead, he stood up and took my mother by the arm and walked out of the room.

"My father covered my bad checks, paid off all my credit cards, and kept me out of jail. He never lectured me, scolded me, or criticized me. I would have preferred a verbal or physical lashing to his silence.

"I flunked the whole last semester of my senior year. I did not return home. I stayed in the university town and worked two jobs. Every week without fail, I mailed a money order to my father for fifty dollars. I never included a message with it. I did not speak to my father nor try to contact him. Although my mother was also silent during this time, I knew she was supporting her husband, and I knew her heart was broken.

"When I decided to stay in the university town, I also began attending Gamblers Anonymous meetings. I totally surrendered to their suggestions and I attended the meetings religiously. The members in my GA room were the ones who recommended I send money home to my father to try and build up trust in me again.

"The following fall, I reregistered for my final semester. I did not give up my jobs. I attended classes from seven in the morning until noon. At one in the afternoon, I worked in the post office until eight in the evening. When I left that job each day, I went straight to my GA meeting. On Saturdays, I worked eight hours in the community hospital, in the maintenance department. And you could find me on any given Sunday in the university library doing my assignments for the week.

"This heavy schedule was actually suggested by the recovering gamblers in my GA room. They told me it was very important to keep busy during the early part of my recovery. I must say, I found that to be true. I hardly had time to think at all about gambling. I'm exhausted every day, and I sleep soundly every night.

"I have been abstinent from gambling for six months. I don't know if I will ever get my father back in my life, but right now I am trying not to make that the focus of my days. Each day I concentrate on one thing and one thing only—not placing a bet. Every time I go to sleep, knowing I haven't gambled that day, I know I've won.

"Gambling is a great preventative. It prevents you from reaching your goals, nurturing your spirit, having successful relationships, and savoring your own personal values. All I want today is to stay clean from gambling, and perhaps someday hear my father say, 'I'm proud of you, Son.'"

Facts on File

Most of our youths' views on gambling are the result of what they hear from the adults who surround them. When parents and other family members focus their conversations on the excitement of gambling and on big wins, young people often begin to fantasize about what a wonderful way gambling is to obtain money without having to work. Underage gamblers rarely hear how often gamblers lose large amounts of money or how much debt they are in as a result of their gambling. One reason for this is that most gamblers strive to get one point across: They are winners.

Most underage gamblers do not know the serious downside of gambling. Few adolescents are able to recount stories of adult gamblers who were totally devastated by this addiction.

Questions

- Have you found that winning at gambling is the most effective way to raise your self-esteem?
- Does gambling eliminate your feelings of frustration about not being able to change things in your life that are controlled by others?
- Do you live with feelings of guilt because you have lied to and stolen from your family to support your gambling?
- Are you shouldering heavy, painful secrets as a result of your gambling?

7

Senior Citizen gamblers

SENIOR CITIZENS MAKE UP the fastest-growing segment of compulsive gamblers in the United States. By the time most senior citizens retire, they have worked for more than four decades, they have raised their children, and some have buried their spouses. Now they find themselves living alone without family members nearby, dealing with loss of self-esteem since leaving their job, suffering with some physical ailment requiring ongoing treatment, and having to find new ways to eradicate the boredom of the long and empty hours they face each day. It seems reasonable for them to want to fill their leisure time with something that makes them feel good and removes the loneliness. For many, that something is gambling.

Seniors, at times, defend their gambling by claiming they are no longer physically able to do the things they did when they were younger. The options open to seniors for having fun are limited. For these reasons, the daily bus rides to casinos are very popular. From the day they opened, casinos said they could fill their seats during off-peak hours with senior citizens, if they made it easy, inexpensive, and comfortable for them to get there. In response, not only did the seniors come, but they also said they felt very special because they were given coupons for a free lunch and vouchers that they could exchange for gambling chips.

Seniors are probably the most vulnerable group of gamblers because they live on a fixed income and cannot afford to risk losing money gambling. In addition, they are not in a position to recoup their losses and start over.

LEISURE TIME AND GAMBLING

When seniors come to realize that gambling helps them escape the pain of their reality, they become more and more drawn to it.

Nate's Story

"Why shouldn't I gamble? I worked hard for more than forty years, my wife never wanted for anything, and my son got whatever he needed and most of what he wanted. Today, he owns his own plumbing business, his wife is a waitress at an upscale restaurant, and their fifteen-year-old twin daughters are in high school.

"Since my wife died two years ago, my son or his wife calls me every month or so to come and visit them. They live almost three hours away. I still drive, but most often I turn down their invites. Since I lost my wife I feel I don't fit in when I'm with them. I think they only invite me because they feel they should and because they feel sorry for me. When I'm with them, we have very little conversation. We have nothing in common. I don't even know what to talk about with the girls. I'm seventy-eight years old. Most of their friends' grandfathers are in their late fifties or early sixties, still involved in their lives and able to do things together. I cannot even walk without the aid of my walker, so I'd rather stay home.

"Where do I fit? At a card table or at a sporting event. My friends there greet me with happy faces—they are truly pleased to see me. That's where I get respect and attention. I feel appreciated whenever I am with them. So what if they all gamble? They are my family now. I always heard money can't buy happiness. That's not true. I know what makes me happy, and it requires money. I'm happy when I hold a straight or a flush. I'm happy when my team is winning. Me stop gambling? Never.

"I tried to tell my son, Stu, that I am not lonely. My days are full, and I have good friends with whom I spend my time. Stu's objection is that my friends are all gamblers. He blames them for my increased interest in gambling. It's true we all like to gamble, and we indulge in several kinds of gambling. My favorite is cards. I've been playing cards all my life, it's fun, and there is no better way to pass the time. When I get tired of card playing, I will follow the sport of the season and place bets on my favorite teams.

"I have never missed paying a bill or taking care of myself as a result of my gambling. My bets are not large, and the losses are such that my lifestyle is not affected. My son just thinks that I should fill my time with other activities. I don't tell him how to live his life. I wish he would just leave me alone."

When Stu speaks, we hear a different story.

Stu's Story

"If you know any persons with gambling problems, then you know they are not only gamblers but also liars. My dad has lived a good and honorable life. I have never known him to be a liar; that is, until he started making gambling the center of his universe.

"I know he is lonely since my mother passed away. I also know that because of his physical condition (he can only get around with the aid of a walker) he is limited in the number of activities he can still enjoy. He uses his condition as an excuse to spend all his time hanging out with his gambling buddies and placing bets.

"Dad claims that his love of gambling hasn't resulted in any financial problems. That is just not true. Two years ago when he had prostate surgery, I had him sign a limited power of attorney. That gave me access to his bank accounts and his financial holdings. I know he is dipping into his capital to feed his habit. Within the last year alone, he has gone through twenty thousand dollars in casino gambling alone. Yet he denies ever having been in a casino.

"He is so hooked on gambling he doesn't take care of himself. He is on several different medications, and when his monthly income runs out, he will tap his savings account to get money to gamble, but he will not take a penny to renew his prescriptions.

"On many occasions when he could spend time with me and my family, he refused because he didn't want to miss a day of being in action. He always says he doesn't have many more years left on this earth, so he has the right to spend his time as he sees fit. I want him to spend time with me for just the same reason he wants to continue to gamble—it doesn't occur to him that we don't know how many years either of us has on this earth.

"I wish my dad would stop gambling or at least make it fit into one of his other activities. Most of all, I wish he had more time for me and his granddaughters. Although he might deny it, my daughters love him, and they too wish he was more interested in them. We are all hurting, but Dad can't or won't stop gambling."

GRIEVING AND GAMBLING

Each year, the number of female gamblers grows because women today are employed, bring home a paycheck, have their own credit, and are overall more independent. At the present time, many older women are the first generation likely to have inherited money not only from their deceased spouses, but also from their parents who survived the Depression by living frugally, thereby passing their savings on to their children. These widows are the first generation of elders who enter the golden years with more financial security than ever before. Their economic situation gives them the freedom to fill their days with whatever suits their fancy. They have ample funds to cover monthly bills. Most of these widows are in good health and have enough energy to fill long hours each day without burning out physically.

When a woman is widowed, for the first several months or years she will fill most of her days and hours thinking about her lost spouse. As she moves through the grieving process, she will one day find herself looking at options as to how she can fill each day. Unfortunately, for those who have money, it is easier to turn to more expensive avenues of adventure.

Jan's Story

"Scott was always a health nut. He watched his fat and sugar intake, and he was physically active and a competitor with the Masters Track and Field events. Scott ran track in high school and never gave it up.

"Because Scott was adopted, we never knew his genetic family history. Even though he had yearly checkups, which showed him to be in excellent health, he was diagnosed at age fifty-two with congenital heart failure. His heart became so weak he was put on a transplant list. While on the list, he passed away early one Wednesday morning with no one at his side.

"Even when Scott was ill, I never believed he would die. Having lived such a healthy life, he seemed to have more going for him than most. The doctor told me that because he was still young and in such good condition, he was high on the list of those awaiting transplants. Despite all our optimism, Scott passed away two months after entering the hospital.

"For the year following Scott's death, I hardly did anything. I had no interest in life. I quit my job as a paralegal and spent most of my time at home alone. I never had any children, but Scott had one daughter by his first wife. Kami and I were friendly whenever we saw each other, but that wasn't very often since she lived almost two thousand miles away.

"The first time I entered a casino, I was alone. At the time, I adamantly refused to spend time with anyone, even close friends. I did not want to socialize or act in any way that would indicate I had gotten over Scott's death. I knew I would never get over losing him. I was almost six years older than Scott, and I assumed I would die first. I never once entertained the thought that he would precede me.

"I gambled a little over four hundred dollars on my first visit to the slots. I did win a number of times, but I don't remember how much. I didn't care if I won or lost. My goal was to be by myself and kill time. When I returned home that evening, it was nightfall, and I was glad. It meant the day was almost over. During those months, as much as I wanted to sleep, I couldn't. I could not find peace. I could not get Scott out of my mind. I was angry that he died, depressed living without him, and lonely knowing I would never again have him by my side.

"In the weeks that followed, I did not think about returning to the casino. Then one day, in the mail, I received a coupon book from the casino I visited offering me a free bus trip, a voucher for lunch, and fifteen dollars. In addition, they enclosed a credit card that would allow me to play the slots without having to ask for change all the time. I liked that idea. The trip to the casino would take two and a half hours. That meant I would fill five hours just sitting on the bus. Adding to that the hours I would spend at the slots, I knew I would kill another whole day. I decided to take them up on their offer.

"Within a couple of months, my trips increased to three times a week. On one of those trips, I won the jackpot on the three-quarters machine. All tolled, I collected almost four thousand dollars. That night the casino offered me a free room and meals so I wouldn't have to take the bus home. Because that was a stormy night, I accepted their offer. The room was beautiful, and they treated me like a queen. Twice an officer of the casino came to see me to ask if there was anything I needed or wanted. I couldn't remember ever feeling so special.

"The following day I lost all my winnings and then some. Nevertheless, I chalked it up to a good day since I never once felt lonely.

"Because I never liked driving long distances, I continued to take the bus to the casino. Then one day, the casino offered to pick me up in a limo. I enjoyed that more than the bus. There were three other women sharing the limo with me. It was interesting to me that each of us was a widow. We became quite friendly. What I liked was that they knew nothing about my background. Not that there was anything to hide, just that they didn't ask me about my marriage, my husband, or other relationships in my life. I was beginning to adjust to life without Scott, and I didn't want to continually talk about him. Two of the widows seemed to feel the same way. The third widow talked about her deceased spouse all the time, and frankly, none of us were interested.

"About six months after I made these new friends, one of them, Iris, decided to stop gambling because her children were angry with her. At first she didn't tell us why. Then she said she asked two of her children to help her pay her utility bill and a couple of her credit cards, which she had maxed out. We were shocked because we understood Iris was quite wealthy. She explained that she had been gambling at the casino for more than four years, and in that time she went through all the money her husband left her plus most of her own savings.

"That night I thought so much about what happened to Iris. I swore that would never happen to me. Although I didn't care if I won or lost, I certainly didn't want to end up penniless.

"By the time I had been playing the slots for about a year, I was so hooked on gambling it was the only thing in my life. I went there originally to help me deal with my grief over losing my husband. For the last few months I hardly ever thought about Scott. My focus four days a week was getting ready for the limo to pick me up. I never gave any thought to what happened to the widows I met on my first trip. Each one seemed to quietly drop out. I never wondered why. When a new widow entered the limo, I just accepted her.

"Probably my greatest downfall was visiting other casinos and gambling there in addition to my favorite casino. One year after beginning gambling, I had in my possession eight casino credit cards. These cards gave me the freedom to play the slots whenever I wanted and for as long as I wanted.

"Because of my devotion to the slots, my personal responsibilities at home were put on the back burner. I had no interest in anything other than sitting at the slots and moving quietly and succinctly away from my reality. I never felt lonely when I was in action, I never felt depressed, but what I did feel was relief and peace. The slots had very special meaning for me. I trusted them. They took care of me. Even when I wasn't winning, I could count on these machines to take care of my feelings—to numb them, to protect me from pain. The slots never let me down. Each time I sat in front of them I knew I was about to go to nirvana, and that gave me peace.

"My bottom came when each of my casino credit cards was canceled and my free limo trips were withdrawn. At this point, I was no longer opening my mail or paying my bills. I had become totally irresponsible. I guess in my mind I thought I could gamble forever and never have to stop. I certainly wasn't rich, but sporadically I did win big. However, on those occasions I invariably fed those winnings back into the machine. My gambling had gotten completely out of control. I could not fight off my never-ending urge to gamble.

"Despite how much and how often I was gambling, no one in my life was complaining about it. I had done such a good job of distancing myself from my friends that they got my message loud and clear. They left me alone.

"On my own, I reached out for help. I had no choice because my pockets were almost empty, and I didn't want to lose what little I had left. With the help of Gamblers Anonymous, I slowly began to get my life back on track. After having been retired for over three years, I had to go back to work to pay off all my credit cards and overdue bills.

"I began gambling to escape from loneliness, but the price was so high that I wound up with nothing in my life but feeding a machine that I thought cared about me. It was only after I began my recovery program that I learned to deal with the pain of losing Scott. And it was only with the help of Gamblers Anonymous that I was able to arrest my gambling addiction."

DISABILITY AND GAMBLING

One of the major problems facing senior citizens is how to fill their endless empty hours. Although there are centers that cater to seniors, these facilities often do not satisfy seniors' needs or wants. To wake up each day dreading the morning light is depressing and leads to feelings of hopelessness.

Because many senior citizens are living with some kind of physical ailment, they need to adapt to an existence that no longer includes their pleasures of the past. Accepting this situation requires a great deal of adjustment and a positive attitude.

Ward's Story

"When I turned fifty, I started to take note of the physical condition of some of my peers. I saw, for the most part, men who were invariably overweight and who had lost much of their zest for life. A couple of my friends had bypass surgery, and one of my brothers had a fatal heart attack. This shocked me into believing that if I didn't embark on a program of physical fitness, I might be next to join their group.

"I made a contract with myself to get into the best physical condition possible. I began playing racquetball three nights a week after work and every other Saturday morning. I grew to love it.

"In time, I made friends with three other guys who loved the sport as much as I. One of them, Ted, a sixty-seven-year-old retiree, was in better shape than any of us. He was kind of my role model. I thought if I could look as good as he at that age, I would be very happy.

"I also wanted to look good for my wife, Beth, who is eleven years my junior. Beth takes pride in looking great. She used to be an aerobics instructor, and even after she stopped she continued to exercise regularly. Beth leads a full life. She has many interests and a ton of friends. She has never been a clinging spouse, nor one who tells me what to do or not do. When I started playing racquetball, she was so pleased.

"Three years ago, I began having problems with my knees. I would be in tremendous pain each night when I returned home from playing. Within a few months, I could no longer play. I never once thought of giving up the game; instead, I focused on finding the best treatment available. At first I entered physical therapy, but after three months of that I was only in a little less pain, and I still could not play racquetball. My doctor suggested the best treatment would most likely be surgery. After speaking to a couple of others who had had the surgery, and because Beth said she couldn't stand seeing me so miserable, I decided it was my last hope.

"I did everything I was directed to do, but to no avail. Oh, the treatment definitely helped; I was able to do many things without pain, especially walk. However, I was still unable to return to the sport I loved.

"Within a short time I succumbed to depression. Every night I just sat at home. I pushed Beth away. I suffered with severe insomnia. No matter how hard I tried, I could not sleep. I moved into the guest room with the excuse that I did not want to disturb Beth's sleep. Instead of being grateful that I could walk without pain, I could only focus on the fact that I could never again play racquetball and be with my friends.

"As a result of not exercising and eating more than ever, I ballooned to well over two hundred pounds. The extra weight put additional stress on my knees, so the pain worsened. I had become old, fat, depressed, and very unhappy. With each passing day, I missed racquetball and the guys with whom I shared that sport.

"Beth was beside herself. She tried to be there for me, but I would not let her get close. My depression worsened. I wanted to leave my job and just stay home and isolate. So one day, without telling Beth what I was considering, I walked into my supervisor's office and handed him my retirement papers. When I got home and told Beth what I had done, she was furious, not because I retired but because I did not discuss it with her first. Beth made me listen to her for more than an hour. She told me how she had been patient with me and tried everything to help lift my depression, and how disappointed she was that I was wallowing in self-pity, and most of all how she had felt completely shut out of my life. She said she had kept all of her emotions locked up for fear that if she shared them with me, I would only get worse. She cried, and for the first time in months, I held her.

"At the end of the hour I promised Beth I would begin looking for a substitute to fill the hours I used to spend on the court. She suggested I start by attending some of the activities available at the senior center attached to our complex. To satisfy Beth, I was willing to accept any suggestion at that moment, so I agreed.

"It took me three days to go to the center. I did not want to spend my time with old people. I hated it there until one day when I met a man I had spoken to a few times prior. He told me he only went to the center to pick up his wife, who spent many hours there. Jake told me he spent his time playing cards with other men who did not frequent the center. He said he sometimes played for money and sometimes just for fun. The choice was up to him.

"This idea interested me because when I was in the navy, I played poker all the time, and I was a good player. The following day Jake took me with him to the card room, which was located in the basement of a small barbershop within walking distance of our complex. I never believed in love at first sight, but love of gambling at first sight I definitely believe in. I can't tell you how my mood lifted after I began playing cards on a daily basis. In the beginning, I never gambled more than I could afford. But then I don't know what happened. I've always been a man of great control. I never wanted anyone or anything to control me. When my gambling started to do just that, I couldn't see it. Or I didn't want to see it. All I wanted to do was gamble. When I started losing, I wouldn't leave the room until I won back my losses. I became obsessed with chasing my losses. Many times I not only didn't win back my losses, I lost more.

"Within a few months I was tapping our savings for money to keep me in action. Now, when I look back, I can see that I was addicted to the action, and neither winning nor losing had anything to do with why I wanted to gamble. I never once cared about how much money I was going through in order to gamble. My only desire was to keep alive the feelings I had when I was in action. I now know those feelings were caused by the adrenaline that flowed through my veins. Gambling was my answer to depression, insomnia, and continuous feelings of isolation.

"For the next few months, I focused on only two things: gambling and keeping Beth from finding out how much money I was 'investing' in it. I told myself that because I often won big, I could easily replace the money I was 'borrowing' from our accounts. The truth is that when I won big, it meant only one thing—I could place larger wagers and gamble for longer periods of time. I never replaced a penny of the money I was 'borrowing.'

"Within one year of daily card playing, I had gone through all of our savings, emptied out my 401k, and gambled all of Beth's inheritance from her parents. At that point we were totally broke. Did this stop me? No. I proceeded to take out a home equity loan by forging Beth's name on the application. I told the lender that my wife was handicapped and unable to leave the house. As a matter of fact, I told him I needed the money badly to get Beth additional medical care. The lender was very cooperative and even compassionate.

"Everything came to a screaming halt one day when I just couldn't stand myself anymore. My uncontrollable urge to gamble was more than I could bear. There were days when I swore I would not go to the card room, but I went anyway.

"At this point, Beth was still completely in the dark as to how much I was gambling. When I finally made up my mind to tell Beth everything, I immediately felt better. I knew Beth would understand and help me.

"Beth listened compassionately as I told her all. She said she knew there were people who couldn't control their gambling and that it was a sickness like alcoholism. It was when she asked me how much I had gambled and where I got the money that she did a complete turnaround. When I told her about emptying my 401k, spending her inheritance from her parents, and forging her name for a home equity loan, she lost it. I had never seen her so angry. For some reason, I thought because I confessed everything to her she would appreciate my honesty. I couldn't have been more wrong. Without hesitation, she told me to leave our home immediately. I did, and I didn't go back for three days. When I returned to try and explain further what had happened, Beth refused to listen. She told me she was divorcing me, not because of my gambling, but because I was not the man she had loved. She couldn't come to grips with the fact that I had deceived her so completely. She said there was no way she could ever trust me again. Added to that was the fact that now she was penniless when she thought she would have her inheritance to fall back on should she or I ever come upon bad times or serious illness.

"I never anticipated Beth would react so drastically. But she did. She walked out of my life without even looking back.

"I still have bad knees, I still suffer with insomnia, I am still grossly overweight, and I am still depressed. However, thanks to the men and women in my GA room, I am no longer gambling. The pain of losing Beth is something I will never get over. No matter how euphoric the feeling of adrenaline was flowing through my body, it could never replace the warmth and love I once had with Beth in my life."

DEMENTIA AND GAMBLING

Today, very few people live in an extended family household. Americans are uprooting and relocating on an ongoing basis. Grandparents are more likely to live far away from their children and their grandchildren than ever before. Distance makes bonding difficult for young children, and for adult children, it makes it very difficult to ensure that their elderly parents are safe and in good health.

As senior citizens age, their adult children become more and more concerned. Being involved with the care of an elderly parent is sometimes impossible purely for financial reasons. It is costly to get on a plane or have someone step in and take care of their families in their absence. For this reason, adult children live with unending guilt that should some tragedy befall their parents, they will not be there to help.

Ely's Story

"Until my father retired, my parents and I lived in the same small suburban community thirty miles from New York City. Because it's so costly to live in this area, my father decided he and my mother would relocate to Las Vegas. He knew they could purchase a less expensive home there and that the taxes would be lower. I was not happy about them living so far away, but I did nothing to discourage them.

"My parents lived in Las Vegas for almost twenty years before my father died. Although Dad liked to gamble at the casinos, it never caused a problem. He was careful with his money and never gambled more than he could afford. Mom had no interest in gambling. She did not like casinos nor the crowds walking on the strip nor the fact that tourists always seemed to be in a hurry. As Mom aged, she became unsteady on her feet, and twice she fell while walking along the street. She was embarrassed, so she blamed her mishap on the rushing tourists. Not having been there at the time, it was difficult to know how much of what Mom reported was factual.

"Three years ago, Mom had a mild stroke that left her limited on the right side of her body. She was fortunate in that she did not lose her ability to speak, and although she was still able to walk, her right leg would drag behind so she resorted to using a walker.

"My husband and my two daughters were second in my order of importance because Mom needed my attention. After her stroke, I tried to get her to move back home with us so I could be of more help. She adamantly refused, stating that Las Vegas had been her home for so many years she did not want to leave.

"Up until this time, Mom filled many of her afternoons playing bridge with her friends. This was something she enjoyed. Unfortunately, this came to an end the year following her stroke. She developed a serious eye disease, macular degeneration. The disease affected her lifestyle much more than the stroke. Mom's vision was now greatly impaired. She could no longer play bridge. Her friends were very supportive of Mom, but there was nothing they could do. Once again, I flew out to be with Mom and help rearrange her home to make it easier to get around without tripping over furniture. In addition, I redid all her closets so she could find the things she needed without being frustrated. After spending two weeks with Mom, I returned home feeling more concerned about her than ever.

"Things were quiet for the next few months. Then one day, after speaking to Mom on the phone, I found myself feeling a lot better. She told me she took a walk around the neighborhood by herself. She said she walked very slowly, was out about three-quarters of an hour, and felt tired when she returned. After napping, she made dinner for herself. She sounded uplifted and proud of what she had accomplished.

"When summer arrived, Mom was faced with a new problem: It was too hot for her to take her daily walk. Once again, she began staying home all day. After a couple of weeks of total boredom, she ventured out. She walked less than two blocks to a small neighborhood casino. Mom spent almost three hours there playing the nickel slots. When she got home, she called me and told me about her day. I was elated. I couldn't stand the thought of her sitting in her small house day in and day out. I remembered how much Dad enjoyed gambling, and it was never a concern or a problem.

"As the months passed, Mom continued her daily routine. Her mood lifted since she started visiting the 'locals' (her name for the small casinos).

She felt at home there, she was welcomed by the owner, it was nice and cool there, and they often gave her a free lunch. Most of all, Mom liked the fact that she could walk there and that it was a safe place for her to be. Then Mom mentioned something to me that had never crossed my mind. When she used to play bridge with her friends at her home, she had had to feed them, entertain them, and, most of all, wait for them to leave. Many times after bridge, she was tired and wanted to go to bed, but she had no choice but to wait for the last one to leave. When Mom went to the locals, she didn't have to do anything, and she could leave whenever she wanted. It was recreational, it was fun, and it came with no expectations or responsibilities.

"For the first time, I was less anxious about Mom. Once again I began to focus on my own life and family. What a relief!

"Just before Christmas, Mom had another stroke. This one was much milder than the first. She had no additional limitations, and within one week she was back to where she was prior to this second stroke.

"At the end of January, I received a call from one of Mom's friends. She said Mom was often confused, at times not even knowing where she was or where her daughter lived. I flew back to see her.

"I found her a little confused, but not all the time. In order for me to observe Mom better, I encouraged her to go back to her daily routine, and I would tag along to make sure she would be all right.

"She visited her locals. While there she went straight to the quarter slots and began to play. Three hours later, I could not get her to leave. She absolutely refused to go home. She must have spent hundreds of dollars in that one afternoon.

"When I finally did get her home, I tried talking to her, but she would not listen. She accused me of not wanting her to have fun. Because she was tired and it was late, she began to get more confused, frustrated, and annoyed with me. At that point, I just didn't know what to do. I knew I had to return home. I couldn't stay in Las Vegas any longer. I called her friend, and asked her to please get in touch with me again if Mom seemed to worsen in any way.

"When I got home and told my husband about Mom's condition, he suggested I have her declared incompetent before she went through all her life savings at the locals. That was exactly the thought I'd had coming back on the plane.

"I called our tax attorney, the only attorney I knew, and after I explained the situation, he suggested I get a Las Vegas lawyer to help me. I did just that. The Las Vegas lawyer gathered all the information from me and Mom's doctors and then set everything up for us to take Mom to court and have her declared incompetent.

"At the competence hearing, Mom was as sharp as any of us. Her performance was amazing. Mom accused me of just wanting her money so I could buy a larger house and put my daughters through college. She was so clear and coherent anyone listening to her would never have thought she was incompetent. The judge didn't think so, either. He threw out my incompetence claim and found in favor of Mom. She was free to continue the life she claimed she loved. Discouraged, scared, and feeling helpless, I returned home.

"Seven months later, we placed Mom in a Catholic Charities nursing home. Her dementia had worsened, and she was no longer able to take care of herself. By this time she was penniless, having given all her money to the locals.

"It took me a long time to understand that Mom's love of gambling came directly from her need to fill empty lonely hours, to be in a safe place where she felt comfortable, and to be with other senior citizens. And despite her increasing forgetfulness and the progression of her dementia, she never forgot how to gamble."

Facts on File

The reason most seniors give for gambling is to fill the long, empty hours they face each day. Many are not involved in the lives of their children and grandchildren because their families live a long distance away. Seniors rationalize that they don't see their adult children very often because these adults live extremely busy lives. Not only are they employed, but also their children are involved in after-school activities that require parental involvement and support.

Young adults can often be heard saying that time flies, while their elderly parents are saying that time moves so slowly.

Questions

- Has gambling become the most common way to fill your empty hours?
- Have you turned to gambling because you have a disability that zaps your energy and/or makes physical activities painful or impossible?
- Has gambling become your only form of socializing?
- Has your gambling jeopardized your financial situation?

8

Internet gamblers

IN 1999, FORTY MILLION PEOPLE had access to the Internet. By the end of 2001, that number will climb to one hundred million. The Internet is open twenty-four hours a day, seven days a week. As a result, people don't have to leave their homes to play casino games; all they need is a computer, a credit card, and a limited knowledge of how to surf the Web. Gambling on the Internet is equivalent to living in a casino.

Gambling on-line is one of our country's fastest-growing industries. In 1997, Americans had approximately thirty gambling sites from which to choose. Presently, there are more than seven hundred gambling sites that offer casino-style games or sports betting.

Internet compulsive gamblers are looking for two things: fast action and to get rich quick. Internet gamblers are usually young males who want to be self-employed and make a great deal of money in a short period of time. This is the only sphere of business they can enter and claim success in without having had any prior experience.

The attraction to on-line gambling is the possibility of hitting it big after investing only a small amount of money, and the feeling of being in action, which produces a heavy flow of adrenaline and other neurotransmitters that give the gambler a high equal to that achieved by snorting cocaine.

DAY TRADERS AND GAMBLING

Day traders are men and women who buy and sell stocks, hold them for a few hours or minutes, and hope they will move up or down rather quickly, thereby producing a sizable profit. Day traders jump in and out of the stock market many times each day. When these gamblers win big, they give all the credit to their own intellect. Their ego is very much involved in each transaction. Day trading often produces the same feelings a gambler has while gambling at a baccarat table with high rollers.

This form of investing is always very risky. A study conducted by the Security and Exchange Commission found that sixty-seven out of sixty-eight day traders were losers and that seven out of every ten day traders lost all their money.

Rob's Story

"Anyone who knows me knows how tight I am with a dollar. I guess I follow after my dad, who fathered six children and never made more than a living wage. I hated doing without when I was a kid. I wanted everything my friends had and more, but that was not possible. I was lucky I got most of the things I needed.

"By the time I was twelve I was able to earn money on my own. I ran errands, shoveled snow, and cut lawns, but I never spent a penny. Whenever I wanted to buy something, I would find a reason why I shouldn't. Somehow it was impossible for me to spend money. Having money in the bank made me feel secure. Even at a young age, I feared a crisis might strike and I wouldn't be prepared. I think I got this from my father, who was forever worried about our lack of financial security. In reality, we were never struck with a misfortune, so my parents managed just fine.

"All through college I managed to pay my expenses. I took out student loans, and I was awarded grant money as a result of my academic achievements: I graduated from high school with honors and I took third in the high school national debating competition. I was what some kids called a nerd. I didn't care. My accomplishments made me feel good about myself.

"When I look back, I can see how my love of money influenced my choice of a girlfriend. I dated girls who loved the outdoors. Camping, hiking, and fishing were my loves. Having an attractive woman at my side who would join in these activities made me happy. I'm an excellent fisherman. What cheaper date could I find than a woman who would eat what I caught and sleep in a tent?

"Whenever people ask me who I take after, I answer my mother. I feel I have many of her traits. She is compassionate, kind, giving, and other-focused. That totally describes me. The biggest difference between us is that I am a controller and she is not. Mom is there for whoever needs her. She doesn't impose her opinions on others, and she doesn't try to control the outcome of their situations. She just listens. That is not me. When people I care about find themselves going through a difficult time, I am the first one to jump in and try to fix everything. I don't give up until they choose the option I feel is best for them.

"From the time I was twelve years old, I knew I wanted to be an attorney when I grew up. I never deviated from that goal. At age twenty-three, I graduated from the university with a law degree. I immediately went on a ten-week camping vacation in the Hawaiian Islands. I had planned this trip well in advance because I knew that once I started practicing law, it would be some time before I would be free to travel again. It was on that trip that I met Kalani.

"From the first time I saw her, I knew she was for me. She was the most natural beauty I had ever seen. She had long, black, shiny hair and eyes that appeared to be dark blue. Her skin was tanned from the sun and as smooth as a baby's. What most attracted me to Kalani was how in tune she was with nature. She ran on the beach, ran up the mountain roads, paddled a canoe, and surfed the waves as well as any native-born Hawaiian. She attracted a great deal of attention from both men and women. Although I saw her every day, I did not know where she worked or lived. Because she was on the beach seven days a week, I at first thought she was unemployed. When I got up the nerve to speak to her, I found out she worked nights in her parents' restaurant. Her mother was Japanese and her father was Hawaiian. Their restaurant was a favorite among natives and tourists.

"I met Kalani's parents when I picked her up for our first date. Her father was polite but not overly friendly. Her mother, who was raised in Japan, was warm and friendly. Kalani was their only child, and I could see right away how protective they were of her. They especially did not like Kalani to date tourists.

"Following our first date, Kalani and I spent every day together. She and I had many things in common. Most of all, she loved nature as much as I did. When my vacation was coming to an end, I asked Kalani to marry me.

Without hesitation, she said yes. I extended my stay two weeks so we could marry in Hawaii and her parents could be present. That Kalani was marrying me after such a short relationship was difficult for her parents. Her leaving Hawaii was even more difficult.

"Right after we celebrated our second wedding anniversary, our son Kyle was born. He immediately became the center of our universe. I had always wanted to have a son, and his arrival brought nothing but joy.

"After practicing law for a decade, I received an offer of a partnership from a colleague whose senior partner had passed away. Peter and I had consulted on a number of cases together. I admired his work, and the two of us worked well together. We both specialized in elder care law. Most of our work involved managing the inheritances of widows who were left estates they could not manage by themselves.

"I was successful in managing my clients' accounts simply because I had a heavy interest in investing in the stock market. Unlike me, Peter never wanted his nor his clients' financial futures dependent upon the moves of the Street. Like his father, Peter invested in real estate.

"Although it was a few years since Peter and I had had computers installed in our offices, I still didn't have one at home. I never saw a need for one. Anything I needed to do on a computer, I could do in the office. Why should I spend money for something that was not absolutely necessary?

"When Kyle turned five years old, I could see the need to start introducing him to computers, so I purchased one for our home. At first, the only thing I did on the computer was play children's educational games with Kyle. I wanted him to develop a thirst for learning and to do well in school.

"When Kyle was six years old, he joined Little League. Baseball was the only game he wanted to play. Kalani and I attended all his Saturday morning games. By the time Kyle entered middle school, he was one of their best players. We were at his last game of the season when he was seriously injured. He was hit in the head with a fastball and knocked unconscious. He was taken by ambulance to the hospital, where he remained for four days with a severe concussion. Within a couple of weeks of returning home, everything returned to normal. Or so I thought. Two months following the accident, Kyle had a convulsive seizure. Following medical testing, he was diagnosed with epilepsy. As the weeks went by, doctors labeled his convulsions grand mal epilepsy.

"Despite switching medications several times, the convulsions continued. Kyle was often too ill to attend school. The school placed him on home study until his seizures could be controlled. That didn't happen. Kyle had an average of three seizures a day. After giving Kyle six months of traditional treatment that wasn't helping, we decided to try alternative treatment. The costs of this treatment would not be covered by insurance; we would have to pay for it ourselves. In addition, it meant Kalani and Kyle would have to go to New Mexico for four months, because that was where the treatment was being offered.

"One day while they were away, I began to explore the Internet. I was amazed at how much information was available on the World Wide Web. I was attracted to some of the chat rooms. Within a very short time, I was visiting the chat rooms regularly. Different rooms had different interests. I came across a room that sparked my interest—investing in the stock market. I had been doing that for years, and although I was conservative, my portfolio was valued at over one hundred thousand dollars. I didn't know anyone my age with those kinds of holdings.

"Some investors, in one of the chat rooms, were continually talking about some biotech Internet companies that were about to take a big jump forward. Because my interest was sparked, I began to take a closer look at some of these stock recommendations. I picked six of the stocks they were promoting and followed them for a week. I was amazed at how well they did. If I had invested one thousand dollars in each of those stocks I would have realized six times my initial outlay.

"What I learned in that one week scared me; it also excited me. I decided to invest more imaginary dollars so I could see if the trend continued. It not only continued, it got better. The paper records I kept for those two weeks showed I could have quadrupled my money in less time than it would take me to increase my present portfolio by 1 percent.

"I immediately began investing in these high-risk stocks with the belief that, in a very short period of time, I would be able to secure our financial future. I kept my newfound interest to myself.

"Up to this point, my day-to-day trading didn't interfere with my life. I was still able to take care of my clients and focus on my son's treatments. Kalani had always been passive in our relationship, and I never appreciated it as much as I did at that time. Kalani never asked about our financial status. From day one, she let me take care of it all. The only time she ever asked if we could afford something was when she and Kyle had to move to New Mexico. And I reassured her we could afford it without any problem.

"After months of alternative treatment Kyle was still having eighteen to twenty seizures a week. Nothing seemed to help. Kalani and Kyle moved back home. We got a private tutor for Kyle because he was still unable to return to school.

"Very soon after all this transpired, my world fell apart. Most of my portfolio was filled with tech stocks. I had made well over a million dollars investing them. Although the fee for each of my trades was only $16 compared to $125 with my former broker, I was paying out thousands of dollars each month because I was making as much as thirty trades a day.

"I no longer had a life. Every minute of each day was spent preparing for the day's trades and searching for new investments that would reward me well. There was no room in my head for anything but jumping in and out of the market. It was now affecting my career. I tried to keep everything under cover, but it became impossible. I wasn't giving my clients the time they needed; I wasn't helping them with decisions necessary to protect their holdings. My distraction became so bad Peter began to notice and confronted me. I reassured him that nothing was wrong; I was just tired and needed a vacation.

"Because many of my holdings were on margin, I began to panic when the market made a complete turnaround. I could see all my money disappearing, and there was nothing I could do to stop it.

"While all this was going on, Kalani and I were fighting every night. She didn't know our life savings were quickly disappearing, so when she needed something for herself or Kyle, I would give her ten reasons why we couldn't afford it. She did not understand why I would refuse Kyle anything when she knew I had plenty of money, and Kyle had so little pleasure in his life. Our biggest fight came when she wanted me to buy Kyle a computer of his own. She reminded me that although we had a computer, I was on it all the time, and Kyle had no chance to use it for himself. I accused Kalani of being demanding and not at all appreciative of all the good things she already possessed. She backed off that day, but it wasn't long before we fought again.

"Money became my number-one problem. As a person who always

needed to feel secure, I was living with continuous feelings of anxiety. Each day I would get a margin call meant I had to once again come up with thousands of dollars if I wanted to secure the few holdings I had left. It wasn't only that I was losing money every hour of each day, it was also that I wasn't making any money. The money I had for our future was gone; the money I had for any further treatment Kyle would need was gone, and the college fund I had for Kyle no longer existed.

"Kalani and I continued our daily arguments, always over money. Then one day in the middle of all this, Kyle attempted suicide. Kalani had been trying to tell me for a couple of weeks that something was wrong with Kyle, and I minimized everything she said. Kyle was everything to me, but my heavy involvement in high-risk investing made me blind to his needs. I knew he was down and distant, but he never complained about anything. Fortunately, his attempt was unsuccessful, and he recovered. Both Kalani and I tried to get Kyle to talk about what was bothering him and why he tried to kill himself. Kyle absolutely refused to speak about what was bothering him. I couldn't get him to talk at all. I knew I wasn't as close to him as I had been, and he did seem angry about that. No matter how I tried, he wanted nothing to do with me. The psychiatrist in the hospital wanted Kyle to continue to see him as an outpatient, but Kyle refused. Although I wanted the best for my son, a part of me was glad Kyle refused because that would have been very expensive and I couldn't afford it.

"Within two weeks after the market folded, I began manipulating some of my clients' accounts. Most of these clients were elderly widows who had very little knowledge of how to handle money, so they put their complete trust in me. Up until then they had no reason not to trust me.

"Because I had power of attorney for a number of my clients, I had no trouble transferring money from their accounts to mine. No one was the wiser. Six weeks later, I was in the hole for $700,000 of my clients' money. I was desperate, out of control, and panicking, thinking that if things didn't turn around I would never be able to recoup.

"It was all over when the son of one of my elderly clients noticed, while checking her monthly statement, that a large sum of money was missing. He went to my partner, Peter, to ask for an explanation. Peter was shocked. He had no knowledge of what I was up to, so he had no answers for the client.

He did assure the client that he would do a full investigation and get back to him in a few days.

"Unbeknownst to me, Peter had a full audit done of all my accounts. The result clearly showed I'd been transferring money from clients' accounts into mine.

"Peter never said a word to me. Instead he spoke to his attorney, who referred him to the police. When I arrived at the office the following morning, the police were there and I was arrested for grand larceny.

"My focus was so much on money, I let the importance of my relationship with my wife and son go unattended. Kalani, who had always been loving, caring, and faithful, was so crushed by my actions and so devastated by my betrayal that she divorced me almost immediately. My greatest pain came when my son refused to speak to me or to visit me while I was awaiting trial. I could not understand why he was so angry. I had seen to it that he had everything he needed. Before I became consumed with my day trading 'career,' I was there for Kyle, and he knew that. When Kalani brought me the divorce papers to sign, I insisted she tell me why Kyle was so angry at me when I'd never done anything on purpose to hurt him. She said she tried to get Kyle to open up to her, but he refused. She said he was angry with everyone and everything. She too was having a difficult time staying close to him. But she said she was sure the thing he was most angry about was my gambling. I didn't buy that. Kyle didn't even know I was gambling. No one knew about my high-risk investing.

"My feeling was that Kyle was angry more at Kalani than me. Kalani had become so negative and irritable; she had developed a short fuse. I saw her verbally abusing Kyle over some small, insignificant things he was doing. And Kyle saw Kalani screaming at me every day. We always fought over money. Kalani had become very demanding. She would nag me and put me down. She wouldn't let up. But no matter what she said, I never gave in; I couldn't, I had no money.

"The day I was arrested I lost everything in my life. My partner sued me for the money I stole, which resulted in a lien on my house and the loss of my car. When our home was sold, there wasn't enough to pay off my debts, so Kalani and Kyle ended up penniless.

"No matter how hard I tried, I could not understand Kyle's anger toward me. Despite all the problems I caused, I thought my being his father would give him some compassion for what I had been through, and for the fact that I was to spend the next twelve years in jail.

"Kalani stayed in our hometown so Kyle could finish out his schooling and graduate from high school with his friends. One month later, Kalani moved back to Hawaii to work in her parents' restaurant while Kyle attended the university. Just before she and Kyle left, she asked Kyle to visit me and tell me the truth about why he was so angry and why he never wanted to see me again. After thinking it over for a few days, Kyle agreed. When I got the call that he was coming, I was overjoyed. To me it meant I would have a chance to explain everything to him, and then he would no longer be angry.

"Kyle arrived on a Saturday afternoon. Kalani did not come in with him. She waited outside. Kyle did not want her to hear what he had to say.

"A large thick glass wall separated me from Kyle. When he entered I was all smiles. Kyle was solemn. I said to him I just needed him to listen so he could understand why I was in so much trouble. Kyle interrupted and said he didn't want to hear anything I had to say. He said the only reason he came was to tell me where his anger was coming from and why he never wanted to see me again.

"Kyle said he could not have wanted a better father than me when he was a little kid. He stated his early childhood gave him many happy memories. However, one evening all that came to an end. Kalani and I were having a shouting match. Kalani was asking me to pay one of Kyle's medical bills. She said if we didn't pay our back bills they would have to cease treating Kyle's epilepsy. They suggested she take him to the county clinic. I responded with a loud voice that it was Kyle's treatments that were costing so much money there was nothing left for anything else.

"At the time of this incident, Kyle was fifteen years old. He never said a word to Kalani nor me about overhearing our conversation. Two nights later, Kyle attempted to end his life. As soon as Kyle told me this, he got up and walked out without saying another word.

"My lies and deception pushed my son to try to end his own life. He believed he was the cause of all our pain. I still hear Kyle's words every day. How could I have put my son, whom I love with all my heart, in such a position? Today, I know the answer. I never would have done such a thing, but my disease of pathological gambling would do it without blinking an eye. My gambling addiction stole from me more than my money and my family. It stole my ability to hold on to my convictions, my morals, and my beliefs. It stole who I am.

"My desire to get rich, to feel omnipotent and to be 'king of the hill,' left me penniless and without any self-esteem. My high-risk trading, the time and energy I gave to beating the market, and my pathological optimism left me living in total isolation alongside criminals. My present associates are muggers, rapists, abusers, molesters, burglars, and murderers. And I am one of their peers.

"I have been incarcerated now for seven years. But today I am grateful. Since I have been here I have attended GA meetings regularly. I have worked the Steps and am continually working on my character defects. GA has not only helped me stop gambling, it has also helped me see I have a serious, progressive, and possibly fatal illness. My knowledge about compulsive gambling has strengthened my desire to remain abstinent."

COLLEGE MAJOR: INTERNET GAMBLING

When young people go off to college, parents find many things to be concerned about. Their concerns include their child's ability to make new friends, to use a washer and dryer, to manage an allowance, to keep up with studies, to avoid the temptations of drugs and alcohol, and to practice safe sex. The one thing most parents do not worry about is the possibility that their child will succumb to the temptations of gambling. This is not a concern because gambling requires money, and students are known to be paupers.

Even if parents become aware that their child has developed an interest in gambling, they usually do not become concerned, simply because they do not know the downside of this activity. Rarely are parents aware that gambling can become addictive and that when that happens, the gambler will be unable to control when, where, and how much he or she gambles.

Andy's Story

"You can be born with a silver spoon in your mouth even when your parents don't have a dime. I found this out before I turned eighteen. I am the fourth child of a homemaker and a carpenter. My oldest sister, Anna, is eleven years older than I, my second sister, Sara, is nine years older, and the youngest of my three sisters, Grace, is seven years older.

"When I was born, I was seen as a prince from day one. My father always wanted a son to share his love of sports with, to do 'men' things with, and to have as a best friend. My father had two close friends: 'Uncle' Paul, whom my father knew since he was a child, and my Uncle Artie, who is married to my mother's sister. Each of these uncles had a son, and I think my father envied them because they could do so many things with their sons that my father couldn't do with his daughters. Not one of my sisters was interested in anything that Dad wanted to do.

"By the time I was four, my father was teaching me how to throw a baseball. I loved baseball, but I loved most sports. When my father went to live games, he took me along. I was quick to learn the names of the players on the professional teams. To add interest to watching the games my father would bet me a quarter on the game. I was getting two dollars a week as allowance, so I had to put up my own quarter in order to place these bets. In his whole life, I don't think my father ever bet more than a dollar on any sporting event.

"Being the only boy in a family of three girls was never easy. Because I was the youngest, I was forever being told what to do and when to do it. I felt like I had four mothers. I never really got along with Anna or Grace. They were very close and they had no use for me, especially Grace. She had been the baby in the family for seven years, and then I came along. She couldn't understand why my parents wanted another child. She thought the family was just fine the way it was. I know from my father that my arrival made quite an impact on my sisters. The topic of conversation began to focus on me and turned away from them. Anna seemed least affected by my birth. She was the oldest, and by age twelve, she became a self-proclaimed parent. She was always kind of bossy and liked telling us what to do.

"By the time I was fourteen I found myself closest to my sister Sara. Because Anna and Grace were so close Sara had no one else to turn to. Sara was also different in looks from the rest of us. She looked like my father and had suffered since birth from poor vision, so she needed to wear glasses with rather thick lenses. Anna, Grace, and I looked a lot like my mother, who was Scandinavian; we were tall and blond with blue eyes. Sara had black hair and brown eyes, and she was short and a little pudgy.

"All through school, my gambling on sports continued. The first time I lost money on a game and was unable to pay, I went to my father for help. He bailed me out and then lectured me never to do that again. He said it was not necessary to place a large wager in order to enjoy a game. I kept quiet and listened, but in my head I was saying to myself, *He's wrong.* I knew it was much more fun to place a decent-sized bet on a game than to bet only a dollar. My father was very serious when he told me never to do that again; so I never again spoke to him about my gambling. He did ask me about it a couple of times, but I lied to keep him happy, so he wouldn't worry and so he would stay off my back.

"The next time I had to borrow money to pay a gambling debt, I turned to my sister Sara. Of course I didn't tell her why I needed the money. I told her I lost the CD player Mom and Dad had given me for my birthday, and I didn't want them to find out. Without thinking twice, she gave me the money. Sara was the most compassionate and generous one in the family. She rescued me more times than I care to remember. Many times during my high school years she did reports for me, helped me study for tests, and let me submit papers she had written years before on the same topic. I could count on her. The only time she refused to cover for me was when it required that she lie to Dad or Mom.

"All my life I was told I was handsome. I believed it and I used my looks whenever I needed something. I bartered on many an occasion. The first big barter I got involved with was when I was a junior in high school. I owed two hundred dollars to Hal, my school bookie. I could only come up with seventy-five dollars, which I got from Sara. He wasn't satisfied. However, he proceeded to offer me a deal I didn't like, but I had to accept. Hal said he had asked a girl at school whom he didn't know very well to go to the senior prom with him, and she accepted. Then he found out, through a friend, that another girl, whom he liked a lot, was hoping he would take her. He told me if I could get the first girl to break her date with him, and go to the prom with me, he would wipe out the balance of my debt. I did not want to accept his offer, but I did. I needed to get relief from my debt before my dad found out. On prom night, I picked up the girl, took her to the prom, danced with her once, and took her home as soon as the prom ended.

"Later that night, I thought about what a great lesson I learned from that experience. When I divided the amount of my debt by the number of hours I spent at the prom, I figured that I was paid forty dollars an hour for doing something stupid. That was pretty good money.

"By the time I was a senior in high school, I was barely passing my courses. My love of gambling was so strong I had no interest in anything else. I did manage a social life, but the only time I asked a girl for a date was when it was to a house party or a school football game. I wouldn't spend a penny on anything but gambling.

"Sara was my greatest enabler, and I was her confidant. Whenever she needed someone to talk to, she would come to me. I would feign listening to her but never concentrated on what she had to say. I just put in a little time so when she was finished speaking, I could hit her for more money. We had a kind of a barter going. She paid me for being her friend.

"When I got to college, I decided to major in science and math because through research I found out there were more federal and university grants available for students with these majors. By my third year in school, I was actually majoring in Internet gambling. In my sophomore year, I discovered the multitude of gambling sites on the World Wide Web. I viewed those sites as the answer to my wants.

"In the middle of my senior year, I was forty-seven thousand dollars in debt. I had applied for and received a third of that from grant monies. The other thirty-two thousand dollars I got from eight unsolicited credit cards that were sent to me starting in the fall of my senior year. Each card had a cap of either four or five thousand dollars. I thought I was in heaven when those cards started coming in the mail. I had absolutely no problem getting cash advances from each of them. When one card maxed out, I got cash from another card so I could begin making payments on the first. I kept this round robin going for more than five months.

"Two months before I was to graduate, everything hit the fan. The forms I was supposed to fill out near the end of each semester were never done. I was required to account for the grant money I had received and to send documentation that I had completed those courses. Well, that was impossible. How could I complete and submit those forms when I didn't complete even one of my math or science courses? I had let everything slide. I did nothing in my final year except gamble on sports over the Internet. I was twenty-one years old and I had wasted two years at a university where I not only accomplished nothing, but also I developed a great number of problems and a mound of debts. There were many times when I won big and could have lowered my liabilities, but I didn't even consider it. When I was gambling all those months, I often won, and sometimes I won big so I actually became a pathological optimist. I convinced myself I would win big again and then I would pay off some of the heavy load I was carrying. It never happened.

"My uncontrollable urge to gamble made it impossible for me to think clearly or to be able to see that my love of this enterprise was destroying my life. I had spent years pursuing an impossible dream. I wanted to win all my needs: to be admired, to be accepted, to be seen as someone whose success is the result of high intelligence and creative abilities.

"When my class graduated, my parents were home, and I was on a bus headed for Palm Beach, Florida. The only things I took with me were my clothes and my roommate's laptop computer. I needed the computer as much as I needed my clothes. I had to have access to the Internet so I could continue to gamble. I told myself I was turning a new leaf. My immediate goal was to win enough money to repay my debts and return the grant money I had received for education. I felt I could prevent being prosecuted if I made restitution before they found me.

"I had been chasing that goal for years. The only thing that changed is that now I was gambling on any sporting event, even sports of which I had little or no understanding. I'd won many thousands of dollars, but I'd lost even more. I always kidded myself into believing I gambled to make money; it is only with hindsight that I can see that I gambled for only one reason—to be in action, to feel the fast and heavy flow of adrenaline inside my brain. I was just like a junkie. I needed my fix as badly as they do. And despite all the years that have passed, I have not repaid a penny to anyone.

"I chose to move to Palm Beach because I knew there were a great number of wealthy people living there. When I arrived, I was surprised to find out how many of these wealthy people were female, single, and lonely. Within a couple of days of my arrival, I thought of something that could be a successful business for me. I began my own escort service. It didn't take me long to find out wealthy, lonely women do not squabble over a sizable fee for service when the escort is handsome and attentive. Some of my clients were so grateful for the attention I paid them, they would give me a tip twice the size of my fee.

"In time I came to realize it would be more profitable to be in a relationship with one of these women than to be an escort. Each time I chose to have a relationship, the woman gave me everything I needed and then some. I had my own credit card provided by my lady, a checking account with unlimited funds, and recognition in the finest restaurants in the county. I used all the funds available to me to continue gambling on the Internet. When my lady would begin to get on my case and question me about every bill that came in, I would just walk away and begin a new relationship with another lonely, desperate woman looking to fill her hours.

"The last woman I used was forty-four-year-old Erica, widowed four years and the mother of a ten-year-old daughter, Pam, and a severely handicapped eight-year-old son, Kenny. Kenny had special aides who took care of him seven days a week. When Erica's husband died, she was still financially able to continue the lifestyle to which she had become accustomed.

"I treated Erica and her children very well. Her little girl was both charming and intelligent. Her son, whose speech was so poor it took me months to understand anything he said, was happy and always displayed a positive attitude. He was confined to a wheelchair and had to be fed. There was virtually nothing he could do for himself. Without all the aid he was receiving, he would surely have had to be institutionalized.

"After I moved in with Erica, I no longer worked. I stayed home and spent most of my time placing bets over the Internet. Since Erica gave me my own credit card, I had access to more money than I could ever spend. If spending was all I was doing with the card, I would still be in Erica's life. Erica trusted me and loved me. She never questioned what I was charging. Because she had an accountant pay all her bills, she never saw any of the credit card statements. Once, when the accountant called her to question the amounts being charged in her name, she lashed out at him and told him never to question her business again. She told him to forward her a copy of her monthly statements and to continue paying them unless she told him otherwise. When her statements came each month, Erica never opened them. It was then that I knew I had it made. I figured out that Erica's greatest fear was that I would leave her, and she was willing to pay anything to keep that from happening.

"The only thing Erica ever asked of me was, each day, to pay some attention to Kenny. I grew to like Kenny. He was so easy to please, and he enjoyed everything we did together. Sometimes the only thing we did was to go over to the park so he could watch the other kids play. Kenny's ability to enjoy life was so limited, yet he was always happy and grateful for any bit of attention he received. On a rare occasion, I would pick up a little something for him, and he would react like I had just given him a magnificent gift.

"Two and a half years after I moved into Erica's home, I had almost completely drained her finances. My gambling cost Erica a total of $1.2 million. At the time, I had no idea how much I was gambling, nor did I care. But I was shocked when I found out that I had wiped out Erica's funds. For the first time in my gambling career, I felt extremely guilty over what I had done. At that moment, I would have given anything to reverse that situation. But I had nothing to give.

"Erica did not press charges. Why, I don't know, but I believe it was because she was too humiliated and ashamed of what she had allowed to happen.

"Erica moved back to her hometown and into her sister's house with her daughter. Kenny is living in a state institution eighty-four miles away. He has regressed and is not expected to return to live with his family.

"I have never felt anything for anyone. For years I have used and manipulated people to get what I needed in order to feed my habit. Despite all the times I won big, I never once gave anything to those who loved me. I never once put their needs before my wants.

"With the help of Gamblers Anonymous, I have been in recovery from compulsive gambling for two and a half years. I have come a long way, but no matter how hard I try, I will never fully let go of the guilt I feel for the devastation my gambling brought to Erica, and especially Kenny. Kenny's quality of life depended upon the degree of Erica's wealth. That never once mattered to me. My own illness prevented me from caring about a little handicapped boy who smiled whenever I walked into a room."

RELIGIOUS GAMBLER

How is it possible that an activity of any kind could force people to abandon the values and traditions they hold to be most precious? It is easier to understand that people suffering with a substance abuse problem might, under the influence, do things they would never do when they are straight. To make this same statement about an activity that does not include ingesting mood- or mind-altering substances is beyond the understanding of most.

Most people know compulsive gamblers are capable of stealing, lying, and manipulating. However, it is more difficult for them to grasp the idea that addicted gamblers would willingly and deliberately engage in behaviors they believe to be wrong and sinful.

Bridget's Story

"In all my years of childhood, I never heard the word *gambling*. Even if I had heard it, I would have had no idea what it meant. The state I grew up in did not have any form of legal gambling. To this day I have never been inside a card room or a casino. I have never been to a horse race or dog race. I've never bought a lottery ticket, and of course, I have never placed a bet on a sporting event. Even if these things were available, I would have had no interest. To me, gambling was something that fancied only the male gender. No one was more surprised than I was when I placed my first bet at age sixty-two.

"When Hal and I married, we carefully planned our future. He was a lumberjack and loved working outdoors. Because Hal didn't want me to work, I stayed home and devoted some of my time each day to volunteering at our church.

"Within three years of marriage, we bought our home, and by the time we were married five years, we had two daughters, Emily and Julia.

"Because Hal and I had similar values, we wanted to pass them on to our children. The Christian work ethic was one thing in which we strongly believed. We started right from the beginning to teach Emily and Julia that they would have to earn the things they wanted. Even at a young age, they each enjoyed saving for a new toy or for the money needed to go on a special trip. We could see that the anticipation of having a wish fulfilled made each of them very happy.

"The second most important thing we wanted to give our daughters was a strong faith in God. Hal and I were both raised as Roman Catholics, and we believed the greatest gift we could pass on to Emily and Julia was the faith we cherished.

"When Emily and Julia were in high school, Hal was killed on the job when a large tree, being sawed down by a novice lumberjack, fell in his path and killed him. On that day, all the joy in our small family disappeared. Emily immediately blamed God for the loss of her father. She refused to go to church, and she turned her back on the many friends who tried to support her. She isolated herself from everyone. I tried so hard to comfort her and help her see that what happened was a random act for which no one was responsible. I could not reach Emily.

"Julia, on the other hand, mourned her father's passing and turned to every friend she had to help her through that painful time. She also turned to her spiritual advisers for help when she felt she needed it. Within six months, Julia was doing all the things she did before Hal died. She was still mourning, but she cried less and talked about her father more often. She made a point of reminiscing about the many happy times we shared together. She even started to share feelings of gratitude for the years she had her father in her life.

"While all this was happening, I was going through my own period of adjustment that I never imagined I would have to face.

"I did not have much of an education, but before I married Hal, I did work for two years as bookkeeper in a local doctor's office. Although that was a long time ago, I believed I could get that kind of a job again. However, when I went searching for such a position, I experienced quite an awakening. I found that most of today's businesses relied upon computers and not hand bookkeepers. I felt there was nothing out there for me. As a last resort I turned to my pastor, Father Felix, who had known me for more than twenty years. He knew my situation and the difficult time I was having because of Hal's death. Father Felix told me he had no openings in his office. He said the only job open at that time was for a cleaning lady for the church and rectory. I had no choice, I took it. It paid less than what I needed to meet expenses, so I knew I would also have to search for a part-time job to make ends meet.

"The next twenty years were good and bad. My happiest time was when Julia married Jed. He was a member of our church and well liked by everyone. A year later, when Jed got a job offer in Chicago, they relocated. It was there that their son, Jack, was born. I didn't get to see Jack until he was five months old because I couldn't afford the trip.

"As for Emily, she went to college with a partial scholarship from the lumberjack's union. She was not a great student because she partied too much. She did manage to graduate with a degree in business management, but she did not work in that field. After graduation, she got a job as a bartender in a local tavern, a few miles from her alma mater.

"It has been over twenty-two years since Hal passed away. Julia and Jed have divorced. Julia remained in Chicago because she has many friends there, as has her son, Jack, who is a senior at the university. He is majoring in psychology and hopes to become a school guidance counselor.

"Emily is on her third or fourth relationship. She has never married. She is a supercaretaker who tries to fix everyone. The man she is presently with only works on occasion but never for very long.

"When Emily was very young she would often speak about how one day she would have a baby of her own. She has never had a child, but I do know from Julia she was pregnant a few years ago, by a former boyfriend, and she had an abortion. Emily blames everything in her life that has gone wrong on the loss of her father. She cannot see how her use and abuse of drugs and alcohol is responsible for anything.

"As for my life, I had no complaints. After working as the church cleaning woman for eleven years, Father Felix offered me a position as a bookkeeper in his office. I was thrilled. The woman who held that position for many years was retiring.

"Fortunately, Father allowed me a one-month training period so I would be familiar with all their accounts before the other bookkeeper left. I held that position for over ten years. I was very proud of the job I was doing. Even though I was employed at the church, I continued to volunteer several hours each week helping other parishioners who were in need. I had made many friends in my parish, and I was happy.

"Whenever I did feel some sadness it was always related to my daughters. Julia's divorce hit me hard. They seemed like the perfect couple; I never thought they would split up. I was glad Julia stayed in Chicago because all her friends lived there.

"As much as I loved my grandson, Jack, I was not very involved in his life because my financial situation did not permit me to see him very often. Whenever he would call me, he did seem happy to hear my voice, and he would share with me whatever was going on in his life.

"Three years ago, when I turned sixty, I began thinking about retiring. I didn't think about it for too long because I quickly came to realize if I took early retirement, I would not have enough income to sustain myself. Even if I waited until I was sixty-five, I would have a very hard time making ends meet.

"The best thing about my decision to stay on the job was that I had terrific co-workers. We got along so well together and had grown to become best friends. Father Felix used to comment on what a pleasure it was for him to have competent, dependable, and honest employees on his staff. It was true. Over the years he had given me more and more responsibility. I knew all the companies and owners who serviced our needs in the office and in the church. I would submit bills and pay our invoices without question. Many times I signed Father's name when he was busy or out of town. For more than ten years, there was never a question nor a problem with how the office was run, and for that, all the credit was given to me.

"Years ago I used to wish my daughter Julia would ask me to move to Chicago and live near her and my grandson, but that never happened. If she would have asked me after I got the job with Father, I would have refused. I had the best life possible. Being very active in my parish meant everyone knew me. Three years ago when I fell on the ice and broke my foot, I received dozens of cards and phone calls from parishioners offering me all kinds of help. While I was convalescing, I received many homemade dinners. My life was full and I wanted for nothing.

"Following a successful three-month fund-raiser, Father Felix bought a new computer system for the main office. The old one was slow and outdated, and left much to be desired.

"When the new system was up and running, Father Felix came and offered to give me the old computer. At first I refused it, but then he explained he was planning to buy another computer soon so that the bookkeeping could be done in a more modern and efficient way. He thought if I took the old computer home and familiarized myself with it, the transition to the new system would be easier. Realizing I would probably still be working for him the following year, it made sense to start learning how to operate a computer.

"One of our parishioners hooked up the computer in my apartment and got it running for me. For the first month, I hardly touched it. I was intimidated by it and afraid I would do something that would eradicate whatever was already stored on it.

"When Father asked how I was progressing, I told him the truth, and he immediately reassured me that there was nothing I could do that would cause a problem. He said they had already transferred everything they needed from the old computer to the new one. Right after that I began experimenting and exploring.

"One of the first things I found upon exploring the Internet was games. I always loved playing solitaire and I found I enjoyed playing it on the computer even more.

"As I became more confident with the computer, I started to further surf the Internet. I came across a site that offered games of chance that did not require money to play. They were strictly for fun. I began playing them every evening for a couple of hours. They helped me relax and pass the time. I loved them.

"One night I noticed a box in the lower corner of the game site that said to increase your pleasure, click here. I did, and that click turned my life around. It took away every single thing in my life that mattered: all the love, respect, approval, regard, and recognition that had been mine for so long. That click put me on a site where I could continue to play my game of choice—video poker—with a chance to win big bucks. All I had to do was submit a credit card number.

"Being a person who controlled every penny she spent, and having been extremely careful with my personal budget, I had no concern that I might gamble more than I could afford. I could not have been more wrong. All I could comfortably afford to bet was three dollars a day, because after I paid my bills each month, I didn't have more than ninety dollars left over for entertainment. By the end of two weeks I was playing video poker for three hours every night. I was spending between fifty and seventy dollars a week. I wasn't worried how I would pay for this new expense; since I had excellent credit, I applied for three more credit cards to help me meet this uncontrollable urge to play video poker every single day.

"Six months after I received my new credit cards, I was maxed out on each of them. My hobby, playing video poker on the Internet, cost me more than my whole life's savings. In addition, I was in heavy debt. I had no choice but to borrow from the church's accounts, which I managed. In order for Father Felix not to find out what I was doing, I opened a new service contract with a nonexisting computer company that would maintain our computers on a quarterly basis.

"When I explained this new account to Father, he didn't question it all. He trusted me 100 percent. I put my name on the new account and made checks out to it on a regular basis. I was home free. Believe it or not, I didn't feel at all uncomfortable about what I did because in my mind I was only borrowing the money. I knew I would replace it as soon as I had a big win and then terminate the account.

"That never happened. Four months after I began borrowing from the church I suffered a heart attack followed by triple bypass surgery. I spent two weeks in the hospital and six weeks at home recuperating.

"I can't tell you how many cards I received from co-workers and parishioners filled with their concern and prayers. In addition, I had daily visits from Father Felix. I felt so loved and so fortunate.

"During my recovery I never once gave thought to the possibility that anyone at the church would discover the phony account for the nonexistent computer company.

"Since my recovery was expected to take quite a while, Father Felix asked one of our parishioners who was a certified public accountant to take over my books. Father's goal in making that request was to keep the workload up-to-date so I wouldn't be swamped when I returned. Father did not tell me he was doing this. He did not want me to even think about work while I was ill.

"All the while I was at home recovering, I continued to play video poker on the Internet. I felt it was helping me get well. I had no idea how much I was 'investing' in this game. I do remember at that time there were days when I would promise myself I wouldn't gamble, but no matter how sincere I was, I gambled anyway. I knew my debts were mounting, but it didn't matter. Nothing mattered. My only concern was that I would be able to play video poker every single day.

"The first few weeks following my heart attack, when I was unable to gamble, I was miserable. I was anxious, irritable, and very unhappy. That was the first time I became aware of just how important playing video poker was in my life. But I never questioned it. And I certainly didn't have a clue I had become an addicted gambler.

"Four weeks into my at-home recovery, Father Felix came to see me. He brought with him the CPA who had been working on the church's accounts. He knew everything I had been doing, thanks to the CPA. When a total audit was completed, Father found out I had 'borrowed' almost eight thousand dollars from the church.

"Did you ever hear the expression 'pillar of the church'? That was how many parishioners saw me. That was how Father Felix saw me. I had worked and volunteered at my church for more than twenty years. I was the first one to step forward if a family was in need. I helped our elderly when they were ill, mothers who were unable to care for their young, and new mothers who needed help. I cleaned houses, baby-sat, and ran errands. I was Miss Fix-It, the number-one caretaker, and I was happy to do it all.

"When Father Felix and the CPA left my apartment, I cried for hours. I cannot tell you the severe guilt, shame, and humiliation I was feeling. What made it even worse was that Father showed no sign of anger. He didn't yell at me, chastise me, or judge me. He just asked me why I needed so much money. I knew he was asking because he was willing to help as best he could if I needed it for a legitimate reason. That thought made me feel even worse. At that moment, I wanted to die. How could I ever face my friends, co-workers, and parishioners who offered me their love and prayers while I was so ill?

"Less than an hour after Father and the accountant left, Father Felix returned to speak to me privately. For what he did for me at that time, I could never show enough gratitude. He told me he was well aware of how gambling could grab a person so hard they couldn't get away. He told me he knew other parishioners who suffered with the same demon, and those who truly wanted help got it when they began attending Gamblers Anonymous meetings.

"Father asked me if I was willing to go to GA and work their program of recovery. I cried and cried and told him I would do whatever it took to stop gambling. I told him how often I tried to stop but I just couldn't. No matter what, I could not stop gambling. I knew I was addicted to video poker and I hated it.

"In exchange for my sincere and full cooperation, Father agreed not to tell my co-workers or anyone else what I had done. The only other thing he directed me to do was to return the computer he gave me. I did everything he asked. I was so very grateful.

"Father Felix kept his word and I kept mine. I am back at work once again doing the bookkeeping for the church. I balance the church's books every month with the aid of the CPA, who, I later found out, is also a recovering compulsive gambler.

"I hope I will never lose the gratitude I feel today for all of those who understand my addiction and who support my recovery. I never want to gamble again, and with the help of GA, Father Felix, and God, I'll never place another bet."

Facts on File

The goal of on-line gamblers and stock market traders is to buy fast action and achieve a life of privilege. The thought that this might be possible has seduced many of our adolescents and young adults to take steep risks gambling over the Internet. When adolescents continually hear about people who strike it rich gambling on sports or churning stocks, they cannot resist the thought that they too can do the same. The Internet is like a magnet for youths. They are more familiar with it than their parents are, they are not intimidated by it, and they do not fear the degree of risk using it involves.

If underage gamblers try to gamble at a racetrack or in a casino, there is a good chance they will be turned away at the door. However, almost any underage gambler can access gambling on the Internet with nothing more than a valid credit card. If this is all that is required and if we have become a nation of gamblers, how then are we to protect our young from gambling on the World Wide Web?

Questions

- Which Internet site do you visit most frequently?
- Do you become angry when your computer is down or frozen and you are unable to place your bets or trade your stocks?
- Does the ease of using cyberbookies entice you to gamble on the Internet?
- Have you ever accepted a high interest rate, short-term loan to meet a margin call?

Part 3

RECOVERY

How do compulsive gamblers, affected so severely by compulsive gambling, start to rebuild their lives once the illness has been arrested? Where do they start? Does the mere fact that the gambling has ceased right all the wrongs that have occurred? Are there warning signs that signal a block on their path to recovery? If so, how can they overcome these roadblocks?

What are the needs of a couple who, in the beginning, shared so much hope and then, years later, share only despair—despair so deep it prevents either from being there for the other? A despair that tells each of them that *there is no way out; there is no one else with this problem; we are totally alone?*

If nothing else, compulsive gamblers and their loved ones need to know that their pain is the result of a mental illness. They can discover that they are not to blame, that there is help, and that recovery, happiness, and intimacy are not only possible but also attainable.

9

On the Steps

FOR COMPULSIVE GAMBLERS and their loved ones to receive the help they need, they must reveal to others exactly what is happening in their lives. They need a knowledgeable professional (a therapist, doctor, clergyperson, or counselor) who will direct them to the Twelve Step, self-help programs of Gamblers Anonymous (GA) and Gam-Anon. To date, this is the most successful treatment available for compulsive gambling. These programs offer both the afflicted and the affected the help, strength, support, and hope that can return them to sanity and health.

GA and Gam-Anon are simple. They are based on the member's willingness to be honest; to focus on himself or herself; to follow suggestions; to stop trying to change other people, places, and things; and to allow a Power greater than themselves to guide their lives. Couples who surrender and stop trying to do things their way can, and do, recover.

TREATMENT OF CHOICE: GAMBLERS ANONYMOUS

When compulsive gamblers "hit bottom" and ask for help, many different suggestions may be offered. Some may suggest they begin by speaking to their clergyperson, a social worker, a psychologist, or a psychiatrist. Still others may recommend an addiction specialist. Any one of these may be a good referral, because often, when people first reach out for help with a problem, they are more comfortable sharing it on a one-to-one basis as opposed to sharing it with a group of strangers. The hope is that, whichever professional the compulsive gambler chooses, it will be one who is well versed in this addiction and who knows only too well the importance of the afflicted being involved in the Twelve Step recovery program of Gamblers Anonymous. Past experience has shown that the odds of a compulsive gambler remaining abstinent from gambling without being involved in this fellowship are such that no gambler would bet on it.

HISTORY OF GAMBLERS ANONYMOUS

The fellowship of Gamblers Anonymous is the outgrowth of a chance meeting between two men during the month of January in 1957. These men had a truly baffling history of trouble and misery due to an obsession to gamble. They began to meet regularly and, as the months passed, neither had returned to gambling.

They concluded from their discussions that, in order to prevent a relapse, it was necessary to bring about certain character changes within themselves. In order to accomplish this, they used for a guide certain spiritual principles that had been utilized by thousands of people who had recovered from other compulsive addictions. The word *spiritual* can be said to describe those characteristics of the human mind that represent the highest and finest qualities, such as kindness, generosity, honesty, and humility. Also, in order to maintain their own abstinence, they felt that it was vitally important that they carry the message of hope to other compulsive gamblers.

As a result of favorable publicity by a prominent newspaper columnist and TV commentator, the first group meeting of Gamblers Anonymous was held on Friday, September 13, 1957, in Los Angeles. Since that time, the fellowship has grown steadily and groups are flourishing throughout the world.

How the Program Works

When compulsive gamblers are in action or deep escape, they cannot see that they continually look outside themselves for solutions to their difficulties. For years they live with the belief that, if they win big one more time, their problems will be solved. In truth, they have won big many times, only to use their winnings to return to gambling.

The help compulsive gamblers need in order to turn their lives around can be found in Gamblers Anonymous.

It is in this fellowship that the afflicted feel supported and understood. It is in these meetings that they no longer feel alone or isolated. Once entering GA, the newcomers are exposed to a kind of hope they never knew existed. This hope, along with the strength they receive in the GA room, is the catalyst in their willingness to return.

It is in GA that the afflicted will find that this addiction is one of equal opportunity. They will be exposed to men and women of all walks of life. They will learn very quickly that regardless of how successful or unsuccessful people have been in life, here they all have one thing in common: They have been unable to resist the impulse to gamble.

Some compulsive gamblers who want to stop gambling resist going to Gamblers Anonymous because they mistakenly believe it is a religious program. Those who put this belief aside and attend find that the program is spiritual, not religious. In these rooms are members who believe in God, members who question the existence of God, and members who fiercely deny God's existence. By following the precepts of Gamblers Anonymous, motivated compulsive gamblers, regardless of their religious beliefs, can experience a miracle—they can resist the urge to gamble.

The GA program is based on the Twelve Steps of recovery, the same steps developed by Alcoholics Anonymous. (For a list of the Steps used by AA and GA, see pages 247–248.) These Steps help compulsive gamblers look inside themselves and examine their behaviors, their thinking, and their values. By working the Steps, compulsive gamblers are able to let go of their denial, recognize that all their problems are gambling-related, and admit that they, by themselves, are unable to remain abstinent from gambling.

The Steps help compulsive gamblers take a serious look at their personal assets and liabilities and become willing to have the liabilities removed (liabilities that contributed to their gambling). Members of the group will support newcomers to help them take the steps necessary to accomplish this. In addition, the group will help each compulsive gambler to work out a way to repay the debts accumulated as a result of gambling.

As the afflicted move along the Steps of recovery, they will eventually work on the diseased values that have led them to misery. They will learn to recapture the values that once enriched their lives, values that will help them become more flexible in their thoughts and less controlling in their manner. This program of recovery will show newcomers how to turn their negative attitudes into positive ways of thinking and will help them make amends to their loved ones for all the pain gambling has caused.

As the newcomers climb the Steps, they will eventually reach the point where they will be able to see how doing things their way led them to a life filled with turbulence, chaos, and pain.

Working the Steps of recovery is a process, and how long this takes is not important. What is important is that compulsive gamblers who want to recover work this program without hesitancy or question. They do not need to concern themselves about what is behind each question asked or each suggestion made. As a matter of fact, in the very beginning, the new members of GA need to do only two things: not gamble, and go to meetings.

DOING IT FOR YOURSELF

Many compulsive gamblers begin attending Gamblers Anonymous meetings with a "footprint on their fanny." A spouse, a parent, a job, or a court has given them an ultimatum: get help or get out. Unless these gamblers attend meetings with an open mind and are willing to listen when their gambling behavior is confronted, it is unlikely that they will remain abstinent.

At times, the compulsive gambler is strongly confronted by someone concerned about him, a person who wants him to stop gambling and start attending Gamblers Anonymous meetings. Should he comply with that person's wishes and go to GA meetings but not work the program, he may find his life unbearable. Without gambling, he is miserable and resentful of the one who pushed him to abandon his "love."

Harlow's Story

"The first time I gave up gambling, I was only twenty years old. I had just received a general discharge from the navy. Actually, they had threatened to give me a dishonorable discharge because my card playing had gotten me into so much trouble. During my two-year stint, I hustled, manipulated, connived, lied, and stole in order to play poker. In addition, I wired my parents for money on three occasions because I had not only gambled away my paycheck, but also a few hundred borrowed dollars as well.

"When my parents found out I had spent three months in the brig for stealing from a shipmate, they started to get on my case about my gambling. When I returned to their home to live, they made me promise I'd never gamble again, and, in return, I wouldn't have to repay my dad the eleven hundred dollars I owed him. I was clean for almost a month. It was one of the longest and most unhappy months of my life. I was bored every day and filled with resentment at my parents, who did that to me. So, sure enough, I returned to gambling.

"In less than a year, my gambling had become so heavy, my debts were larger than the day I left the service. I couldn't keep up with the loans I held from two loan sharks. I had to turn to the sharks because every other legal avenue of borrowing was closed to me. I was overextended on all my credit. I tried everything to buy time from the sharks, but I ran out of excuses. One loan shark called my parents and told them that if I didn't pay him thirty-four hundred dollars in forty-eight hours, I would have my skull fractured. My mother became hysterical. My father became enraged. They bailed me out. My mother became ill as a result of that incident. I was willing to do anything to reassure her that I wouldn't gamble again. I was so filled with guilt, I couldn't stand myself.

"My mother asked me to go to GA to get help with my gambling problem. I agreed. I didn't gamble for ten months. That's *all* I did—not gamble. I did not have a sponsor, I did not make telephone calls to the members of my group, nor did I follow their suggestions about working the program. I just didn't gamble.

"Needless to say, I was once again miserable. I blamed the loan sharks for making my mother so upset. I convinced myself that it was all their fault. I also convinced myself that gambling had never been a problem; it was just that every once in a while I had bad luck.

"After ten months of not gambling, I felt I had learned my lesson, and I would never get into a hole because of gambling again. I told myself I could control my gambling if I was careful.

"I did control it for about three weeks. Then I found myself calling another loan shark for money to cover a heavy loss of the prior day. Still, I wasn't worried; I was secure in the thought that I would never let gambling control me again.

"Within eighteen months of resuming gambling, I was fired from my job for absenteeism and poor job performance. I couldn't concentrate on my work because my gambling was too much of a distraction. Despite that, I still felt I had it under control, so I stopped attending Gamblers Anonymous.

"Four years and hundreds of poker games later, I found myself married to Lori and awaiting the arrival of our first child. I was still gambling and, as before, lying all the time to cover it up. Lori knew I liked to play poker, but she had no idea I was playing daily on my lunch hour at work.

"I was truly looking forward to Lori giving birth. I wanted a child very much. However, the night he was born, I was nowhere to be found. I was on a poker binge. By the time I got to the hospital to see my son, he was thirteen hours old. Lori was furious. I tried to explain to her that I was on a roll that turned bad and I just couldn't leave the table. She didn't want to hear it. I couldn't eat or sleep that night because I felt so guilty; I wasn't with my wife when our son was born.

"Three days later, when we took our baby home, Lori spoke to me only to say if I didn't stop gambling, she would leave me and take the baby with her. I felt she meant it. Lori didn't need me; as a legal secretary, she could well support herself and our son without me. I was distraught by what she said. I did not want to lose my family. Without them I had nothing to give me happiness.

"I made Lori a promise, and I meant it. I would do whatever it took to keep from gambling. I never viewed her decision to leave me as a threat. Lori knew what she wanted, and a compulsive gambler wasn't it.

"I returned to Gamblers Anonymous and, for the first time, I went to the meeting because *I* had a desire to stop gambling. I don't know how it is for other gamblers, but it took me years to be able to refrain from playing cards and not be miserable. I truly believed that each time I relapsed into gambling, it was because I had maintained abstinence because someone else wanted me to. I never did it for myself, and that kind of abstinence cannot last; nor can it result in happiness, contentment, or serenity.

"I soon found out I had never accepted the First Step of recovery (We admitted we were powerless over gambling—that our lives had become unmanageable). The day my wife told me she wanted to leave me and take our son with her, I knew my life had become completely unmanageable, and I knew exactly what made it that way—my gambling.

"I now realized working Step One requires the compulsive gambler to say and mean every word of that Step. It means nothing if someone else says it and means it. Lori and I could never have a happy marriage if I kept gambling. I needed to accept my illness and want to stop gambling in order for us to begin to get close."

UNDERSTANDING THE ILLNESS

Partners often have difficulty accepting compulsive gambling as an illness. Unlike alcoholism, no substance is taken into the body. But compulsive gambling is an addiction in which the abused substance is already in the body. The compulsive gambler is addicted to the feeling of being in action or in escape—of being "high." He is dependent on the feeling of adrenaline racing through his system or of being focused on something other than reality.

When holding a bet and awaiting the results, the compulsive gambler's blood pressure surges, his heart beats faster, and his desired feeling of being high (removed from reality) is present and secure. As the afflicted is about to get the results of his wager, the feeling of excitement becomes euphoric. This is especially true if he is about to win big. Winning big guarantees the gambler the ability to purchase the same feeling the following day.

Like many other addictions, compulsive gambling is chronic and progressive. As it continues, the gambling must take place more often and for longer periods of time. Larger bets must be placed to obtain the same sense of excitement. Like alcoholism, compulsive gambling results in many physical problems. Compulsive gamblers suffer from chronic headaches or migraines, chest pains, heart problems, stomach problems, skin rashes, and severe depression. Two out of three contemplate suicide.

Usually when a compulsive gambler is stricken ill, his partner is the first to learn as much as possible about the illness. She wants to be supportive and helpful. Unfortunately, this is not always true when the illness is compulsive gambling.

Perhaps the partner is naive about addictions and rejects the idea that an activity can become an illness. Or maybe she is resistant to the addiction concept because she has seen her loved one control his gambling on many occasions. Or she may believe that, if this activity can become so destructive, it would be legally curtailed. Because gambling is not only legal but also supported—and even encouraged—by our government and some religions, she is convinced that gambling cannot be a problem.

A compulsive gambler can have no greater support in abstinence than a partner who not only understands the illness but also who is in recovery for herself. An untreated partner remains stuck in yesterday and continually feels the pain caused by the gambler's illness. Once the gambling is arrested, the partner may find her desire to get close to the gambler roadblocked, not by the gambler, but by the fact that she still lives with the belief that *if he loved me, he would not have continued to gamble.*

Heather's Story

"When I think back to what I put Don through the first months he was abstinent from gambling, it's amazing he didn't leave me. For years, all I wanted was for Don to stop gambling, but instead of feeling relief and gratitude when he finally did, I continued to feel a great deal of anger.

"Even as Don started to pay off his gambling debts and we started to catch up on our bills, I couldn't seem to get beyond the outrage I felt over all the hurt his gambling had caused. He had lied thousands of times. He had manipulated and used members of both our families. He had lost several jobs. He was arrested for forgery and almost went to jail. We had to sell some of our property to pay the legal fees, and we had to take out a second mortgage to repay the money he stole from one of his employers. He was so deep in debt when he stopped gambling that we were going to be strapped for money for a long time, and I resented that tremendously.

"Underneath my rage and fury was the fact that I believed that if Don truly loved me, he would have controlled his gambling and would not have let it get out of hand.

"When Don started attending GA meetings, he asked me to go with him. I could not agree to that. I didn't need meetings. I didn't have a problem, and I resented *his* meetings. He was going to two and sometimes three meetings a week. On days when he wasn't at a meeting, he was on the phone with people I didn't even know. I hated it when he would talk on the phone for forty minutes to a stranger and then refuse to tell me what the conversation was about. As the weeks passed, I grew more resentful of his recovery program and his strong involvement in it. For years I had felt cut out of his life because his gambling came first; now, in recovery, I felt even more distant because he was sharing a great deal of his life with someone other than me. At least when he was gambling, I knew he was alone and not with someone else.

"During all the years I fought with Don over his gambling, it never occurred to me that we would still be fighting once the gambling stopped. Actually, I was the one who was fighting. Don was quite passive and patient. He never started an argument; since he wasn't gambling, he had little reason to.

"I started the arguments as a way of getting out my anger. I didn't want to forgive him for all the pain his gambling caused. Somehow I felt that forgiving him would mean I was letting him get away with all the hurtful things he did. I just wasn't willing to do that. I guess I somehow wanted him to make up for everything. No matter what I thought, my bottom line was always the same: If he loved me, he would have controlled his gambling.

"Every once in a while, Don would approach me in a romantic, loving way, and I would reject him. I was so mixed up. On one hand, I wanted us to return to the close relationship we once had, and on the other, I would not give him *me,* because he didn't deserve me. He had to pay for what he did.

"Nine months after Don made his last bet, he asked me for a very special fifteenth wedding anniversary present. I was willing to give him anything because I did love him and because our wedding date had always been our favorite day of the year. Don asked me to attend a self-help meeting with him for family members of compulsive gamblers (Gam-Anon). I agreed to go, but I secretly wished he had asked for anything but that.

"I was so uncomfortable the day of the meeting. I spent some time trying to think of an excuse why I couldn't go, but nothing would have been acceptable to him. I could tell by the way he spoke to me that this was very important to him.

"While I couldn't come up with an excuse, I was unable to come up with the real reason I didn't want to go to the meeting. I truly believed Don gambled the way he did *because of me.* He had often told me that, and I bought it. I was so unhappy with his gambling that I nagged him, I scolded him, I threatened him, and I even hated him. Once, in an outrage, when I found that he had sold my mother's brooch, which she had given me, I hit him. That night, I remember saying to myself that, if I were married to me, I would leave and never come back. Don's gambling made me a person even I couldn't stand. I went to the meeting.

"The first thing I found out at that meeting was that my anger and resentment were perfectly normal reactions to what I had experienced. No one there told me not to feel that way. As a matter of fact, almost everyone present told me they felt exactly the same when they attended their first meeting of Gam-Anon. The care and support I received in that room that night was something I never expected.

"The night Don received his one-year pin (clean from gambling for twelve months), I had been attending Gam-Anon for three months, and in that time, I learned my husband was the victim of a mental illness. I also learned that his addiction could remain arrested as long as he attended GA meetings, followed the precepts of the program, and worked the Twelve Steps of recovery.

"Most important, I then understood that Don's gambling did not mean he didn't love me, but rather that the gambling controlled him and he was powerless over what it was doing to him and to us.

"Understanding the gambling addiction made a great difference in *our* recovery. I have learned to direct my anger at the illness and not at Don. In doing so, our relationship has greatly improved, and I feel more gratitude each day."

CHANGING ATTITUDES

Compulsive gambling is an addiction that causes its victims to act directly against their life values. Lying to, stealing from, and manipulating others result in loss of self-respect and diminished self-esteem. Gamblers who find themselves in this position will develop a false ego, become grandiose, develop many negative thinking patterns, and work hard at reducing the self-worth of those around them. In addition, the gambler will demand the center of attention and will become self-righteous and intolerant of contradictory opinions. Once the addiction is arrested, these negative attitudes do not fade. Since they have become almost ingrained in the personality of the compulsive gambler, removing them will require hard work in recovery.

Vinny's Story

"Compulsive gambling has been referred to by some as a disease of attitudes. It took me a long time to fully understand that. My gambling almost destroyed me and my relationship with my wife. It removed not only the few pleasures we used to enjoy—dinners in nice restaurants, theater, vacation—but also the necessities of everyday living. It resulted in our second car being repossessed, our telephone being disconnected, and our diets being limited to rice, pasta, and beans for months.

"Tiffany and I fought constantly over money, my gambling, and my lying. There was never a day without a battle. We were both suffering badly.

"She actually believed we could have a happy marriage if I'd stop my gambling. I began to believe it too, because I had become so miserable gambling every day. I made a commitment, finally, to stop the gambling, and to help me keep the commitment, I started attending Gamblers Anonymous meetings. I soon found that stopping the gambling was not as difficult as I believed it would be, but I found changing my attitudes virtually impossible.

"Compulsive gamblers are very self-centered and demand that they get what they want. That description certainly fit me. I was never one to put others first. It was rare that I would even compromise. I would do whatever was necessary to get my way. Most of the time, I just demanded it. When my wife fought back, I would hammer at her self-esteem until she surrendered. I never doubted I would win. This was one area where I always won.

"Stopping gambling did not deflate my false ego. I was still the big shot. I didn't want others to believe I lacked anything or that I couldn't afford the best. I defied many of the suggestions of my GA brothers. I refused to surrender my credit cards or turn my finances over to my wife. I needed my credit and money to continue the lifestyle to which I had become accustomed. Although I was paying off heavy debts, my grandiosity caused me to run up all my credit cards to the hilt. I would not give up my big-shot image. I continued to invite my friends out to dinner and, not only did I pick up the tab, I made sure I left a hearty tip. I never missed an opportunity to show off in front of anyone I thought would notice.

"I knew my behavior meant I was not working the program, but I couldn't see what charging my needs on my credit card had to do with placing a bet. I felt GA had no business interfering in my personal lifestyle. When it came to this, I refused to listen to the suggestions in my group, because no one there would listen when I tried to tell them how giving up my credit cards would hurt my dignity.

"At the time, I could not see that my behavior was directly related to my need for immediate gratification. I just thought I was a spontaneous person, and I admired that in myself. My spontaneity led me to purchase things I not only didn't need but also didn't want. In no way did I connect my spontaneous nature with my need for immediate gratification. And I certainly didn't connect either of these with my uncontrollable urge to gamble. In my mind, GA was there for one reason only—to keep me from making another bet.

"I absolutely refused to see that my impulsive nature and my inability to delay gratification had anything to do with my gambling, even though these unwholesome attitudes kept Tiffany and me from getting close. Tiffany had no trouble relating my behavior to my addiction. She often spoke of my self-determination and self-centeredness as being part of my attitude, which made me nearly impossible to live with. When I was actively gambling, she hoped that, when my illness was arrested, my attitudes of entitlement, arrogance, grandiosity, and selfishness would leave me. Just listening to her express that infuriated me, because I felt that many of these characteristics were positive, implying manhood and maturity.

"Besides my negative attitudes, I continued to gamble in ways that had nothing to do with placing a wager on anything. For example, I would drive on a long stretch of highway with the fuel gauge on empty, even when I knew the next exit was thirty miles away. I got a kick out of seeing if I could make it without running out of gas. Also, I would deliberately put off paying utility bills on time, so that when I got home from work each night and threw on the light switch and the house lit up, I would get a high. It was just like being in action. I would say to myself, *I won again.* I got a thrill every time. My wife got angry.

"Arresting my gambling did little or nothing to bring Tiffany and me closer. Things weren't much better than when I was active in my gambling.

"Attitudes? I refused to look at them. I denied for months that they had anything to do with my gambling, that they were irrational or destructive.

"However, by continuing to attend my meetings, and by taking the cotton out of my ears and putting it in my mouth, I was eventually able to hear how my attitudes were part of my illness, and how, by not changing them, I was still gambling even though I was not wagering any money.

"Only when I swallowed some of my pride and asked a fellow group member for help did I have some idea of what I needed to do to improve my relationship with my wife and to truly be in recovery from my compulsive gambling.

"My friend suggested I start seriously working Step Four of GA's Twelve Steps of recovery (Made a searching and fearless moral and financial inventory of ourselves).

"Working this Step helped me to see how my strong feeling of insecurity drove me to become power-hungry. Every time I won, I felt powerful, important, and secure in my relationship with others. But each time I had money in my pocket, my false ego thickened. When I entered GA, I brought with me absolutely no humility. That was one of the reasons I refused to follow many of the suggestions of the program. Although I did go to GA to ask for help to stop gambling, I was not going to ask them to help me change myself so I could function in an emotionally healthy way with others. I was sure I was already doing that. My only problem in that area was that other people in my life were not cooperating with me. I felt I needed to be better than everyone. Working Step Four helped me to see it would be almost impossible for me to recover if I wasn't willing to give up my irrational need for perfectionism and move toward humility. In the end, it was because of my willingness to become humble that my self-pride was deflated, and I was free.

"It was by working Step Four that I was able to see how many of my character defects were the attitudes I savored. My group helped me to see how the attitudes I carried and nurtured were anything but healthy and certainly didn't do anything to unite Tiffany and me.

"I found it amazing that when I stopped being grandiose, let go of my pride and false ego, and admitted I was not *entitled* to anything extraordinary, Tiffany began to move toward me. The things I thought would endear her to me were precisely the things that kept her away.

"The Twelve Steps of recovery, especially Step Four, definitely improved my attitudes, my behaviors, my marriage, and my life."

LEARNING TO TRUST AGAIN

How does any couple have a relationship when one partner does not trust the other? If the spouse of a compulsive gambler has no knowledge of the gambling but finds out about it as a result of some economic, emotional, or legal catastrophe, it is likely that trust will not return for a very long time.

Compulsive gamblers are secretive, careful to keep their spouses from finding out about their passion for action. The ecstasy they receive from gambling is so enticing and creates such a high that they do not want anyone to know what is going on. They fear that someone will try to remove their love.

Drew's Story

"There is something much more devastating about having a wife who gambles compulsively than having a husband who does; at least that's what I believe. I never knew my wife gambled. By the time I found out, we had been married twenty-two years and had one daughter married and a younger one in college. Holly, my wife, was forty-one years old, tall, blond, and attractive. I had no knowledge that she had any interest in gambling.

"One Thursday afternoon, I was in my office dictating a letter to my secretary when the phone rang. I answered it. It was the bank that held the mortgage on our new home. The caller identified himself as one of the vice presidents.

"He told me that because I did not respond to the two warning letters he sent me, he was proceeding with the foreclosure of my home. I asked my secretary to leave, and I began to explain that there must be some mistake because I had received no such notices. Mr. Briggs said he had spoken to my wife about this matter several times over the past two months. He said Holly had explained we had a serious illness in the family and were in dire financial straits. I asked Mr. Briggs why he hadn't called me sooner; he said that Holly told him I was depressed and couldn't handle additional stress. I asked Mr. Briggs to give me forty-eight hours to straighten out the situation. Reluctantly, he agreed.

"I called Holly; she wasn't home. I left the office and went home to wait for her. When she walked in a short time later, I told her of the phone call and everything Mr. Briggs had said. She was furious, calling him a liar. She said that he had never spoken to her, that she knew nothing about anything he had said to me, and that she was going to sue the bank. I never saw her so enraged. I thought she was going to have a stroke. Trying to calm her down, I told her I would take care of everything.

"The following morning, before going to work, I went to see Mr. Briggs. I started my conversation with anger, chiding him for causing Holly to become so emotional. Mr. Briggs was patient and listened to all I had to say. When I finished, he asked me to sit down and look at our payment record. The statement he laid in my hands indicated our last mortgage payment had been three months prior. No payment was recorded for the last two months. I still tried to convince him there had to be a bank error somewhere. Mr. Briggs asked me to return home and speak to my wife again. He assured me he had spoken to Holly several times about this matter. I was confused and starting to feel a little scared.

"I went home. Holly was in bed. She looked terrible. She said she wasn't feeling well and was too sick to discuss the bank matter. I told her it could wait a little while but not too long. I was uncomfortable, very uncomfortable. I went to the office, but it was a wasted day. I could not concentrate on the things that needed my attention. My mind focused only on our home situation.

"When I returned home, Holly had made a light dinner, but I couldn't eat. I told her we had to talk. Just by looking at her face, I knew something was seriously wrong. I truly thought some family member was very gravely ill and that she hadn't told me to keep me from worrying. But if that was the case, what would that have to do with our unpaid mortgage?

"I put my hands on Holly's shoulders, looked her in the face, and told her to tell me what was going on. She began to cry. She became hysterical. I couldn't make sense out of what she was saying. She talked about being heavily in debt and owing thousands of dollars. I asked her how that was possible, since I had a great salary and we didn't live beyond our means. She said, 'I've been gambling.' Gambling? I couldn't believe my ears. Then I reacted with anger. I started to shout at her and demanded she tell me everything. She did.

"As Holly started to speak, I found I had to force myself to listen with an open mind and try to understand why she did what she did. Holly explained that for most of our married life, she had enjoyed an active, busy, and involved life managing our home and raising our daughters. She had been a member of the PTA and the Mother's League for all the years our children attended school. Even when Lauren married and moved twelve hundred miles away, Holly continued with her busy life because Kara was still at home. However, when Kara went away to college, Holly began to feel a large void in her life. Within a year after Kara left, Holly was severely bored. Just hearing Holly say that was a shock to me. I always thought we had excellent communication, but I never knew she was bored. She had never said a word, and it didn't occur to me that she might be feeling that way.

"Holly told me that one day she had met a woman whom she hadn't seen in almost two years. Bea was in a situation similar to Holly's in that she too was no longer involved in PTA, nor was her day filled with motherly duties. Bea's husband had died seven years earlier, leaving her financially well off.

"Holly and Bea talked over a long lunch, and when it ended, Holly was convinced that Bea had the answer to her boredom—join a midday card club. Bea had been playing for over a year and found her interest in the club eradicated her boredom completely. Bea explained she never let her betting get out of hand, and for no more than fifty or seventy dollars a week, she could fill many hours playing cards with interesting people. Holly was open to anything, and she had always liked Bea, so she decided she would join the club.

"Holly's first day at the card room was an eye-opener. The room was occupied by approximately fifteen women, no men. They all had one thing in common—they loved to play cards. In the room were three tables. Two of them were three-dollar limit games; no one was permitted to bet more than three dollars on any one hand. Bea played at these tables. The third table, the occupants of which seemed to be members of the upper middle class, had no limit. Holly joined Bea. When Holly left the card room on the first visit, almost four hours had passed since she had entered. Holly couldn't believe she had been there so long. At dinner that night, Holly was more talkative than usual, but she never mentioned to me that she had joined a card club. She only told me she had an interesting afternoon with Bea.

"After playing at the limited table for almost a year and a half, Holly decided, against Bea's advice, to move up to the no-limits table. After being an active member of this table for only a few months, Holly knew she was in love with gambling. In the beginning, Holly was quite lucky. On one afternoon she went home with almost twelve hundred dollars, and she couldn't wait to return.

"It didn't take long before her gambling got out of hand. She soon found the meaning of the no-limit table: She could bet any amount of money. As a matter of fact, the more she bet, the greater the thrill. In what seemed a very short period of time, Holly was no longer controlling her gambling; rather, it was controlling her. She didn't care how much she bet nor how much she lost. She had only one concern, and that was to stay in action.

"For all of our married life, we have had all of our personal possessions in joint ownership—our home, our cars, our investments, and our savings. When Holly became controlled by the gambling, she began to dig into our security. Little by little over the last ten months, she sold everything without my knowledge. In addition, we were almost $31,600 in debt. Holly asked for forgiveness and understanding. I had neither to give.

"Right after Holly bared her soul to me, she began attending Gamblers Anonymous meetings. After a month or so of attending meetings, she was helped by them to develop a plan to repay all the money she owed in gambling debts. Their plan included Holly getting a job. Holly hadn't worked in almost twenty years, but she was willing to do whatever was necessary to make restitution and to follow the suggestions of successfully recovering compulsive gamblers whom she had met in the program.

"I started attending Gam-Anon meetings, but I didn't like them. For one thing, most of the meetings were composed of women, and I was most often the only man in the room. As a matter of fact, I was about to drop out when another man began coming. I could see he was more devastated than I was when I began attending, so I stayed to help support him. In reality, we supported each other.

"It didn't take long to feel grateful that Holly was no longer gambling; however, I became obsessed with another problem after she was abstinent: I could not find it in my heart to trust Holly again.

"By the time Holly received her one-year pin, she was trying hard to renew our relationship. I really wasn't doing my part. I was confused and living with mistrust. For as long as I had known Holly, I had trusted her;

but when I found out about the gambling, I lost it completely. I found myself developing negative and painful fantasies. Of course, these thoughts prevented us from becoming intimate. I started telling myself that if she could be that devious, then perhaps there were other secrets she was keeping from me. The one I entertained most was that perhaps at some time she had had another man in her life. I allowed these thoughts to torment me. It was only when I was open and shared them with Andy, the man in my Gam-Anon meeting, that I could see how I was allowing this negative thinking to keep me from what I wanted in my life—Holly.

"Andy also helped me to see how a great deal of the anger I was experiencing was directed at myself. I was angry because I didn't see what was happening in my own home. He was right. I was very angry at myself for being so blind. I felt inadequate and stupid because I believed I should have been the one overseeing our securities. My openness with Andy led me to see that much of my anger was based on guilt. I honestly felt that had I done my job as a husband and provider, our life savings would still be intact.

"Because Andy fully surrendered to the Gam-Anon program, he had started working the recovery Steps right from the beginning. I had been to a few Step meetings, but I can't say I ever worked Step Two (Came to believe that a Power greater than ourselves could restore us to a normal way of thinking and living). Andy suggested I work that Step with him, and I agreed. Up until that time, I had only accepted Step One because I had no trouble admitting I was powerless over Holly's gambling and that my life had become unmanageable. However, because I was a successful executive in a high-pressure corporate position, I was unwilling to turn to another— Higher or otherwise—to help me find the answer to my pain. I was determined to handle it like every other problem I had ever faced—by myself. It was only because I liked and respected Andy that I finally agreed to go with him to a Step meeting and take a closer look at Step Two.

"Despite my resistance, my willingness to listen made it possible for me to admit that perhaps there was something to Step Two. By continuing to attend Step meetings, I let go of my belief that I could handle my pain and started to admit how the things I heard there were mirror images of my situation and my feelings. Soon after that, I began to work Step Two. For me, this Step opened up my rigid way of thinking—I did not have to have all the answers for everything that touched my life.

"Eventually I was relieved of my pain. Slowly I was able to let go of my mistrust of Holly. In time, because I needed something—anything—that could restore me to a normal way of thinking and living, I grasped this Step fully. For me, a Higher Power was exactly what made it possible to remove my obsessive negative thoughts of Holly. In time, my thinking returned to normal, and I was able to put Holly's behavior in its proper perspective and renew our relationship, from which I had detached.

"Though I once wanted to drop out of Gam-Anon, it was by staying with it that I found the relief to my pain. My refusal to trust my wife after being hurt by her addiction was costing me more than any amount of money she could have lost had she remained active. With support from my group in working Step Two, I was able to let go of my strong feelings of mistrust and work on building true intimacy with Holly."

WORKING SKILLFULLY WITH ANGER

Anger is such a simple word. Most people know its meaning and, even when it is not expressed verbally, they recognize its presence. It's easy to understand why compulsive gamblers are angry so often. When they are actively gambling, they are under great pressure with little relief. They are continually torn between guilt about their gambling and their inability to control it.

Once the compulsive gambler arrests his gambling, it might be expected that much of the anger would leave him. Most often it does, but not until he surrenders to his GA program and works the recovery Steps.

At times, the recovering compulsive gambler may find that he is dealing with issues in recovery that existed before the gambling began. He is a sensitive human being who felt abandoned in his early years. Once abstinent, he may fear building an intimate relationship because he knows he is again risking rejection and abandonment. Moreover, he is living an unnatural lifestyle. For him, life without gambling is boring and stressful.

As difficult as it is to live with a compulsive gambler, at times it can be more difficult to live with an abstinent gambler.

Kyle's Story

"I stopped gambling because I wanted to. Nobody made me stop. When I started attending GA, I was determined to follow their suggestions and do whatever was necessary to stay clean. I worked very hard at the Twelve Steps of recovery. By the time I received my one-year pin, I was making appropriate amends daily.

"Once I stopped gambling and began faithfully working the Twelve Steps of recovery, Jill and I started to get closer, although not as close as I'd have liked. I knew the reason was my anger. I was angry all the time, and Jill bore the brunt of it, even though her behavior didn't spark it. My fury kept her distant from me, because even when we were intimate, my sense of contentment never lasted long. As a matter of fact, there were times when Jill would reject me because my approaches to her were at the end of a day when I had done nothing but scream at her.

"At my GA meeting, I was Mr. Nice Guy. Everyone there knew me as pleasant and helpful. They certainly didn't see me as an angry man. I saw myself as a man with a short fuse, but I saw nothing wrong with that.

"Many times Jill tried to get me to see just how much yelling and screaming I was doing, not only around the house, but outside, too. She gave me examples, such as the day I tore into the mailman about delivering the mail thirty minutes later than usual, and the evening our fifteen-year-old daughter sobbed hysterically—she was so embarrassed over the way I screamed and cursed at the tire salesman who didn't have the tires I wanted.

"I was blinded. I thought my anger was justified and that everyone else was unreasonable. Even when I would apologize for my anger, my wife didn't want to hear it. I started to question the validity of my recovery program. If Jill and I weren't close and neither of us was happy, then what was abstinence all about? I was feeling confused, frustrated, and more angry—until my son helped me see the light.

"Scott was home on leave for ten days from the marines. He had just finished a tour of duty in the Philippines, and I was happy to see him. But my happiness didn't last. On Scott's third day home, my next-door neighbor started erecting a six-foot-high cedar fence around his property. The sight of that fence going up caused me to lose my cool. I did everything but tear it down with my bare hands. Scott witnessed my outrage. He listened as I swore at my neighbor. With an expression of obvious disgust, Scott got in his car and drove away.

"When Jill came home, all I could talk about was the fence, but she was concerned only about Scott. He called that night to say he was staying with a friend for the rest of his leave.

"It was two days before Scott came home. He walked into the den where I was sitting in my chair reading the newspaper and began talking to me. He told me his perception of my behavior. He told me he felt I had never learned to accept a basic fact of life that he had to accept when he joined the marines. Scott pointed out that he joined the service to become a computer programmer but, since that school was overcrowded, he was trained as a carpenter. In addition, although he had enlisted with the promise of being stationed in Hawaii, because no carpenters were needed there, it never came to pass. And then, when he was sent to the Philippines, he had only forty-eight hours' notice instead of a promised two-week leave. Scott told me that, if he fought against everything he had no control over, he would be in the brig by now, dishonorably discharged, or crazy. He pointed out that if we don't accept the fact that there are some things in life we cannot control, we will be miserable and angry all the time.

"Everything Scott said was true. All my life I had done my best to have things my way. I couldn't stand it when something or someone interrupted my plan and altered the destiny I had mapped out for myself.

"That day, through my son, I was finally able to see the light: As hard as I worked my recovery program, and even though I always said the Serenity Prayer at meetings, I had never been willing, nor had I even tried, to accept things in my life that I could not change.

"Following my son's confrontation, and after getting honest with myself, I returned to my GA group and asked for their help. I told them I had never been totally honest with them because I kept my anger out of my meeting and in my home. I let them think I was Mr. Nice Guy, when I was anything but that.

"I guess the key words in Step Six are *entirely ready*. I know now that I never was entirely ready to make major changes in my personality. I was satisfied that I wasn't gambling and was well accepted in my GA group. The need to have my major character defects removed was beyond my understanding. Even when I accepted this Step, I have to admit I was scared. If my

defects were removed, who would I be? I had no idea. If I were very different, would people close to me still like me? But that was a crazy question.
The people I cared most about being close to were not close at all.

"The thing I liked most about Step Six was that *I* didn't have to remove
my character defects. All I had to do was be ready to have them removed.
That was such a relief. Once I allowed that to happen, I could feel myself
letting go of much of my anger. After that I could say and feel every word of
the Serenity Prayer, acknowledge its value, and, eventually, by living life one
day at a time, begin accepting the thing I could not change.

"Today my anger has greatly subsided, and Jill and I are moving closer.
Now I know it was my anger that kept us distant."

LETTING GO OF THE PAST

Couples recovering from compulsive gambling have many issues and emotions to work through before intimacy can be restored. It is imperative that
the hurts from yesterday be dealt with honestly, be forgiven, and be left in
the past.

Once abstinent, the gambler begins to live in a world that is foreign to
him. He has avoided dealing with reality from childhood. As abstinence begins, he will find himself an adult with the coping mechanisms of a pre-
adolescent boy. In this situation, he does not need a partner who keeps
bringing up the past—a partner who continually reminds him how his gambling hurt her. Guilt is one of the foremost feelings the gambler needs to
work on in abstinence, and reminders of prior inappropriate, negative behavior make it difficult for him to move ahead. When the partner of a compulsive gambler continually brings up the past, it is because she has not
internalized the fact that the compulsive gambler has an illness—one he did
not choose, could not control, and did not know could be treated. He did
not deliberately hurt her; he was consumed with the gambling fever, for
which he knew no antidote. If gambling had not controlled him, he would
have had the fortitude to behave differently.

Continually bringing up the past is not only unhealthy for the gambler,
it is unhealthy for the partner.

Dawn's Story

"It is not easy to admit it, but the obstacle that kept Brett and me from having a good relationship after he stopped gambling was me. For some reason, I could not let go of the past. I took advantage of every opportunity to throw in Brett's face how much damage his gambling did to me and to our relationship. I never let an occasion slide by without mentioning it. Maybe I wanted him to pay for all the pain the gambling caused.

"I remember that when my two sisters and their families were renting a house on the beach for the summer and they wanted us to join them, we had to decline because we were in the process of repaying gambling debts, and the last thing we could afford was a vacation. That whole summer, on every hot, humid day, I reminded Brett that it was because of him that I had to stay in the city and suffer.

"Another time, I insisted he drive over forty miles in a blizzard so I could visit my mother on her birthday. Ten miles from her home, we got a flat tire. We had no spare, so Brett removed the tire, carried it a mile to a garage, and had it repaired. He returned, put the tire back on the wheel, and, with near-frozen hands—he had no gloves—continued the drive to Mom's.

"I spent the rest of that day nagging him about how cold I had been, waiting in the car, and how if it weren't for his gambling debts, we would have had a spare tire. I let him know, in no uncertain terms, that he was to blame for my discomfort.

"Brett was so guilt-ridden that he never became defensive when I put him down like that. He would just listen. Down deep, I knew I was being revengeful, but I didn't care. I believed he deserved it.

"Because I was only attending Gam-Anon meetings and not working the program, I was getting sicker, nastier, and more resentful. I was angry all the time. In reality, I was resenting the fact that we did not recapture the closeness we shared before Brett began gambling. However, I never told Brett that. Instead, I continually brought up the past to punish him.

"I had no gratitude and no forgiveness in my heart. I continued to seethe and put down Brett to make him pay for all the bad things *he* had done to me.

"The meanest thing I did to Brett was on the day our son Jimmy was hit by a car while riding his bicycle to the park. The police came to my house and took me to the emergency room at the hospital. My next-door neighbor called Brett at work to tell him what had happened. He got to the hospital in forty minutes, although the trip should have taken at least fifty minutes. By that time, Jimmy was in surgery, and I was beside myself with fear. Instead of accepting Brett's support and the concern he was showing for me, I told him to get out of my sight. I accused him of never loving Jimmy because for years he preferred to go to the track rather than one of Jimmy's Little League games. I was so focused on my own pain and fear that I couldn't see the terror on Brett's face, nor could I see the hurt in his eyes, caused by my cutting words of anger.

"After the doctor assured us Jimmy was going to be fine, we went home. About an hour later, Brett came to me and said, 'If I cut off my right arm, will that make up for all the pain my compulsive gambling has caused? I am beside myself. I cannot live anymore with your anger and hatred of me. I cannot change the past. I cannot go on living with daily reminders of how I've hurt those I love. I can only not gamble one day at a time.'

"Brett began to cry. I began to cry. He told me that, once he became abstinent, he had expected he would live a normal life and have a fairly happy marriage. He reminded me that, for years, all I ever wanted was for him to stop gambling, and now that he had, he was more unhappy than when he was gambling. Brett explained that when he was gambling, he could set my anger aside and not have to feel the pain it caused him. However, without that faithful painkiller, he was in greater distress than ever before. He added that many times he wanted to gamble again because I wasn't changing, and if it hadn't been for his sponsor and his GA group, he would have.

"Brett went on to say that my anger and rage had kept him distant from me, and he had now reached the point where he could no longer endure it.

"I listened quietly, sobbing, and for the first time, I felt compassion for Brett. I had to admit he was right. Down deep, I wanted our marriage to work, and, as unbelievable as it may sound, I was shocked to learn that my behavior was the barrier.

"My sisters in Gam-Anon suggested I review the character defects I had found in my Fourth Step inventory, and then be willing to work Step Five (Admitted to ourselves and to another human being the exact nature of our wrongs) with them.

"When I did, I found the three main character defects that I was still living with: resentment, anger, and feelings of revenge. That summed up me. When I read Step Five, I knew why I had never proceeded beyond Step Four. I had totally rejected Step Five. I honestly felt I had no wrongs. I refused to own my negative feelings, and I had no intention of revealing them to another human being.

"If I hadn't attended Gam-Anon regularly, I would never have resolved the strain between Brett and me. Only with the help of my group was I eventually able to admit to another the exact nature of *my* wrongs. When I was finally able to do that, I could see how self-righteous I had been. My false ego must have been as large as Brett's when he was gambling.

"Working Step Five ended my self-deception. I could no longer keep blaming Brett and his gambling for my behavior. Regardless of how badly I had been hurt, Step Five made me realize I am responsible for my own behavior. Once I shared Step Five, a feeling of humility, unlike anything I'd ever felt before, came over me. Then I realized that, no matter what happens to me, I am responsible for how I react. I can no longer blame another for my feelings. They are mine alone, and I am responsible for changing them.

"My sincere effort to change made it possible for Brett and me to move closer. I am convinced that the spouse of a recovering compulsive gambler must let go of the past before the couple can renew their relationship."

OVERCOMING SELF-CENTEREDNESS

Few people are more rigid, stubborn, or self-centered than addicts, and compulsive gamblers probably top the list. They like to think they call all the shots in their lives. No matter what they do, they always want to do it their way.

Perhaps this is because many of them had difficulty with the first authority figures in their lives—their parents, especially their fathers. Often, compulsive gamblers describe their fathers as cold and distant. The way their fathers treated them was not what they wanted or needed as children. Some gamblers started to gamble to prove something to their fathers. Some, perceiving their fathers as materialistic, started gambling to accumulate a great deal of money and thus obtain Father's attention and recognition. Still others saw their fathers as workaholics who did not have time for them. Some of these gamblers admit that they set out to develop a successful gambling system in order to prove to Dad that they could obtain a great deal of money *without* working. The basis of the goal of these compulsive gamblers is resentment of their fathers' devotion to work, which always seemed to come before their needs during childhood.

If Father was a gambler, it is not unusual that his offspring would turn to gambling as a means of connecting with him. Even at a young age, a child can see what is important to a parent, and if the parent loves only one thing, then the child will likely strive to learn about the father's passion in order to have a relationship with him. Whether the result was negative or positive did not matter; all that mattered was his attention.

Should the compulsive gambler be unsuccessful in his pursuit of Dad's attention but find that his gambling brings him money and material things, he may put aside his original goal. He may then begin to gamble to fill the internal void left by not having his innate needs met.

As the illness of compulsive gambling progresses, it is the gambler's grandiosity, along with a large false ego and arrogance, that makes him difficult to live with. These attitudes create extreme barriers to recovery and are especially detrimental to a relationship that needs to heal.

Alex's Story

"My desire to stop gambling started about two months before I reached out for help. I was thousands of dollars in debt, my job was in jeopardy, my children weren't talking to me, and my wife, Alana, had gone to a lawyer for a legal separation. My reason for wanting help was that I was beaten financially, spiritually, emotionally, and physically. Every day I lived with knots in my stomach. I suffered from ulcers and was nauseous all the time. Whenever the phone rang, I had heart palpitations. One day I thought I was going to have a stroke. I hadn't gone to work, and my boss called me at home. When my wife told me he was on the phone, I had to run to the bathroom and vomit.

"I hated how I was living. I dreaded each day, knowing I had to lie to more people to raise the money I needed to pay gambling debts from the previous day. I couldn't stand the fact that I would promise myself I wasn't going to gamble, and then I'd find myself placing another bet. It was impossible to resist the urge to gamble. I was sick and tired and willing to do anything to cap my gambling fever.

"I found out about Gamblers Anonymous and called their hot line. That night, a member came to my house, picked me up, and took me to a meeting. I listened to the men and women tell stories about how their lives were ruined by gambling and how they were helped by the GA program. I couldn't believe that so many people felt exactly as I did. I felt so at home. As each person spoke, my sense of being alone with my gambling problem gradually left me. At the end of the meeting, I felt such hope. I knew I had come to the right place, and I looked forward to attending the next meeting.

"When I went to my second meeting, my wife came along to attend the Gam-Anon meeting—self-help for family and friends of compulsive gamblers. She got so much help in her room that her anger and resentment of me, and of my passion for gambling, subsided within a few weeks. Once she understood that I had an illness and that I was not gambling and lying and stealing to hurt her, she started to soften and began to communicate with me more openly. Her attitude changed completely. She said that as long as I was abstinent and continued to attend GA, she would stay and try to work out our problems.

"I had no trouble understanding that my problem was gambling compulsively, but other than that, I believed I had no problem. I understood that so well because I heard nothing else that was said to me in my meeting. Being a person who resists authority figures or anyone who makes suggestions about how I should change or conduct my life, I made sure I closed my ears to any suggestions that I didn't agree with. And many came under that category.

"Within two months of attending meetings, it was suggested that I get a pressure relief group so the men in my room could work out a budget that would allow me to provide for my family and slowly pay back the debts I had accumulated. I totally balked at the idea. I had always taken care of my family, and no one was going to tell me how to spend my money. Nor was anyone going to tell me I couldn't have access to my credit cards or bank accounts. Couldn't they see how my manhood was attached to my ability to control my money? I wasn't going to turn all my finances over to Alana and have to ask her for my every need. I wasn't a child. I insisted on doing it myself.

"Within five months, I was debt-free; soon after, I cut back on my meetings because there were a few real jerks in my group—poorly educated men who, I knew, were simply jealous of my success in my profession. They were always trying to tell me I had an ego problem and that I needed to go to Step meetings and work on some of my character defects. They had their nerve to tell me I had character defects. I didn't go to GA to change who I was. I only went to stop gambling.

"Sometimes Alana was just like the men I disliked in my room. She would call me arrogant and self-centered. She would accuse me of not growing and improving my personality once I stopped gambling. She started to add on many other things she didn't like about me. Her list was long.

"I couldn't understand it. I was clean from gambling and feeling better physically, yet I was very unhappy.

"Alana and I were growing further and further apart. Again, she started talking about separation. She seemed to be doing fine herself. She had even improved her relationship with her mother.

"I didn't know what to do. Finally, I opened up at my meeting and told them what I was feeling and asked them to help me. It was the first time in my life I ever asked another for help, and I got what I asked for. Several men, who had all been clean for over three years, suggested I start working the Twelve Steps of recovery. Although every ounce of me resisted, I agreed to do whatever they thought I needed to do to improve my relationship with Alana and, even more important, to make me feel better, more comfortable with myself. I finally knew what I really wanted: peace of mind.

"I started with Step One. It quickly dawned on me that I had already done the first part of Step One (We admitted we were powerless over gambling), but I hadn't done the second part (that our lives had become unmanageable). I could never admit that. Managing my life was always important to me. I had always been very stubborn about letting anyone tell me what to do. I had been resistant to authority figures all my life. My father never met *my* needs, and I was determined never to meet *his* or *anybody else's* needs.

"From the beginning, I had refused to listen to the successful recovering gamblers in my group. I did not want to do it their way. I had to prove to them, just as I had to prove to my father, that I could do it my way. It was only with their support in working Step One that I started to internalize the meaning of my illness. It was only through working all Twelve Steps of recovery for myself that I was able to work on my marriage and eventually move closer to Alana."

LEARNING TO SUPPORT — NOT CONTROL

When the addiction is active, most partners of compulsive gamblers try to control it. Needless to say, whatever approach they use, they fail. Most illnesses progress uninterrupted along a predictable path unless effective intervention is applied. Because many partners do not know they are dealing with an addiction, they believe they can control or even cure the problem. When someone is devastated by her partner's gambling, especially financially, she becomes even more controlling in the gambler's abstinence.

When a compulsive gambler is in early recovery, it is suggested that he not carry any significant amounts of cash. It is also recommended that he not have access to credit, because he has not yet abstained long enough to be able to handle this freedom. The compulsive gambler's partner is often happy to be supportive during the early months of recovery and readily assumes responsibility for the family budget and the purchase of cash items. But her fear of his relapse leads her to do things that the compulsive gambler needs to do for himself. Not only does she hold on tight to their money, she turns the TV off when the gambler is watching a sporting event; she tears out the sports pages of the newspaper before he can read them; and she interrogates him each time he makes a phone call or leaves the house. This kind of behavior makes the compulsive gambler feel he is not being allowed to work his own program, to grow up and become responsible for himself. His self-esteem, which was already low, plummeted because of his gambling, and there is no chance for it to recover if he is prevented from making positive decisions and taking positive steps on his own. Needless to say, the controlling done by the partner prevents him from even trying to get close emotionally. In recovery, the compulsive gambler doesn't need a "mother"; he needs a supportive partner who is in her own recovery, focusing on herself, but willing to work along with him on rebuilding their relationship.

A partner who continues to control a compulsive gambler in recovery keeps him distant from her and prevents their relationship from healing.

Marie's Story

"My sister was married to an alcoholic, and when she thought she was losing her mind because of the way he was drinking, she started attending Al-Anon. There she learned to change some of her behavior, behavior that was enabling him to avoid the consequences of his drinking. She was always bailing him out by calling his boss and reporting him ill when, in fact, he was hung over; or she would make excuses for him when he got drunk at social functions. I used to think she was lucky to be married to a man who gave her his paycheck every week, except for the money he needed to drink. Even when he got drunk, he was at home and would just fall asleep and go to bed. I thought I could live with that.

"My husband, Mark, is a compulsive gambler, and no matter what I did, I could never get money from him. His gambling always had to come first, even before necessities. He would not allow me to handle any of the family finances.

"When Mark stopped gambling, we were in debt for six months of his take-home pay. I didn't know how we were going to pay it back; however, with the help of some of his GA friends, a schedule of repayment was worked out. It took more than three years to get debt-free. During that time, we had to watch every penny we spent. There was money only for essentials. Although I was relieved that Mark was no longer gambling, I feared every day that he might relapse. One relapse could result in a debt that we might never be able to repay.

"My fear of relapse turned me into a stranger in Mark's eyes. Because his addiction made him irresponsible, a pathological liar, and an emotionally distant husband, I became a controlling, untrusting, nagging wife who wouldn't let him move unless I knew where he was going, whom he would be with, or what he was planning to do. In addition, I wouldn't trust him to purchase anything on his own. I would fill his car with gas. I would buy his railroad ticket, his cigarettes, and any other item he would normally purchase on his own. Although Mark had been clean for three years, I wouldn't trust him with the smallest amount of money. He was still carrying only the money he needed on a daily basis. I did this while he was struggling with his recovery, his abstinence, and his nongambling lifestyle.

"Many times Mark and I would argue over my controlling ways, but I was adamant. My fear was so great that I would not give in to his requests. I thought that if I let go, he might take advantage of my backing off and return to gambling. Needless to say, our relationship hadn't improved much at all since he stopped gambling.

"With hindsight, I see it as amazing Mark didn't leave me. My behavior made him miserable. Mark complained occasionally, but only when I was unbearable. His guilt kept him silent.

"It was when I began to see Mark going to more meetings and becoming more involved in Twelfth Step work (Having made an effort to practice these principles in all our affairs, we tried to carry this message to other compulsive gamblers) that I started to feel his absence and his distancing from me. To tell the truth, the fear of losing him frightened me more than the thought of his returning to gambling. I knew I had to do something. That 'something' was going back to my own Step meetings and sincerely working Step Three (Made a decision to turn our will and our lives over to the care of this Power of our own understanding).

"Working this Step brought me to fully accept the fact that nothing I do can prevent Mark from relapsing into gambling. All the controlling ways of all wives of all recovering compulsive gamblers in all of the world will not prevent one of them from relapsing. Only the recovering person can prevent relapse.

"It was difficult for me to believe that after three years in the program, I still hadn't accepted Step Three. Working this Step helped me see just how controlling I had been in almost every area of my life. I was raised to be a very independent woman, and the idea of surrendering to anyone or anything else was as foreign to me as trying to speak another language. I believed my self-will was responsible for all the good things in my life. The only area where it didn't sustain me was in my husband's gambling. When it came to dealing with that, I called upon the only God I had known. I prayed to Him often, but I felt He ignored me because He did not answer my prayers. In addition, I had come to believe my God was somehow punishing me through my husband's gambling. That made me angry. I didn't believe I deserved that kind of treatment.

"My sponsor helped me to understand that what I had previously done was ask my Higher Power to do what I wanted Him to do. In Step Three, I am only asked to make a decision to turn over my will to this Power. Making that decision took me several months. What helped me most was to observe the members of my group who had accepted this Step without reservation and to notice the changes that resulted. With the support of my Gam-Anon sisters, I finally did accept Step Three.

"Saying and meaning '*Thy* will be done' gave me such a sense of freedom. It lifted the weight of the world off my shoulders. Although taking this Step didn't remove all my problems, it reduced my desire to control the problems that crossed my path.

"Without a doubt, it was my controlling ways that kept Mark and me from growing closer together, once the gambling stopped."

REBUILDING RELATIONSHIPS WITH CHILDREN

Compulsive gambling requires time and energy. To supply both, the compulsive gambler must ignore his family. When the family includes children, the children suffer from Father's absence, which is both physical and emotional. These children consider their father's lack of interest as rejection more than do the children of alcoholics or drug addicts. When children have a substance addict for a father, they can, even at an early age, understand the reason for their father's absence: He is under the influence of a substance. Children of a compulsive gambler cannot have this understanding. They do not see the physical evidence of the addiction, and they do not realize how the addiction destroys the afflicted emotionally. In addition, should these youngsters ask their mother why their father does not spend time with them, she may fabricate reasons. She does this in order to avoid telling the children that their father is a compulsive gambler. The children are at a loss to understand and thus can come to only one conclusion: *My father does not want me.*

Abstinent compulsive gamblers feel guilty when they look back and see that the only relationship they ever had with their children, especially their sons, was a gambling-related one. Unlike an alcoholic, who, even in the late stages of his illness, would probably not offer his son a bottle of liquor, it is common for compulsive gamblers to teach their sons how to gamble; they believe they are spending quality time with their children, and they consider this time together fun time. What's worse, the children often love it. If the only connection a child can have with his father is through love of sports or betting on horses, for instance, the child will try very hard to be good at sports or at betting on horses.

Tony's Story

"I was a fortunate compulsive gambler. When I entered recovery, I had few debts. My desire to stop gambling was not due to financial pressures but due to emotional exhaustion. No matter how hard I tried, I could not stop gambling. There were endless days when I promised myself I would not make another bet, but I would keep that promise only a day or two. Even a period of forty-eight hours without placing a bet was unbearable. Not gambling made every cell in my body cry out for action. I was addicted to action. I needed it to get through the day.

"My mind was being destroyed by a kind of brain cancer called gambling. I was obsessed. Nothing else mattered to me. For years, I enjoyed sports—watching games, betting on games, and going to games. Then the gambling fever got me and *I* no longer existed. I *became* gambling. I thought of nothing else, wanted nothing else, lived for nothing else. My mind was racing every day. At one point, I thought I was going crazy. I even considered suicide. Instead, I reached out for help and stopped gambling. Slowly my sanity started to return, and I was able to straighten out my life.

"Despite all the gambling I did, I still had a pretty good relationship with my wife, Mary Ellen. Although communications were strained, they were not destroyed. Since I wasn't in debt, we were able to pay for necessities and start being sociable again. Mary Ellen was attending Gam-Anon and was a great support.

"When I was a little more than four months into recovery, Mary Ellen and I went away for a week's vacation. How I looked forward to that week. The first four days of our stay in St. Martin were wonderful. On the fifth day, everything turned around. Mary Ellen brought up a subject I did not want to deal with—our son.

"Aaron was twelve years old and a sports fiend like I used to be. I made him like that. When he was six years old, I started to take him to football games. I can remember warning him that if he ever whined or pestered me at a game, I would never take him again. Of course, he never did. Aaron knew that when I was gambling on a game, I was away from reality and wouldn't tolerate anyone disturbing me while I was in fantasyland. Once when Aaron was attending a game with me, he had to go to the bathroom badly, but he didn't want to risk telling me—he was seven years old—so he wet his pants and sat in forty-seven-degree temperatures for two hours. He never let on. He wanted me to continue to take him to the games.

"By the time Aaron was ten, he had memorized most of the names of the players on several teams. He also had their statistics at his fingertips. By that time, I had taught him how to figure the point spread on the games. So he and I were very close. He was never an annoyance. All he ever wanted was to be with me. When I look back, I can see how hard he tried to follow in my footsteps. But I discouraged Aaron from getting involved in Little League or midget football. If he did, I felt I would then be obligated to attend his games, and then I'd miss the action I longed for at the pro games.

"When I began attending Gamblers Anonymous meetings, I had already accepted Step One, even though I had never heard of the Twelve Steps. From the beginning, I stayed away from all sporting events, live or televised. I dared not risk watching even an amateur game for fear it would lead to a relapse. But although I didn't want to face it, removing all sports from my life also removed my son from my life. Aaron had learned to love sports and gambling because it was the only way he could have a relationship with me.

"I didn't know if anything else interested Aaron. I never asked him. If he did have an interest in anything other than sports, he put it aside because he knew I would reject it.

"So, on our vacation, when Mary Ellen brought up the subject of our son, I was angry. It ruined the rest of the vacation for me. Being honest about how my gambling affected my son was too painful for me. It made me feel very guilty.

"Mary Ellen asked: 'Don't you see how quiet and withdrawn Aaron has become since you stopped gambling and how much time he is spending alone in his room?' No, I couldn't see it; but even if I could, what could I do about it?

"She was relentless in her effort to make me reach out to our son. When we returned home, things got worse. Mary Ellen had awakened the sleeping 'elephant' in our family—how my gambling had affected my son—and she refused to let it lie. Becoming aware of just how affected Aaron was made me uncomfortable. After that, every time I was alone with him, I found the silence between us deafening. I was in anguish; I felt so much guilt.

"As the weeks and months passed, I could feel Mary Ellen withdrawing from me. One night she told me she didn't see how we could be happy as a couple unless I made a sincere effort to rebuild a healthy relationship with our son. I thought things had been going well between us, and I couldn't understand why she was making Aaron such an issue. In my mind, Aaron was doing fine in school and he had a few friends. Sure he was quiet, but so what? I felt that in time he would get over the emptiness in his life brought about by my abstinence. But he didn't. He grew more withdrawn. The more he withdrew, the worse I felt. The pain finally got so bad, I decided to talk about it with my sponsor.

"I don't know why I waited so long. He, my sponsor, was a godsend. First he got on me for not mentioning my feelings of guilt at my meeting. Then he told me it was perfectly understandable that I couldn't talk to my son. Aaron was now a threat to my abstinence. Gambling had been our common bond, and that was fine while I was in action. However, the few times Aaron tried to talk to me after I stopped gambling, it seemed like my addiction was talking to me. Aaron spoke only about sports, and listening to him brought out my urge to gamble. I couldn't allow that to happen. I didn't want to relapse and return to gambling, so I pushed Aaron away. My sponsor helped me see how confused and hurt Aaron felt. Mary Ellen and I had a good understanding of my illness and a support group. Aaron had nothing.

"My sponsor began spending more time at my house. He got to know Aaron, and Aaron began to trust him. Little by little, my sponsor began educating him about compulsive gambling. Aaron was an interested listener and slowly began sharing his thoughts and feelings with my sponsor and with me.

"Not too long after, I asked Aaron what he thought the two of us could do together that didn't involve sports. To my surprise, he had an answer. One of his friends at school had gone deep-sea fishing with his father, and Aaron was fascinated. He wanted me to take him, too. So on Labor Day weekend, Aaron and I spent six hours on a boat at sea. Some of that time I spent working Step Nine with my son (Made direct amends to such people wherever possible, except when to do so would injure them or others). I told him I was wrong to keep my addiction and its ramifications from him. I told him I was wrong not to approach him sooner and tell him I couldn't talk sports with him because it made me so uncomfortable. I told him I was wrong not to have been completely honest about what we'd have to do to build a new relationship. Most of all, I told him how sorry I was that, even in abstinence, I was hurting him by not being honest.

"Today I am grateful for my sponsor's help and guidance and for Mary Ellen's insistence on my making an effort to rebuild a relationship with my son. Most of all, I am grateful for the Steps of GA, for they gave me my son back and helped to heal my relationship with my wife."

Facts on File

Occasionally, when a compulsive gambler arrests his addiction, he will switch to another addiction.

All children of compulsive gamblers are affected by this illness, even if they do not know the parent is a compulsive gambler.

Working the Twelve Step recovery programs of GA and Gam-Anon is successful when the participant *wants* to recover from the effects of this illness.

Questions

Gambler:

- Are your ego and false pride preventing you from progressing in the GA recovery program?

Partner:

- What do you think keeps you from *working* your program of recovery?

10

Beyond the Steps

ANYONE WHO IS A HAPPY and contented member of the Gamblers Anonymous/Gam-Anon Twelve Step recovery program will tell you that the program works if you work it. What confuses some members of this fellowship is that they work the program to the fullest, and yet they remain unhappy and discontented. The compulsive gambler may attend meetings for years and place not one bet, yet remain unsatisfied in his relationship with his partner. Or perhaps his partner believes she is working her program, yet she cannot get beyond her anger and move closer to the abstinent compulsive gambler.

There is probably no greater help available for anyone suffering the effects of a serious gambling problem than the Twelve Step, self-help recovery program of GA/Gam-Anon. Many long-term members will tell new members that working the program turned their lives around. Working the program means attending meetings regularly; getting a sponsor; reading GA/Gam-Anon literature; making phone calls to members between meetings; surrendering to suggestions offered; being honest when sharing; and practicing the Twelve Steps of recovery.

What happens, then, to members of GA or Gam-Anon who follow all the precepts of the program only to find that months or even years later the assurances first offered them are not forthcoming? How can it be that after working their program to the fullest and making positive changes, they are still unhappy with themselves, and their relationships have not significantly improved?

One explanation is that the recovering compulsive gambler or his partner is living with another serious problem that cannot be resolved solely by working the GA/Gam-Anon Steps of recovery. He or she may be suffering from another addiction, a mental illness, the effects of being raised by an addicted parent, unresolved grief issues, a sexual dysfunction, or other serious mental or emotional problems. Should such a secondary problem be present, the compulsive gambler (or partner) may require outside help—perhaps another self-help group or professional therapy—because as helpful as they are, the GA/Gam-Anon Steps are useful in resolving only the gambling problem.

This chapter presents stories of recovering gamblers and their partners who, although devoted to their GA/Gam-Anon program, were neither happy nor contented. They were unable to develop the intimacy they desired in their relationships because of another untreated condition.

IMPROVING COMMUNICATIONS

Ask any recovering compulsive gambler or partner how their relationship was affected by the gambling, aside from the financial problems, and most will answer, "We no longer communicated." When effective communication has been missing for some time, outside intervention may be required to help the couple reestablish their ability to communicate.

As the gambling approaches the devastation state, both the afflicted and the affected are living with similar feelings: loneliness and isolation. Both emotions result from a lack of communication between the couple.

One of the consequences of this addiction is that the compulsive gambler and his partner do and say things contrary to their personalities and their values. Any openness, honesty, trust, or emotional closeness they once had in their relationship is eventually destroyed by the need to lie to, steal from, use, and finally abandon the people they care about most.

In time, compulsive gambling makes it impossible for the afflicted to continue the closeness he and his partner once enjoyed. His guilt, lack of honesty, and inability to stop gambling make it inconceivable for him to face his partner and communicate with her. First of all, he doesn't want to hear what she has to say because he *knows* what she will say; he's heard it all before. She just wants him to stop gambling or stop lying. Before abstinence, he handled his guilt by gambling. (That was true of any emotion he couldn't cope with.) He would just place a bet. Being in action numbed all feelings.

Like the gambler, the partner will stop expressing her feelings after a while, because the gambler doesn't listen to her, anyway, or she is afraid of his response. She feels he is not willing to change. She has to walk on eggshells to prevent him from gambling again.

Regardless, the result is that neither of them is emotionally bonded to the other any longer. Unless the recovering individual and his partner learn to share their deepest emotions, each will continue to feel lonely and isolated. Most couples are able to overcome this situation in recovery by using their program and the help of their group. But for some, outside help is needed to regain intimacy.

David's Story

"Have you ever stopped and listened to the way couples talk to each other? I never used to, but I do now.

"When I had been clean from gambling for a year, I wasn't very happy. When I stopped gambling, I had many expectations of myself, my wife, and our relationship. I wanted Terry to stop behaving like my mother and become my wife again. The problem was that I didn't know what that meant. My idea of what a wife should be was far from the kind of wife Terry would allow herself to be.

"In Gam-Anon, Terry learned that what she had been doing kept me irresponsible and kept her in the parent role. Because she wanted us to recover from the devastation of my gambling, she followed the suggestions she received. As a result, I slowly had to learn to become more responsible as a man and as a husband. Even though I made some positive changes, I still felt there was something keeping us apart, and I believed she was to blame. Often, Terry was short-tempered, and at times she would give me the silent treatment. Whenever I'd ask her what was wrong, she'd typically answer with, 'Nothing,' or 'If you loved me, you'd know what's wrong.' This left me confused, frustrated, and angry.

"One day, when we were away on a three-day weekend, Terry was in good spirits. I decided to find out what was behind her silent treatments. Well, she told me. She accused me of being a male chauvinist, of having a foul mouth, of always talking down to her, and of not being willing to listen. I went into a rage. After all, I hadn't placed a bet in over a year, and I had made many positive changes. And now she was throwing this at me! I began cursing and calling her all kinds of names. She packed her bag and left the hotel. An hour later, I left and drove to my mother's home in Brooklyn. I didn't call Terry, and I didn't tell my mother what had happened. The following day, I had an almost uncontrollable urge to gamble again. If it weren't for my sponsor and the other members of my group, whom I spoke to on the phone, I believe I would have done just that.

"My mother and Terry had always been close, and I know that sometime during the next few days, they spoke to each other. A short time later, my mother, who usually makes a habit of minding her own business, asked me to tell her what was wrong. Although reluctant, I told her everything.

"When I was finished, Mom asked me to sit quietly and listen to her. She told me some things I knew and some things I didn't know. She said that during all the years she and my father were married—he had died six years earlier—their relationship was never equal. He was the absolute ruler in our home. He made all the decisions but held her responsible for carrying them out. Her opinions didn't matter, and her feelings were pushed aside. But, in order to protect the family, she never talked about her situation with anyone.

"As she spoke, I could feel my anger beginning to surface. I felt my mother was comparing me with my father, and that hurt because I had never wanted to be like him. He had raised me with unremitting verbal and emotional abuse. I held my anger in check and continued to listen.

"My mother said my treatment of Terry had been, in some ways, a lot like the treatment she received from my father. She said my father was my role model for a husband and that I had naturally learned his manner of speaking—and his belief that if the man in the house didn't come first, he wasn't a man. That hit me like a ton of bricks. Because it was true.

"After thanking my mother for her concern, I went for a drive down to the beach and sat quietly with my thoughts. After what must have been a long time, I was able to answer my question: 'Why do I so often get angry with Terry?' I realized that I had always felt threatened by Terry. I had felt inferior to her. She has a very good job and had advanced to the point where she no longer needed me to survive. On the other hand, I had done nothing. Except for a few salary raises over the last ten years, I hadn't advanced at all. Living with an intelligent, hardworking woman had me hammering at my already low self-esteem—my heritage since childhood—which eventually led to my feeling very threatened by her.

"Reality was something I had avoided most of my life. I avoided it by gambling. Abstinence brought back reality, and my reaction to it was panic. Until the moment when I realized Terry no longer needed me to survive, I didn't know my sense of panic was based on the fear that she would leave me. By being honest with myself, I realized that I had tried to prevent that from happening by keeping her beneath me. I did talk down to her, I did curse at her, and I did act like a male chauvinist. As much as I didn't want to be like my father, I also never wanted to be viewed as a wimp.

"I didn't even know if I could change, but at that moment, I knew that, if I wanted to keep Terry, I would have to try. So I called her and apologized. I asked if we could talk. At first she hesitated, but then she agreed.

"Terry told me she had such high hopes for our marriage when I stopped gambling. But those hopes faded as I continued to speak to her in a manner she found unbearable. She described it as mental and emotional abuse. She said she would get depressed and find herself questioning why she stayed with me. I could feel myself getting frightened as she spoke, but I encouraged her to continue. She spelled it all out for me: I interrupted her whenever I wanted; I told her what to do instead of asking; I blamed her for anything I didn't like; I put her down in the presence of others; I used foul language at her; I refused to discuss my feelings with her; and when she needed to talk, I either refused to listen or, if I did listen, I negated her feelings.

"Until then, I had no idea that Terry's silent treatments were, in fact, reactions to my behavior. Our conversation clarified for me exactly what was keeping us apart. Because I wanted us to be close, I promised Terry that I would stop treating her in ways that were demeaning and painful and would start improving how I spoke to her.

"I felt great after that honest talk with Terry, but despite my desire to change, I had no idea how to go about it. My patterns of communication were so embedded that I felt it was nearly impossible to learn a new way.

"After two months of strong motivation and a dozen apologies for not changing my method of communication, I reached out for help. I didn't want to wait for Terry to react again, and I could see by her frustration that this was close to happening. I reached out at a Gamblers Anonymous mini-conclave we were attending. There was a couple who ran a workshop, and the recovering gambler spoke of having the same problem as mine at one time. When the workshop ended, I asked Terry to go with me to speak to the couple. She agreed. I did the talking. Terry seemed surprised that I spoke so openly with strangers about wanting to change and being unsuccessful in my efforts. The couple told us that they had received help from a marriage counselor who specialized in communication skills.

"Terry and I went to see that very counselor. Not only did we learn a lot about how we spoke to each other, but also the counselor helped me to identify my feelings. That was a job in itself since I was raised in a family that did not speak of feelings. For me, it was like learning a new language. The only feelings I ever knew were anger and the euphoria of winning big. It took months of intense attention from the counselor to help, support, and guide me to a new way of communicating the core of me, my feelings, to Terry.

"All that happened seven months ago, and we are now talking to one another on a more intimate level. Our relationship has greatly improved, and Terry's silent days are few and far between.

"I definitely found it hard to change my established means of communication, even when it didn't work. But like most things, if you believe the outcome will be worth it, it can be done.

"I like what is happening to Terry and me, and I see good things in our future. For that, I have to credit Terry's patience and my effort in improving communications between us. Effective communication has put us on the road to lasting intimacy."

THE ADULT CHILD OF AN ALCOHOLIC

It is not uncommon for the daughter of an alcoholic father to come to a subconscious decision: *I'll never marry a man with a drinking problem and live a life as miserable as my mother's.* If so, as she begins to date, she will observe closely the drinking patterns of the men she spends time with. When she meets a man with traits she finds attractive, she will make certain he is nondrinker or that drinking is of little significance in his life before she considers him for a husband.

This cautious approach to choosing a life partner works well for many. On the other hand, an adult daughter of an alcoholic father may find, after years of marriage, that her husband is a compulsive gambler. This adult child of an alcoholic will examine and question how this could have happened. Unless she educates herself in each of these illnesses, she may not only miss the answer, but she may very well find her own recovery road-blocked by unresolved childhood issues.

Lacie's Story

"You wouldn't believe how I picked Peter to be my husband. One of the things I liked most about him in the beginning was the fact that he didn't drink. Since my father was an alcoholic—who died a year after I married Peter—my childhood was unbelievably painful. My parents fought all the time; they were never happy, not even content. My two older brothers left home at age seventeen and nineteen. Since I was much younger, I suffered the greatest effects of my father's drinking. Perhaps I could have left home before I married Peter, but I felt responsible for my mother; I knew I could not protect her from my father's violent outbursts, but he seemed to have fewer outbursts when I was present.

"By the time I was fourteen years old, I believed the biggest mistake I could ever make would be to marry a man with a drinking problem.

"My mother told me she realized my father was an alcoholic on their honeymoon. Three of the seven nights they spent in Bermuda, he never came up to bed. He stayed in the bar and drank himself into a stupor. She said that, when they were dating, he would often head for his favorite 'watering hole' after their dates and hang out with his drinking buddies, although she never knew about that until after they married. So, from day one, she lived her entire married life with a drunk.

"From the time I entered my teens, Mom continually warned me not to marry a drinker. When I found Peter, my mother loved him because he didn't drink. Of course, neither of us objected to his spending time at off-track betting parlors. We had never known a compulsive gambler, so we didn't think Peter's interest was a potential threat to my future happiness or security. Actually, I appreciated Peter's interest in horses, their trainers, and their owners. It seemed healthy to me, and I could see it made him happy.

"For the first few years of our marriage, I enjoyed Peter's gambling because he shared his winnings with me. But when Peter reached his late twenties, his gambling got out of control. He used to cut out of work to place his daily bets, often losing his whole paycheck in the parlor. At home we were fighting all the time.

"I couldn't believe how Peter's gambling made me become like my mother. When my father would come home drunk, she would attack him with a blast of anger. I found myself saying the same things to Peter that my mother said to my father; the only difference was that I was addressing gambling instead of alcohol. I believe the gambling was worse. As bad as my father's drinking was, we did have the money we needed to buy food and to pay bills. Peter and I had neither.

"When Peter's gambling was at its worst, I got frantic. I thought he would never stop, and no matter what I tried to do to make him stop, it failed. In the end, Peter almost lost his job because of poor performance. He couldn't fulfill his responsibilities because his mind was always on placing his next bet. I was grateful when Peter's boss stepped in and gave Peter an ultimatum. Thanks to him, Peter started attending Gamblers Anonymous meetings. The more meetings Peter attended, the clearer he could see just how out of control his gambling had become.

"Nothing seemed to make me happy. I didn't even know what I needed to be happy. It was strange. I started to believe that there was something seriously wrong with me. Our home situation was better than ever. I couldn't want more from Peter. Nevertheless, I was uneasy all the time.

"I earnestly worked the Twelve Steps, but something was blocking me, and I had no idea what it was. I only knew that once Peter stopped gambling, I seemed to have a huge void. I know that sounds crazy, but that's the only way I could describe it.

"One night at a Gam-Anon meeting, a member commented on how sullen I had become. She sensed that I had shut down and wasn't saying as much about myself as I had when I first got into the program. The truth was, I didn't know what to say. She suggested I just start talking and trust whatever happened. Fortunately, the meeting was rather small that night, so I felt I could talk freely about my feelings.

"I must have talked for over thirty minutes. I told them mostly about my painful childhood. I told them how I lived with parents who didn't love each other—a father who was violent and abusive and a mother who was so depressed that she was never there for me. I explained how we lived from crisis to crisis, how negativism permeated our home, and how unhappy I was. I let my group know how hard I tried to control my father's behavior and how I became a child with adult responsibilities at the age of eleven. I never attended a high school dance or a football game. I never played with my classmates. I never invited any of my acquaintances home—I couldn't call my classmates friends; I didn't have any friends. I just lived the life that others needed me to live. I could never talk to anyone about what I was experiencing, because I would feel so guilty if I ever hinted that my home was anything but fine. Actually, it was F.I.N.E., meaning fouled up, insecure, neurotic, and emotionally unstable.

"When I had finished, an older, unfamiliar woman began to speak. She said she had once been exactly where I was. She said it had confused her, too, and it had taken her a long time to figure out why she wasn't contented and cheerful once her husband stopped gambling. She asked me which of my parents was an alcoholic. I was shocked. How could she have known that I had an alcoholic parent? I answered: 'My father—but why do you ask?' She explained that when someone is raised in an alcoholic home, that person is used to a lifestyle that includes a great deal of excitement. Some of the excitement is in the form of violence, some in the form of lying and stealing, and a lot in the form of anxiety due to inconsistency and always wondering what will happen next. Because she too was an adult child of an alcoholic, she helped me see how life with my gambling husband resembled my life with my alcoholic father. And now that my husband was no longer gambling, I was living in a totally unfamiliar environment—one that was free of crisis, tension, and commotion.

"She was right. I felt uncomfortable with my 'new' husband. He had stopped lying. He had become predictable in his behavior. And he had begun to show concern for me. All of this made me nervous. I could not get used to these changes. In all my life, I had never experienced anything like that.

"In addition, when Peter was gambling, he seemed to need me more. I did everything for him. When he became abstinent, he began to do many things for himself. I felt displaced until Peter told me that when he was active in his addiction, he needed a 'mother'; now that he no longer gambled, he needed and wanted a wife.

"I had no idea what steps to take to become a wife. I reached out to my Gam-Anon friend and asked her for help. She suggested I do what she did because it helped her tremendously. She suggested I start going to Adult Children of Alcoholics (ACA) meetings in addition to my Gam-Anon meetings. So I followed her suggestion.

"Six months of regular attendance at ACA meetings helped me greatly. There I learned to accept the fact that I too needed help. All my life I had stuffed my pain; in these meetings, I unstuffed it. I could do that because each member of my group understood exactly how I felt. Each shared my pain. Each validated my feelings.

"For as long as I could remember, I blamed myself for my father's drinking and my mother's depression. It never occurred to me that I didn't do anything to cause my father to drink or to make my mother depressed. Actually, I did everything I could to prevent both.

"At my ACA meetings, I first came to understand fully how my father's disease and how my mother's untreated reaction to it resulted in my developing caretaker traits that made me ripe for a mate like Peter. Peter called me his mother, and these meetings helped me see that Peter was right.

"I learned I had to resolve many painful issues from the past in order to be free and to allow myself to let others get close to me and touch my soul.

"Without these meetings, I would never have been able to build an intimate relationship with Peter. They helped me begin to heal my inner child, who was so wounded by her father's alcoholism, she would not allow me to trust, or get close to, another human being. Gam-Anon helped me grow as an adult and become an equal partner with my husband; ACA soothed and nurtured the child inside. Only by working both of these Twelve Step programs could I eventually develop a satisfying, intimate bond with Peter."

NEVER MEANT TO BE

In the early months of recovery, a compulsive gambler will devote a great deal of time and energy to remaining abstinent. Eventually, when she becomes more comfortable with abstinence, the gambler will begin working the Twelve Steps of recovery to work on character defects, develop more realistic thinking, and develop more positive attitudes about life. Sometime after that, the gambler may take a serious look at her relationships and discuss ways to improve them. Occasionally, the compulsive gambler looks at her primary relationship and openly and honestly declares: *It was never meant to be.*

Marion's Story

"When Paul and I married, I was nineteen and he was twenty-one. We were so in love that we decided not to start a family for five years so we could have time for ourselves. About a month after our third wedding anniversary, Paul was killed on the construction site where he worked. I died that day, too. My whole life ended.

"Because Paul's accident was the result of company negligence, I was awarded $170,000 in an out-of-court settlement. For more than two years, I didn't touch a penny of that money. I was too depressed to even think about it. On several occasions, I seriously considered suicide. Eventually, with the encouragement of friends and with pressure from my family, I started to get out of the house. But I had no interests. Without Paul, I cared about nothing. Then I found the Las Vegas of the East—Atlantic City. On my first visit, I was dragged there by my brother-in-law and his wife. Lori enjoyed the slots and would go there for fun anytime she could get someone to go with her.

"That first weekend there was the first time I felt relief from the pain of Paul's death. The hours I stood in front of the one-armed bandits seemed to make time fly. As long as I tried to line up the cherries, I was emotionally numb.

"During the next four months, Lori and I made at least ten trips to the casinos. I was starting to feel better. Then, with little warning, my brother-in-law was transferred to Seattle. Of course, Lori went with him. I was angry and saddened by their departure—mainly because I lost my gambling buddy. At that time, I could not see gambling becoming a problem in my life. I loved it. It removed the pain I found impossible to deal with, and it filled my empty hours without my having to socialize with people in whom I had no interest.

"In less than seven months after I found the casinos, I had moved from the slot machines to the blackjack table. The stakes were higher, the feelings of excitement more intense, and numbness of emotions assured.

"The year that followed was an emotional blackout. I have no idea how many trips I made to the casinos. I do know that I gambled away $136,000. I didn't know where it went or how it happened. For the first time, I started to become concerned about my future. I did not want to stop gambling, and I knew the few thousand dollars I had left wouldn't last long.

"Soon after that awareness, I met Stanton at a casino. He was attending a business conference at the hotel and wandered into a gaming area to play blackjack. He was pleasant and impressed me as kind. The following night, we had dinner together, and he seemed to take an instant liking to me. Although I wasn't looking for a relationship, I *was* looking to solve a problem, and the better I got to know Stanton, the more he looked like the solution. Stanton had been divorced for four years and had no financial responsibilities.

"Less than three months after we met, Stanton asked me to marry him. By then I knew he was right for me. As an investment banker, he was most often out of town on business. He was a very rich workaholic and extremely generous with me. What more could I ask for? I married him.

"Our relationship was well matched. When Stanton was out of town, I spent most of my time in the casino. When he was in town, I was there for him. He seemed satisfied with me, and I felt our relationship was fair and equal.

"No matter how much money I gave to the casinos, Stanton never complained. He used to say some wives spend their husband's money in boutiques or jewelry stores, and if I was happy giving my money to the casinos, that was fine with him. I had it made.

"My contentment lasted almost two years. Then, without warning, I went into a deep depression. My gambling had begun to consume me. I could not stop. Even on days when I was determined not to go to the casinos, I found myself there. I came to realize I had nothing in my life but gambling, and I was miserable. When I earnestly tried to stop and couldn't, I thought I was losing my mind. My urge to gamble was uncontrollable. Desperate, I sought Gamblers Anonymous.

"In the first three months, I attended as many meetings as I could. Sometimes I drove more than fifty miles round-trip to get to a meeting.

Stanton never accompanied me. He had neither the time nor the interest. He continued working seventy or eighty hours a week and allowed me to pursue whatever interested me. On more than one occasion, he said he couldn't understand why I kept running to all those meetings. He couldn't understand why I didn't just stop gambling.

"The longer I was abstinent, the harder I looked at my marriage. Unlike most of my brothers and sisters in my group, I did nothing to try to improve it. Stanton, on the other hand, seemed to think there was nothing wrong with it.

"As I became more honest in recovery, I began to admit that Stanton meant only one thing to me—he supplied the money I needed to feed my passion. Once my gambling was arrested, I no longer needed Stanton. If I wasn't a compulsive gambler, I would never have chosen him for a mate. I didn't love him, and he had never been there for me. Even if he had been, I didn't want him. I wanted Paul.

"Being abstinent from gambling caused all the pain I had over Paul's death to resurface. I thought I had put that behind me when I remarried. I thought I had left it in the past or that the passage of time had stopped it. Neither was true. Less than a month after I entered GA, the pain of Paul's death was as strong as when he was killed.

"The depth of the pain frightened me. I wanted it to stop. I became afraid when I became aware that it was threatening my abstinence. My urge to gamble returned. I went to extra GA meetings and used them strictly to help keep me from gambling. I could not use them to deal with my grief; for that I needed additional help. Once again, I sought and found the outside help I needed.

"I went to see a specialist in grief counseling. After seeing me for four weeks, I joined his therapy group. The group was just what I needed. I was able to overcome the anger I had built up against Paul for being careless on the job, for having the accident in the first place. In time, I came to realize I was angry because he had left me. I knew he hadn't really done that, but that's how I felt.

"Once I got out the pain I had stuffed for several years, I could then let go of Paul and start to focus on myself. Slowly I set personal goals that included renewing old friendships, returning to school, and playing golf— Paul and I had enjoyed that so much.

"Three months after I received my one-year pin, I divorced Stanton. In abstinence, I was able to get honest enough to admit that our marriage was never meant to be."

THE CODEPENDENT PARTNER

As the illness of compulsive gambling progresses, it devastates not only the afflicted, but the affected as well. The partner who attends Gam-Anon will work through the pain that comes as a result of this illness and will recover with the help of the program. Some people who begin this self-help group do not continue; and they do not recover. For couples who want to turn their lives around and reestablish a stable relationship, the decision to discontinue self-help can block that goal completely.

Why would someone with such an important goal leave a support group? Perhaps he feels he cannot carry out any of the suggestions he is offered by the group. If it is suggested that he stop enabling and rescuing the gambler, perhaps he knows he will be unable to do that. He fears that that kind of change could make his partner so angry that she might leave him, and *that* possibility—not her gambling—is his greatest fear.

Even if the gambler has stopped gambling and attends GA meetings before the partner begins Gam-Anon, he may find himself in a similar position. Although this partner does not have to change his rescuing and enabling behavior (because his gambler is already in the program), he will need to start focusing on himself in order to recover.

Many partners become totally focused on the gambler and develop such a need to fix him that they do not look at themselves at all. Every day, the gambler's partner concentrates on what he is thinking, doing, or planning to do. She will think of endless ways to stop him from gambling, yet she'll be the first one to bail him out when his gambling has gotten him in debt. She will continually put his needs before hers and eventually will have no idea what her needs are. She is a codependent partner.

Amy's Story

"Although I went to my first Gam-Anon meeting almost twelve years ago, I have been in recovery for only seven years. During those first five years, I was in and out of Gam-Anon many times. I knew I needed help; I knew I was badly affected by Buddy's gambling. But I felt no one in my group understood me. When confronted with not letting go of trying to control Buddy's life, I reacted with resentment. When I began to work the Twelve Steps of recovery, I was continually being challenged by my Gam-Anon sisters about how I was going about it. I did not feel supported, and I couldn't understand why. If we were all affected by the same illness, why was it so impossible for me to change when others were doing so nicely? I was especially confused because Buddy had no problem moving forward in his program.

"I don't know how Buddy put up with me during those frustrating years when I was stuck. Buddy believed my lack of movement was keeping our relationship strained and thought I was doing nothing to try to change it.

"Two years into recovery, Buddy retired and was at home full time. That's when our problems worsened. He felt I was continually on him for everything he did or didn't do. He told me he felt smothered and resented it. I found him more irritable than not, and I got scared that his negative moods would return him to gambling. I knew I had to do something, so instead of returning once again to my self-help group, I sought professional help.

"One of the first assignments in therapy was to write my autobiography. I really didn't want to do that. I hadn't thought about my past for a long time, and I knew that bringing it up would cause me great pain. But my therapist explained that in order for me to be free to make changes in my life, I had to relive my earlier years.

"I was the firstborn of seven children, including two sets of twins. When my youngest sister was born, I was eight years old. A year later, my father died in an automobile accident. The money my mother received as a result of that accident was not enough to support all of us, so she got a job as a cleaning woman in a nearby hospital, working the midnight shift.

"When my mother was at work, I baby-sat my brothers and sisters. When I think back, I find it hard to believe the kind of responsibility I was given at such an early age. No matter what happened at home, I was instructed never to call my mother at work. And we had no friends in the neighborhood. My mother discouraged it; she feared that if the neighbors found out too much about us, they would report us to the authorities. I was only ten years old and had the job of minding six children, three of whom were still in diapers.

"All of my childhood, I was held responsible for the behavior of six younger siblings. My brothers and sisters resented me. They felt I was privileged because they had to obey me. I felt burdened and never wanted that obligation. But I took it very seriously and never let my mother down. So I entered adulthood focused on others. I never learned to look at myself. I had developed communication patterns that had one goal—to make others do what I wanted them to do. I thought I knew what was best for each member of my family, and I never let any of them forget it.

"By the time my youngest brother left high school, I had four irresponsible siblings. They couldn't make a decision for themselves. They would come to me for help. I was so involved in their lives that I had no time to work on personal goals. The only satisfaction I got out of life was in helping others.

"I met Buddy when I was twenty-seven and he was twenty-three. He was intelligent, ambitious, irresponsible, and somewhat self-centered. It didn't take him long to see that I was a caretaker. He could see how I put everyone I cared for first in my life. He liked that.

"When Buddy and I married, I immediately started to take over all the areas of his life in which he was irresponsible. I made all his doctor and dental appointments, saw to it his car was maintained, paid his parking tickets, bought his clothes, and lied to his family to cover up his forgetfulness.

"Of course, the more he got involved in gambling, the more irresponsible he became, and the more I took up the slack. I know now that I fed my need to be needed. I had learned at an early age that most people like things done for them because it frees them to do other things—like play. I, on the other hand, never played. When I did enjoy myself, I would feel guilty and selfish. But when others did it, I was pleased. They deserved it, but for some unknown reason, I never felt I did.

"By the time I was in my early thirties, I was living my whole life for others. It wasn't just Buddy; my brothers and sisters still turned to me with their smallest problems or needs. I never said no. Not to them or my mother. She was retired and had severe arthritis, and she needed my help with shopping and cleaning.

"I remember times when I was hurting over Buddy's gambling, but I told no one. I recall sitting with one of my brothers, laughing about something that wasn't even funny, and never letting on how much I was hurting inside. When I realized that, I started feeling very angry. Writing my autobiography forced me to look back, and in doing so, I became aware of how often I gave to others and how I refused to let them give to me. No one ever asked me how I was doing. But why should they? I let everyone believe I was complete—no problems, no worries, no concerns. I shared me with no one.

"Writing my autobiography helped me to see how I had gotten to such a state in my life. It helped me to see why I could never have done the Fourth Step successfully. My inventory would have included nary a single defect. Most people who knew me thought I was perfect, and in some ways, I thought so, too. Thinking myself perfect made it easier to lace into Buddy about some of his negative behaviors and traits—stealing, manipulating, being self-centered, and, most of all, his compulsive lying. Writing my autobiography helped me to see how many times in my life I had lied. Whenever I was asked to do a favor, I would say yes. Over half the time, I wanted to say no. The difference between Buddy's lying and mine was that no one ever knew I lied. It was only through therapy that I got in touch with the fact that I'm a people pleaser, and people pleasers lie.

"I could never say no. Even if people weren't close friends, I could not refuse them. I guess I was afraid that if I turned them down, they wouldn't like me. Being liked was too important to me. As a child, getting my mother's approval had been very important to me. I never got it. She never told me I was doing a good job with the kids; nor did she tell me she was proud of me. She took me for granted. I never felt appreciated or accepted. Nevertheless, I kept trying to please her.

"I carried my need to please others into every aspect of my life. My co-workers and bosses liked me because they could use me. Everyone knew whom to go to when they wanted extra work to be done.

"I truly believe Buddy's gambling would have come to an end much earlier if I wasn't such an enabler. I never refused him money when he asked for it. I couldn't. I was afraid that if I refused him, he would walk out on me.

"By the time Buddy's gambling was at its worst, my siblings were grown and busy in their own lives. So they turned to me less often for help. Buddy had become the only one who could satisfy my need to be needed. I truly felt if he ever left me, no one else would ever need me. All my life I had gotten my good feelings by helping others and by meeting others' needs. I had always done whatever was needed to be liked.

"The longer I stayed in therapy and continued to explore my life history, the angrier I felt. No wonder I was so unsuccessful in my self-help program. My Gam-Anon sisters wanted me to focus on myself. They were asking me to do something I had never done in my whole life, and I had no idea how to go about it. Whenever they asked me how I felt about something, I would always give the same answer: 'I don't know.' For me, identifying feelings was like learning a new language, and in my ignorance, I saw no reason for that.

"I'm sure that if Buddy hadn't retired and if he hadn't started pushing me to stop doing things for him that he could do for himself, I would never have sought or accepted help. When Buddy became responsible, he left me with a large void. I found I had no one to do things for. I felt unwanted, useless. My resistance to giving up my caretaker role just made Buddy angrier, and he moved further away from me. When he did, I felt hurt and rejected and began to look for a way to make things right again.

"Looking at my reality was very painful. What I found out was that Amy never truly existed. I never developed my own personality, never expressed my feelings to anyone, never even knew I had feelings. At one point in therapy, my counselor asked me what I needed. I said honestly, 'I need Buddy.' When my counselor asked why, I didn't say, 'Because I love him.' Rather, I said, 'To take care of.'

"At that point, I could finally see how I had brought my own serious problems into my marriage and how they did not involve Buddy's gambling. My role of caretaker, my need to be needed, and my approval-seeking behavior were issues that I needed to work on before I could have a mature relationship with my husband. I could never have opened up and worked the Steps until I dealt with my pain, because I felt I had never really mattered. In therapy I was able to identify my character defects, which hindered both my own recovery and the recovery of my relationship with my husband.

"In therapy I was able to choose healthy goals for myself with the guidance of a professional who confronted me gently with support and understanding. She knew I was too fragile for heavy confrontation. When I exposed my raw emotions, I needed to be in the presence of only one other person. I could never have done it in a group, regardless of how supportive the group might have been.

"When I was a kid, I would complain to my mother about someone else's behavior, and she would tell me to mind my own business. I felt put down. In therapy, however, I heard the same thing from my therapist, only worded differently: 'It's time to take care of *you*, because *you* deserve it.' At that I felt no anger or resentment. It just made me feel special and accepted. And that's what I had been looking for for so many years.

"In therapy I began to make positive changes. I got a new hairdo and stylish clothes. I started to work on forms of communication that were clear—no double messages and no manipulating. I started practicing saying no, so that I could be honest. I no longer wanted to be a people pleaser and feel like a doormat. I was far from being an independent woman, but at least I was no longer without a personality or an identity.

"In therapy I learned that, unless I was willing to change my ways and begin to focus on myself, it didn't matter how hard I tried to get close to Buddy. It would be a wasted effort.

"By the time I returned to Gam-Anon for the fifth time, I was ready and able to work the program. I was able to accept confrontation. I was ready to be questioned and challenged without being defensive. When asked to develop personal goals, I was willing. By doing what I did in therapy, taking it one baby step at a time, I was able to make changes that eventually ended my obsession with, and continuous focus on, Buddy."

SWITCHING ADDICTIONS

Many compulsive individuals find themselves susceptible to more than one addiction. They must be aware of anything that gives them pleasure or "relief." These addicts are most vulnerable to a second addiction while in the process of recovering from their first addiction. Compulsive gamblers who have left behind their addictive gambling behavior may be tempted to satisfy their lingering cravings for a "high" by turning to another mind- or mood-altering substance or activity—for example, alcohol, other drugs, or sex.

Roy's Story

"After almost twenty years of heavy gambling, I was way over my head into loan sharks and bookies. When I hit bottom, I was $113,000 in debt. Approximately half of that was money I had stolen from family, friends, and clients—I'm an attorney. The other half was legal debts—from the credit union, credit cards, and a second mortgage—and debts to what are called heavy-handed lenders.

"Just before I stopped gambling, I was so depressed that I attempted suicide by cutting my wrists. I lost a good deal of blood and passed out, but a short time later, my wife came home and found me. I spent one week in a medical hospital and ten days in a psychiatric hospital. Because my wife knew my gambling was out of hand, she told my doctor that my suicide attempt was due to my gambling losses. The doctor insisted that I call Gamblers Anonymous before he would discharge me. Depressed and without much hope, I made the call.

"Gamblers Anonymous saved my life. Almost from the first meeting I attended, I felt I was no longer alone. Everyone was so kind to me, I no longer felt like garbage. But what was most helpful was that I felt hope. I found out I wasn't the first man to try to kill himself because he could see no way out of the bottomless pit his gambling had gotten him in.

"I took to my GA program instantly. When I had my pressure relief group with three members of my group, my wife, and one of her Gam-Anon sisters, I was very scared; I had to reveal to my wife exactly how much debt I was in and how I had obtained the money. Trusting what I had been told by other recovering gamblers who had been in the same position, I followed all their suggestions.

"With the guidance of my group, I began repaying all my debts. It took me almost eleven years. During that time, I was totally devoted to my GA program. I worked the Twelve Steps of recovery, reached out for help to identify my character defects, and asked for help from the members of my group to keep my attitudes positive. After focusing on myself and my recovery, I began working Step Twelve (Having made an effort to practice these principles in all our affairs, we tried to carry this message to other compulsive gamblers).

"I was happy, very happy. Not only had I managed to keep my job as a law partner, but also I was working three evenings a week as a consulting attorney for another firm. This second job paid well, and I needed the money to repay the debts my gambling had caused. I went to two GA meetings every week, and on weekends I spent time fixing up our home, playing with the kids, and being with my wife. I had every minute of every day filled.

"I was never the kind of person who needed much rest. Even as a child, I got along with little sleep. I remember how my mother used to worry about that. But in time, she just accepted it. Everyone who knew me knew that I was a high-energy person.

"By the time all my debts were paid, I had been a member of GA for eleven years. In my city, I was known as Mr. GA. Everybody knew whom to call if they had a problem or if they wanted someone to go with them to pick up a compulsive gambler reaching out for help. I even devoted four hours a week to the GA hot line. My life was truly full.

"With my debts paid off, my wife and I decided it was time to give up my consulting job and spend more time at home with her and the kids. So that's what I did. Believe it or not, this change in lifestyle was more of a shock than giving up gambling.

"Giving up the extra job left me with approximately twelve empty hours each week, fifty hours each month. As the weeks passed, I found myself faced with an old problem—boredom. I had never been able to tolerate boredom, and I now felt bored every day.

"Because I was viewed as Mr. GA—the man who had it all together, the model recovering compulsive gambler—I told myself that I should not bring up what I was going through with my group because it would discourage new members who were just leaving their gambling behind them. I now know it was my ego and false pride that kept me from being honest, and not my concern for others.

"I was in complete denial of the fact that I could relapse. I was determined not to gamble, no matter what the cost. I felt I'd rather die than place another bet. Nevertheless, I had to look for a solution for my problem. I searched everywhere but in my GA group.

"I spoke to others about finding new interests to fill the void left by the absence of my second job. I got lots of suggestions but found none acceptable. Spending more time at home wasn't very exciting. My daughter had just started attending an out-of-town college, and my seventeen-year-old son was hardly ever home. My wife pushed for her suggestion that we spend more time together and perhaps develop an interest in something we could both enjoy. That seemed promising, but nothing came of it.

"Although I had been abstinent from gambling for many years, I now realized that my wife and I had not grown much closer. She was busy, and I had hardly ever been home. Because I was not motivated to try anything new, I started to watch more television to handle my boredom.

"After becoming a couch potato, I realized that what I described as boredom wasn't boredom at all. It was really just excessive unspent energy churning within me. It's hard to explain this feeling to anyone but a compulsive gambler. The way I had released this energy previously was by gambling compulsively. In abstinence, I released it by working two jobs and always staying busy. I never had quiet time and never relaxed.

"The only remedy I knew I could count on to mellow me out was scotch on the rocks. I never overindulged and it was never a problem. Within a couple of months, I had developed a regular routine, one that accomplished what I wanted and gave me peace and quiet. I would come home from work at a decent hour, have dinner with my wife and sometimes my son, and then retire to the den and turn on an old movie or two. That was my day. I invested in laziness.

"I began to find excuses not to return phone calls from my GA friends, and I cut back on my hours on the hot line. I wouldn't give up my two meetings a week, because I didn't want to gamble, and besides, that was where I got my ego stroked. I couldn't see it, but I had started to slip back into my old attitudes. Today, I believe I wasn't confronted on that in my group because I was the elder member and no one wanted to challenge me.

"The first time my wife commented on my drinking was the day I came home and had a drink before dinner. Boy, did I overreact! I began to think she was back to her old ways of trying to control me. I strongly resented Elaine because I didn't want her to tell me what to do.

"As the months passed, my consumption increased. Although I thought it wasn't noticeable—I hid the bottles—the arguments between Elaine and me continued, and worsened. I mentioned nothing of what was going on at home in my GA group. I was unable to see how my attitudes were sliding back to the attitudes I'd had while gambling.

"Eventually, Elaine and I stopped talking. I could see she was back to her old ways, and I hated living with her when she was like that. I kept telling her that, but she insisted it was my drinking that was separating us. I disagreed. Elaine's attitudes had become a new wedge between us, and she couldn't see it.

"We lived like that for almost a year. One black night I came home from work and found no dinner waiting. I found only a note from Elaine saying she had gone to her sister's house for dinner and suggesting I could fix something for myself. I went into a rage. I ate nothing. I retired to the den with my bottle—no glass, just my bottle. That's the last thing I remember.

"My son must have returned home sometime after midnight. All I remember was someone shaking me and telling me to get up. He was furious, shouting at me like he had never done before. I couldn't understand what he was saying. After a minute or two, he was pushing me and trying to punch me. I had been in such a deep sleep it took me several minutes to get oriented. Then my ability to comprehend clicked in, and I was shocked at what he was telling me. My heart began to pound. My son said he had just taken Elaine to the hospital. When he came home, he found her unconscious on the floor of the den and me asleep in my bed.

"I was never so scared in all my life. He was crying and out of control. Trying to calm him while he was trying to hit me was nearly impossible. My first thought was that someone must have broken into the house and assaulted Elaine. But what actually happened, according to my son, was that Elaine had told the doctor in the emergency room I had hit her, and that she had fallen and hit her ear on a coffee table.

"My son and I returned to the hospital to find Elaine conscious, but she did have a concussion. The doctor wanted her to report the incident to the police, but she refused. It was Elaine who calmed my son, saying it was partially an accident. I couldn't believe Elaine was covering up for me. In all my years of gambling, I never felt as guilty as I felt standing at Elaine's bedside.

"That night, I did what I hadn't done for months. I went to my group and reported openly and honestly what had happened. There was a man in the group that night who'd been coming for only a few months. I vaguely remember when he first came to GA that he had said something about being in another self-help program, but to tell you the truth, I hadn't paid much attention. When I finished with my story, he spoke. He said he'd been in recovery for alcoholism for three years and that after he had stopped drinking, he filled his void by going to off-track betting parlors. Within a year, his betting was completely out of control. He told me he believes he's the type of person who can become compulsive about almost anything. I had never heard that before, but after seeing what I had done to Elaine and having no recollection of it, I became convinced that I must never drink again. I followed my group members' suggestion and began attending Alcoholics Anonymous meetings.

"All that happened a year ago. Although Elaine and I are presently separated, I feel confident that she and I will reconcile. We see each other often, and the longer I am sober, the closer we get. In the meantime, she is working her own program of recovery and I am working mine.

"I have long believed GA saved my life. In AA I am finding out that the reason I turned to alcohol to calm me down and help me to deal with my high energy level is because I spouted—but never worked—Step Eleven (Sought through prayer and meditation to improve our conscious contact with God as we understood Him, praying only for knowledge of His will for us and the power to carry that out). Despite all my knowledge about the addiction of compulsive gambling, I had only browsed through the Eleventh Step and as a result found myself switching addictions.

"Gamblers Anonymous did save my life, because if I had continued gambling, lying, stealing, and isolating, I would have destroyed myself. Alcoholics Anonymous made it possible for me to fill the void created when I left my second job. It didn't help me to find things to do, but it helped me to look within and see how my anxiety and my nervousness were the products of never having felt I was whole within myself or part of the universe. I had never felt connected, and that resulted in feeling unfilled and spiritually dead. I looked for something to numb the resulting spiritual death. For me, the numbing agent was alcohol."

SEXUAL DYSFUNCTION

Any chronic, progressive illness will eventually affect every area of the afflicted person's life as well as the life of his partner.

Compulsive gambling and sexual dysfunction commonly coexist. Any partner of a compulsive gambler can tell you how many times she desired sex, only to be rejected because the gambler wasn't in the mood, or if he did comply, she later realized he did so only to set her up so he could ask for another bailout.

A compulsive gambler's sexual desire can relate directly to his gambling experience. If he wins big on a given day, he may become so elated with his victory that he doesn't need or desire sex. Some of the afflicted have called a big win as good as, or even better than, an orgasm. If the gambler has a day of heavy losses, he may be too depressed to have sexual intercourse. In time, the partner of the compulsive gambler will come to realize that his gambling is more important to him than making love to her.

Most couples can reverse this type of physical separation if both attend self-help meetings and have a sincere desire to renew the closeness they once shared. A gambler and his partner, both seriously working their program and the Steps, occasionally may find that one of them is unable to renew or to develop a healthy desire for physical intimacy. For some, the dysfunction that separated them may have nothing to do with the addiction that has devastated them. At times the separation is caused by an early childhood experience that cannot be resolved in a self-help program that focuses on compulsive gambling. Should this condition exist, the couple may need to enlist outside intervention to fully renew their relationship.

Lorna's Story

"I'll never forget the day Jerry came to me and told me he had just come from a GA meeting. It was the happiest day of my life. At least it was the happiest day in over ten years. Jerry had gambled away everything we owned of any value. For years we had nothing. The gambling fever wore away at Jerry so that I hardly knew him. He had become a burned-out, unkempt, angry thirty-one-year-old who looked fifty.

"When I first met Jerry, I liked him right away. He was clean-cut, interesting, and athletic. He loved sports; his greatest pleasure was watching football games, either live or on TV.

"When we were dating, Jerry was kind and patient. He never pressured me to do anything I wasn't comfortable with. Most of the other men I had dated up until then always seemed to be more interested in sex than in me. Although I was twenty-three, I was not interested in having sex before marriage.

"When Jerry and I married, he continued to be extremely considerate of my sexual shyness. I remember thinking I was fortunate that Jerry expended so much energy at athletics—either playing basketball or bowling or watching his favorite football team. It kept his sexual demands low.

"When I was honest with myself, I could admit that I didn't like sex. In fact, I hated it. I didn't know why. I only knew that even the thought of it repulsed me. When Jerry did approach me to make love, I would cooperate because I appreciated his compassion. In all our years together, we never discussed my lack of enthusiasm nor my lack of initiation.

"I remember I used to fantasize: If Jerry would stop gambling and if we could get our finances straightened out, and if he would continue to be understanding about my lack of interest in sex, then I would be happy. Because Jerry was gambling when I first met him, I had no idea that his lack of sexual desire was directly related to his gambling.

"When Jerry began attending GA meetings, he stopped attending football games and stopped watching them on TV; he even resigned from his bowling league. He began spending a great deal of time in his recovery program.

"After Jerry had been abstinent about three months, he began talking about the two of us doing more things together. I favored that until I realized he meant having sex more often. Nobody was less interested than I was in working on lovemaking. Although I never spoke of this in my Gam-Anon group, I know Jerry spoke of it with his sponsor.

"Ironically, every other area of our lives was improving. But the more Jerry attempted to bring me physically close to him, the more resistant and anxious I became. Jerry was patient, but I tried his patience beyond endurance. At one point, he said my sexual rejection of him was my way of punishing him for gambling. It was untrue, but I could not convince him.

"By the time Jerry had been abstinent about a year, we were further apart than ever. At his last attempt at physical intimacy, I pushed him away as hard as I could—and then I broke down. I became hysterical. He could neither calm me down nor comfort me. That night, I finally told him everything.

"My alcoholic father walked out on my mother when I was seven. Although she hated his drinking, she didn't want him to leave. Three years later, she married another alcoholic. I didn't like him from the day I met him, and since my mother worked nights, I was often alone with him. Before I turned thirteen, right after my body started to develop, my stepfather forced himself on me. From that day on I lived in horror, never knowing which night he would enter my room and rape me again. I was so scared and lonely. I couldn't tell anyone because he threatened to kill my mother if I said what had happened.

"I lived through three years of hell. When I was sixteen he was killed driving while drunk. My mother was so depressed after he died that I couldn't tell her what he had done to me. In fact, I never told anyone.

"Before I married Jerry, I had had only five dates with three different boys. I ended each of these possible relationships because each of them pushed me to have sex. For more than two years, I didn't date at all; then I met Jerry. His compassion, patience, and respect for me were his most endearing characteristics. His gentleness and love for me made having sex with him after marriage just bearable, but never satisfying or pleasurable.

"As a result of Jerry's changes after he stopped gambling, I found him more attractive than ever. I decided to get help with my problem of sexual inhibition.

"I found a female therapist who specialized in treating victims of incest and rape. After just six sessions, she placed me in her group of seven other women who had lived through similar experiences. Never in my life would I have believed it possible for me to speak of my teen years in front of a group. But the therapist was so supportive and the group so understanding.

"Six months of group counseling, combined with six months of treatment at a sex therapy clinic—at times with Jerry involved—made it possible for me to deal with, and let go of, the pain, guilt, and fear I had carried for so long.

"When I entered therapy, I was almost thirty years old, but my feelings were exactly as they were when I first felt them. The confusion, the fear, and the sense of isolation I experienced as a young girl returned as if they had never left me. The process of healing with all that pain was made possible because I was willing to open up and talk about it with this group of women—women I had come to trust because each one of them had lived a life like mine. They reached out to the hurting child within me, comforted me, and held me safe.

"The education Jerry received at the clinic enabled him to understand

the basis of my behavior. The treatment he was given made it possible for
him to be so supportive that I could deal with my fear, disgust, and shame
and eventually welcome him back into my life.

"GA and Gam-Anon turned our lives around and returned us to sanity. GA helped Jerry stay abstinent, and Gam-Anon helped me deal with my
own insanity as a result of Jerry's addiction. However, without outside
intervention, I do not believe Jerry and I could have rebuilt the relationship
we wanted unless I dealt with the pain I carried within."

EMOTIONAL INTIMACY

Emotional intimacy is a special closeness between two human beings in
which each respects the other and shares verbal expressions of love and
concern. Couples who are emotionally intimate trust each other with their
deepest feelings and do not fear that the trust will be violated; they know
their partner will be there to care about their emotional needs in times of
joy or pain. They view their partner as their best friend.

Unfortunately, a couple affected by compulsive gambling cannot live an
intimate relationship because the illness destroys any trust or closeness they
may once have shared. For the compulsive gambler, the lying, manipula-
tion, and deceitfulness that result from his disorder make any truthfulness,
openness, or closeness impossible. And his wife may become so affected by
the gambling that she'll lose all desire to reveal her emotions because she
knows he cannot listen or care.

A couple whose communication ceased as a result of gambling may as-
sume that, once the gambling is arrested, they will be able to communicate
as before and will automatically rebuild a strong emotional bond. This is
not always the case. Developing or recapturing emotional intimacy is never
automatic. It requires a great deal of effort. Each partner must be willing to
become vulnerable by openly and honestly communicating feelings to the
other. Each spouse must have resolved the anger, resentment, and pain
caused by the illness. Each partner must be willing to forgive all that has occurred as a result of the gambling.

If a compulsive gambler or his partner was raised in a dysfunctional
family that lacked emotional closeness, bringing intimacy into their relationship once the gambling has stopped may require more assistance than is
available in their self-help group.

Richard and Carol's Story

Carol

"When I met Richard, I immediately saw two sides of him. One side came across as a macho male who accepted nonsense from no one. He was stubborn, determined, and wanted to do everything his way. He was self-righteous, and because he was intelligent and had good command of the English language, few people challenged him.

"The other side of Richard was warm and caring. Once I got to know him, I had no trouble seeing his sensitive side. If Richard liked you, he couldn't do enough for you. It didn't matter if you were male or female, young or old, married or single.

"After Richard and I had dated only a couple of weeks, he started buying me small presents. I knew it was his way of telling me he was interested. The months passed and the presents continued. Then Richard asked me to marry him. He gave me a beautiful engagement ring as well as a gold necklace. I loved him and wanted to be his wife, so of course I said yes. But the one thing I wanted from Richard, and had never received, was to hear him say he loved me. I said it to him hundreds of times, and when I did, he'd reply, 'Me too.' Whenever I asked him if he loved me, he'd always answer 'Yes' or 'You know I do.' I never questioned his love for me, but I did long to hear him say the words.

"I guess part of me wanted Richard to be more like my father. Dad was a very demonstrative man. He told everyone close to him how he loved them. I heard it all my life. If he felt like it, he would tell my mother he loved her in a crowded supermarket. I was fortunate to have been raised by a man and a woman who remained in love all their married life. Even as a child, I knew I wanted a relationship like theirs."

Richard

"One of the things that first attracted me to Carol was that she had something I didn't. Carol was easy to talk to. She was caring and special. One thing I liked about her was that she wasn't a screamer. I was raised in a home where everyone screamed at each other. Another thing about Carol I found very attractive was that she was very rarely negative in her thinking. Most of the time her thoughts were positive, and her attitudes reflected that.

"I hardly ever had positive feelings. As a matter of fact, before I started gambling, the most common feeling I had was boredom. I couldn't stand being bored. Once I started gambling, I never felt bored again. I gambled compulsively for years, until it made me so depressed I could see only two options: kill myself or ask for help. I called Gamblers Anonymous."

Carol

"Within three months of starting GA and Gam-Anon meetings, our lives were much less stressful. Thanks to Richard's GA brothers, we had a very strict budget that enabled us to repay our debts and gave us enough money to live as a family. Richard and I went to our meetings faithfully, and we both made some very good friends there. Our lives had improved 100 percent in all areas except one—intimacy.

"I wanted Richard to start communicating with me on a deeper level. We didn't talk about 'us' at all. We discussed family matters, our house and cars, and even where we would go on vacation as soon as we could afford one. I think because our lives had been so focused on his gambling for so long, we had forgotten how to talk about more important things. I was guilty, too. It was only when the gambling stopped that I began to realize how the focus of our relationship had narrowed."

Richard

"I began to feel a new kind of pressure after I stopped gambling. I was familiar with the pressure that came from loan sharks, banks, friends, and creditors and knew how to handle that. But the pressure that started to come from Carol was foreign. She was after me to share more of the 'real me' with her—whatever that meant.

"I was so confused. In abstinence I had started to pay a great deal more attention to Carol. But that effort wasn't satisfactory, because she spent most of her free time on the telephone talking to her friends. Many times I would turn on a TV show I knew she liked in hopes she would come and sit next to me on the couch. She almost never did. I didn't know how else to let her know I wanted to be close to her. Many nights I would shower and shave so I'd be attractive to her at bedtime, but she never took the hint. For someone who wanted to communicate on a deeper level, she showed no real effort to do that, in my eyes."

Carol

"As much as I expressed my feelings to Richard about wanting to get closer to him, he made no effort to change. Because I had felt emotionally abandoned by him, I turned to my girlfriends for support and love.

"Richard did continue to bring me small presents, and he was somewhat more helpful around the house, but other than that, he was the same as he was before, when the gambling consumed him: emotionally unattainable."

Richard

"For years, all Carol cared about was the fact that we had no money. As soon as that started to turn around, she started focusing on the fact that I wasn't the kind of husband she needed. I could never understand what she was talking about. I was considerate, I was abstinent, and I was working my program. When I wasn't at one of my two jobs, I was home with her.

"She wanted us to be more intimate, but when I did everything to make myself attractive to her, she didn't respond. I felt like a jerk. She just continued to complain. I felt angrier each day. I didn't want my attitude to slip because that would make me vulnerable to relapse, and nothing, not even Carol, was worth that. I could see no way out. No matter how hard I tried, it wasn't good enough for her."

Carol

"Our relationship was becoming more and more distant. At least when Richard was gambling, we spoke every day, even if it was only to argue about his gambling. Now there was only silence. I was so discouraged. Finally, when I shared my whole situation with my sponsor, she suggested we try a marriage counselor—one knowledgeable about compulsive gambling—because she believed our situation was definitely connected to Richard's emotional illness. When I asked Richard if he would go, he hesitated at first and then agreed."

Richard

"The only reason I agreed to see a counselor was because I truly believed Carol was being demanding and unreasonable, and I thought if I couldn't get her to see that, maybe a therapist could.

"But what the therapist got us both to see was how my gambling addiction influenced, changed, and marred our marriage. She had a way of talking so that neither of us felt at fault for our situation. She continually blamed the illness, not me or Carol."

Carol

"It never occurred to me when we went to the counselor that I was contributing to our problem. I thought the only effect Richard's gambling had on me was that I never had any money and that we stopped making love because he loved to gamble more than he loved me. The gambling made me think that the gambling was our only problem. When it stopped, I took it for granted all would be well between Richard and me. But the gambling had affected me in ways I was unaware of. Before the excessive gambling, Richard and I had many pleasant moments together. Our sex life had been satisfying and pleasurable and at times exciting. But the illness, as it progressed, entered our bedroom. There were times when Richard would bring his little transistor radio to bed so, as soon as we had made love, he could listen to the results of the games he had wagered on. There were times when we had to make love in the afternoon because there were two basketball games on, back-to-back, that evening. Moreover, Richard had some basic rules: We never had sex on Mondays (because of "Monday Night Football"), Super Bowl Sunday, or Triple Crown days. We also never had sex on days when he was depressed because he had lost money, or on days when he won big, because then he had better things to do than make love to me.

"I was able to see how our sex life had been determined by his gambling and by the results of his wagers. As the years passed, the gambling wore on me. I had lost all interest in sex, because no matter what the situation, I was not a priority in Richard's life. In addition, his attitudes had grown extremely negative. He would be angry most of the time, and I would bear the brunt of it. His verbal abuse and gambling had destroyed my desire to make love to him."

Richard

"Everything Carol said was true. One thing my gambling did was to make me totally self-focused. I never put anyone before me. I was the only thing that mattered in my life. Even when I saw how much the people I cared about were hurting, I kept gambling. I felt I should have hit my bottom years before I did. Maybe I never had many feelings to begin with, but what few I had were destroyed by my passion for action."

Carol

"Listening to Richard explain himself to the counselor helped me to see for the first time just what the gambling had done to him. I had thought that except for the debts, he was unscathed.

"I knew when I married Richard that he would not express feelings. Even on our wedding day, he didn't say he loved me. He knew how much I wanted to hear it, but he never said it. I don't know how I ever expected things would change with him just because he wasn't gambling. Through the counselor, I began to better understand the emotional side of his illness. It wasn't just that Richard had an uncontrollable urge to gamble, he was unable to cope with life emotionally. The marriage counselor explained that our situation did not have to continue as it was if we didn't want it to. She said she could help us develop a satisfying emotional bond."

Richard

"I never knew what was meant by emotional intimacy. In my whole life, I had never experienced it. I never saw my father and mother kiss or hug each other. Nor did they ever speak to each other lovingly. My father gave my mother unexpected presents occasionally, but maybe that was all he ever gave her. I wonder if either of them said, 'I love you.' I know *I* never heard those words from them.

"The marriage counselor explained how, in order to develop emotional intimacy, I would have to learn to identify my feelings and start sharing them with Carol. That meant that I would have to start trusting Carol on a level I had never trusted anyone. Perhaps the only one I ever trusted for a while in my life was Lady Luck—but that was many years ago, on an extended winning streak. But that trust was eventually destroyed, and I paid a heavy price for making myself so vulnerable.

"It was incredibly difficult for me to start developing an emotional relationship with Carol—it would have been easier for me to learn to speak

Chinese. First of all, I didn't know a feeling from a snowflake, except for anger and rage. Although occasionally, when I won big, I did feel powerful and important and even loved.

"With support from the counselor and patience from Carol, little by little I was able to identify and express my feelings and needs. I had to take many risks, but each time I did I found the experience both rewarding and rein-forcing. More important, I began to feel truly connected to Carol. It enabled me to trust her further. I learned to tell Carol what I needed or wanted. I stopped playing games. If I wanted Carol to sit on the couch next to me, I would say so. If I wanted to make love to Carol, I would approach her in a loving manner and initiate it. I stopped hinting at my wants and desires. I learned to communicate openly and honestly. I began to move closer."

Carol

"After we had been seeing the counselor for about seven months, Richard invited me out to dinner. It was the week he received his annual raise. We had dinner in a café facing the New York skyline. It was very romantic, and I was feeling closer to Richard than ever before.

"When the waiter brought dessert, Richard gave me a present. It was a locket with my name on the outside. When I opened it, Richard held it in his hand and said, 'Let me read the inscription to you.' He looked down at the locket, and then directly at me, and said: 'I love you.'"

Facts on File

Compulsive gambling is a chronic, progressive, and at times fatal illness. It can never be cured. It can only be arrested.

In order to recover, total abstinence is absolutely necessary.

The only known success in recovery from this addiction is in the self-help fellowships of Gamblers Anonymous and Gam-Anon.

Questions

Gambler and partner:

- Are you *working* your recovery program?
- Do you have a sponsor?

- Do you work the Twelve Steps?
- Do you use the telephone?
- Do you read GA and Gam-Anon literature?
- Have you done an open self-examination?
- Is there anything in your life (prior to the gambling) that needs to be dealt with in order to recover?

11

Notes on Recovery for the New Gamblers

A CLOSER LOOK AT EACH GROUP of our new gamblers—Internet, senior, female, and underage—may help us identify what is motivating each to continue gambling while debts are mounting and disaster lies ahead.

What is needed to prevent people from falling by the wayside by investing compulsively in the stock market? Perhaps if these gamblers were to investigate the strategies used by successful Wall Street investors, they might take a different road. It has long been known that the most prosperous investors are those who are well diversified in their holdings, commit their money to long-term investments, and rely on expert advice in planning and executing their transactions. Day traders, like gamblers, want good odds. If day traders were forewarned that their odds of being successful were only 12 percent, would they be so enthusiastic, work so hard, and risk so much?

What do we know about female compulsive gamblers? We know most of them do not gamble for the action. The most common reason women give for gambling is to escape. When women are gambling, they do not have to deal with feelings of boredom, nor with any other problems in their lives, whether they involve relationships, finances, jobs, or health.

The last thing a woman thinks about when she begins gambling is that it could ever cause a serious problem in her life. In her mind, gambling problems belong to the male gender. How could spending a limited amount of money on the slots or in a bingo hall cause a problem?

Senior citizens also do not see their interest in gambling as ever being a problem for them. They know from their personal history that when

229

adversity of any kind surfaces, they've always solved the problem without help from anyone.

The number-one concern of most senior citizens is that they never be a burden to their children. Having gambling debts they cannot pay puts seniors in a situation they never wanted to have to face. Gambling seniors may have successfully overcome adjustments to retirement, loss of a spouse, and declining health, but for them to reach out to their children and ask for help is something they would rather die than do.

Between 1975 and 1998, the number of male compulsive gamblers requesting help rose 13 percent, the number of females rose 22 percent, and the number of seniors reaching out rose 100 percent. Senior citizens make up the fastest-growing segment of compulsive gamblers in the United States. Should we be concerned as baby boomers begin to enter their golden years?

What about underage compulsive gamblers? A recent study conducted by the National Gambling Impact Study Commission found that just over one million teenagers in the United States are problem gamblers. Most of our young people are not capable of making responsible decisions when it comes to gambling.

The fact that gambling can become compulsive for teens is not well known. A number of high school Parent Teacher Association and board of education representatives across the country have voted to offer their graduating seniors a Las Vegas night in place of their senior prom. Their goal in doing this is to cut back on teens drinking and driving. They do not see gambling as a risky activity for their children.

Because children often mimic the behaviors of their parents, whenever a problem is seen surfacing in a child, the parent needs to look in the mirror. If the problem is gambling, the parent needs to take an honest look at his or her own interest and involvement with gambling.

As parents, we need to teach our children that gambling is not all fun and games, nor is it a means of getting money without earning it. Our young need to know that compulsive gambling is a serious emotional illness that anyone, at any age, can come down with.

Perhaps one powerful antidote may help prevent our youth from succumbing to gambling and other addictive or compulsive behaviors, and it lies in the hands of the parents. Spend time with your child; in effect, make "dates" with him or her.

When adults marry and have children, they sometimes become almost completely family-oriented. This is, for the most part, very good. What gets lost in the concept of family unity, however, is the need for each child to spend private time with each parent.

Such "dates" are best described as times when the child and parent can go someplace together and talk without being disturbed. A movie does not constitute such a date. Sitting opposite each other in a restaurant or walking together in a park does.

This alone time allows the parent and child to communicate with each other without interruptions. This level of communicating and sharing builds trust and fosters emotional intimacy between any two people. In time, this trust will allow the child to be more open with the parent.

This time spent together results in a bonding between parent and child. Bonding builds a sense of security, and security allows the child to share things he or she would not have shared before the dates began. Dating your child may be the most powerful preventative to the devastating disease of compulsive gambling.

Conclusion

SINCE THE PROLIFERATION OF LEGALIZED GAMBLING in the early eighties, many Americans have added it to their list of leisure activities. Eighty percent of those who gamble have no problems related to it; 15 percent have problems related to their finances, family relationships, and/or with their educational/occupational pursuits; and another 5 percent become compulsive gamblers.

Two decades ago, recreational gambling stood in a different light. If you wanted to gamble in a casino, it required some planning. Most people had to drive or fly to Las Vegas to enjoy the slots or the tables. In 1975, Nevada was the only state that offered legalized casino gambling, and only thirteen states had lotteries. In 1999, twenty-one states had legalized casino gambling and thirty-seven had lotteries.

Our youth today represent the first generation of Americans who grew up viewing gambling as an acceptable, exciting, and fun way to spend their money and their leisure time. How could they possibly view this form of entertainment in any other light? Our government and many of our religions not only support gambling but also promote it. This makes it almost impossible for our youth to see it as a high-risk behavior that is capable of destroying not only the gambler, but also his or her family.

Because some bureaucrats and corporations in the gaming industry promote gambling, they are slow to warn gamblers of the risks involved. The evidence of the dangers of gambling can be found in some of the documented statistical information available from the fellowships of Gamblers Anonymous and from state councils on problem/compulsive gambling. For example, in 1999 Americans spent more money on gambling than on sporting events, movies, and theme parks combined. That same year, they spent more money on gambling than on food. Perhaps this is one of the contributing factors in the expansion of our nationwide GA meetings. In 1994, Detroit had six weekly GA meetings. In 2001, there are twenty weekly meetings. Las Vegas has seventy-four weekly GA meetings, and New Jersey has fifty.

Gambling makes its greatest impact on the families of compulsive gamblers in the form of suicide. The number of suicides is higher in states with casino gambling. In the United States, the nationwide suicide rate is eleven per one hundred thousand people. In Las Vegas, the rate is more than double—twenty-five per one hundred thousand people.

Every year, gamblers who have lost all their money, including money borrowed or stolen from friends, family, or employers, end their lives. In Florida, a man who lost fifty thousand dollars ended his life by jumping from the roof of the casino in which he had been gambling. An elderly couple who lost everything gambling did not want to be a burden to their children, so, together, they each took their own lives. In August of 1999, during an eight-day period, three gamblers ended their lives by jumping from casino buildings in Atlantic City.

The reports of these tragic incidents are endless. A nineteen-year-old man, not old enough to gamble legally, killed himself because he had accumulated sixteen hundred dollars in gambling debts. His method of ending his life was what is called "suicide by cop." The young man drove erratically, at a high rate of speed, on a major road in New York. When the police pulled him over, the young man got out of his car pointing a toy gun at the policemen, who did not realize the gun was a toy. When the young man refused to drop the gun, while moving closer to the officers, the policemen shot and killed him.

What can be done for the general public in the area of prevention? The first step in preventing any tragedy or disaster in life is to be prepared. We need to educate ourselves, our elderly, and our youth. The most effective method would be for the media to bombard the public with information about the risks of gambling. It is not to tell them not to gamble, but rather to be aware of the warning signs. If two or more people say, "I'm concerned about your gambling," listen! No one ever makes that statement to a recreational gambler or someone who enjoys various recreational activities in addition to gambling.

Widespread information disbursed by Mothers Against Drunk Driving (MADD) awakened us to the serious consequences of driving while intoxicated. Their efforts resulted in stricter laws and penalties. The surgeon general's warnings about the consequences of smoking made a tremendous impact on the number of adults smoking in the United States. And the information we have about the value of wearing a seat belt has resulted in saving many thousands of lives each year. All of this was accomplished by educating the public.

To prevent further devastation resulting from compulsive gambling, we need the same kind of media support. Without it, history is likely to repeat itself.

When gamblers reach their bottom and are ready to reach out and ask for help, they need to know which road to recovery offers the best odds for success. The programs that have had the most successful long-term help for compulsive gamblers and their families are the fellowships of Gamblers Anonymous and Gam-Anon. It is by accepting and working these programs of recovery that the afflicted and the affected can and will recover.

Appendixes

DO YOU HAVE A GAMBLING PROBLEM?*

Gamblers Anonymous has twenty questions that it asks new members.

Twenty Questions
1. Did you ever lose time from work or school due to gambling?
2. Has gambling ever made your home life unhappy?
3. Did gambling affect your reputation?
4. Have you ever felt remorse after gambling?
5. Did you ever gamble to get money with which to pay debts or otherwise solve financial difficulties?
6. Did gambling cause a decrease in your ambition or efficiency?
7. After losing did you feel you must return as soon as possible and win back your losses?
8. After a win did you have a strong urge to return and win more?
9. Did you often gamble until your last dollar was gone?
10. Did you ever borrow to finance your gambling?
11. Have you ever sold anything to finance gambling?
12. Were you reluctant to use "gambling money" for normal expenditures?
13. Did gambling make you careless of the welfare of yourself or your family?
14. Did you ever gamble longer than you had planned?
15. Have you ever gambled to escape worry or trouble?
16. Have you ever committed, or considered committing, an illegal act to finance gambling?
17. Did gambling cause you to have difficulty sleeping?
18. Do arguments, disappointments or frustrations create within you an urge to gamble?
19. Did you have an urge to celebrate good fortune by a few hours of gambling?
20. Have you ever considered self-destruction or suicide as a result of your gambling?

Most compulsive gamblers will answer yes to at least seven of these questions.

---

*Reprinted with permission from Gamblers Anonymous.

ARE YOU LIVING WITH A COMPULSIVE GAMBLER?*

If there is a gambling problem in your home, the Gam-Anon family groups may be able to help you cope with it.

1. Do you find yourself constantly bothered by bill collectors?
2. Is the person in question often away from home for long, unexplained periods of time?
3. Does this person ever lose time from work due to gambling?
4. Do you feel that this person cannot be trusted with money?
5. Does the person in question faithfully promise that he or she will stop gambling; beg, plead for another chance; yet gamble again and again?
6. Does this person ever gamble longer than he or she intended to, until the last dollar is gone?
7. Does this person immediately return to gambling to try to recover losses, or to win more?
8. Does this person ever gamble to get money to solve financial difficulties, or have unrealistic expectations that gambling will bring the family material comfort and wealth?
9. Does this person borrow money to gamble with or to pay gambling debts?
10. Has this person's reputation ever suffered due to gambling, even to the extent of committing illegal acts to finance gambling?
11. Have you come to the point of hiding money needed for living expenses, knowing that you and the rest of the family may go without food and clothing if you do not?
12. Do you search this person's clothing or go through his or her wallet when the opportunity presents itself, or otherwise check on his or her activities?
13. Does the person in question hide his or her money?
14. Have you noticed a personality change in the gambler as his or her gambling progresses?
15. Does the person in question consistently lie to cover up or deny his or her gambling activities?
16. Does this person use guilt induction as a method of shifting responsibilities for his or her gambling upon you?
17. Do you attempt to anticipate this person's moods, or try to control his or her life?

---

*Reprinted with permision of the Gam-Anon International Service Office, Inc.

18. Does this person ever suffer from remorse or depression due to gambling, sometimes to the point of self-destruction?
19. Has the gambling ever brought you to the point of threatening to break up the family unit?
20. Do you feel that your life together is a nightmare?

If you answer yes to six or more of these questions, you may be living with a compulsive gambler. For further information, please write to Gam-Anon International Services Office, P.O. Box 157, Whitestone, NY 11357, www.gam-anon.org, (718) 352-1671, (718) 746-2571 (fax).

TYPICAL WARNING SIGNS FOR WOMEN*

1. Gambling to escape worry, boredom, or trouble.
2. Suffering from severe mood swings.
3. Believing that life without gambling is impossible.
4. Neglecting personal responsibilities to focus on gambling.
5. Fantasizing about this week's win to overcome last week's losses and dreaming of the big win.
6. Scheming to borrow money from friends and family.
7. Considering illegal acts, such as prostitution, stealing, and forgery as a means of financing gambling.
8. Lying to conceal activity.
9. Jeopardizing employment or schoolwork because of gambling.
10. Having self-destructive thoughts because of problems related to gambling.

---

*Reprinted with permission of the New York Council on Problem Gambling.

QUESTIONS FOR YOUNG GAMBLERS *

1. Have you ever stayed away from school or work to gamble?
2. Is gambling making your home life unhappy?
3. Is gambling affecting your reputation?
4. Do you gamble until your last dollar is gone, even your bus fare home or the cost of a burger and Coke?
5. Have you lied, stolen or borrowed just to get money to gamble?
6. Are you reluctant to spend "gambling money" on normal things?
7. After losing, do you feel you must return as soon as possible to win back your losses?
8. Is gambling more important than school or work?
9. Does gambling cause you to have difficulty in sleeping?
10. Have you ever thought of suicide as a way of solving your problems?

---

*Reprinted with permission from Gamblers Anonymous.

STUDENT GAMBLERS: WARNING SIGNS*

If you suspect a student has a gambling problem, you may want to have this test available. A yes to any of the questions below may indicate a problem.

1. Do you lose time from school due to gambling?
2. Have your grades dropped because of gambling?
3. Does your life center around sporting events or getting the scores/winners of sporting events?
4. Do you call sports telephone numbers or the lottery report often?
5. Have references to gambling or gambling language increased in your conversation?
6. Do you gamble to escape worry or trouble?
7. Is your free time consumed with gambling?
8. Have your family or friends noticed a change in your personality?
9. Do arguments, disappointments, or frustrations create within you an urge to gamble?
10. Did you ever take anything that didn't belong to you or do anything illegal to finance your gambling?
11. Do you gamble until your last dollar is gone, even small amounts of money you planned to spend on "normal" things?
12. After losing, do you feel you must return as soon as possible to win back your losses?
13. Does gambling cause you to have difficulty sleeping?
14. Have you ever thought of suicide as a way of solving your problem?

---

*Reprinted with permission of the Council on Compulsive Gambling of New Jersey.

SIGNS OF SENIOR PROBLEM GAMBLING*

- loss of interest and participation in normal activities with friends and family
- blocks of time unaccounted for
- exhibits a high priority on gambling and gambling-related activities
- changes in attitude and personality
- a sudden need for money/loans
- missing possessions or assets
- neglect of personal needs (i.e., food, utilities, medical, etc.)
- secrecy and avoidance when questioned about time and money
- decline in health
- withdrawal/depression

---

*Reprinted with permission of the Florida Council on Compulsive Gambling.

QUESTIONS FOR ON-LINE TRADERS*

1. Are you trading in the stock market with money you may need during the next year?
2. Are you risking more money than you intended to?
3. Have you ever lied to someone regarding your on-line trading?
4. Are you risking retirement savings to try to get back your losses?
5. Has anyone ever told you that you spend too much time on-line?
6. Is the way you are investing affecting other areas of your life (relationships, vocational pursuits, etc.)?
7. If you lost most of your money trading in the market, would it materially change your life?
8. Are you investing (day trading) frequently for the excitement and the way it makes you feel?
9. Have you become secretive about your on-line trading?
10. Do you feel sad or depressed when you are not trading in the market?

If you answer yes to any of these questions, you may be moving from investing to gambling.

---

*Reprinted with permission of Edward J. Looney and the Council on Compulsive Gambling of New Jersey.

THE TWELVE STEPS OF ALCOHOLICS ANONYMOUS *

1. We admitted we were powerless over alcohol—that our lives had become unmanageable.
2. Came to believe that a Power greater than ourselves could restore us to sanity.
3. Made a decision to turn our will and our lives over to the care of God *as we understood Him.*
4. Made a searching and fearless moral inventory of ourselves.
5. Admitted to God, to ourselves, and to another human being the exact nature of our wrongs.
6. Were entirely ready to have God remove all these defects of character.
7. Humbly asked Him to remove our shortcomings.
8. Made a list of all persons we had harmed, and became willing to make amends to them all.
9. Made direct amends to such people wherever possible, except when to do so would injure them or others.
10. Continued to take personal inventory and when we were wrong promptly admitted it.
11. Sought through prayer and meditation to improve our conscious contact with God *as we understood Him,* praying only for knowledge of His will for us and the power to carry that out.
12. Having had a spiritual awakening as the result of these steps, we tried to carry this message to alcoholics, and to practice these principles in all our affairs.

---

* The Twelve Steps of AA are taken from *Alcoholics Anonymous,* 3d ed., published by AA World Services, Inc., New York, N.Y., 59–60. Reprinted with permission of AA World Services, Inc. (See editor's note on copyright page.)

GAMBLERS ANONYMOUS
THE TWELVE STEPS OF RECOVERY*

1. We admitted we were powerless over gambling—that our lives had become unmanageable.
2. Came to believe that a Power greater than ourselves could restore us to a normal way of thinking and living.
3. Made a decision to turn our will and our lives over to the care of this Power of our own understanding.
4. Made a searching and fearless moral and financial inventory of ourselves.
5. Admitted to ourselves and to another human being the exact nature of our wrongs.
6. Were entirely ready to have these defects of character removed.
7. Humbly asked God (of our understanding) to remove our shortcomings.
8. Made a list of all persons we had harmed and became willing to make amends to them all.
9. Made direct amends to such people wherever possible, except when to do so would injure them or others.
10. Continued to take personal inventory and when we were wrong, promptly admitted it.
11. Sought through prayer and meditation to improve our conscious contact with God as we understood Him, praying only for knowledge of His will for us and the power to carry that out.
12. Having made an effort to practice these principles in all our affairs, we tried to carry this message to other compulsive gamblers.

---

* Reprinted with permission from Gamblers Anonymous. Adapted from the Twelve Steps of Alcoholics Anonymous with permission of AA World Services, Inc., New York, N.Y. (See editor's note on copyright page.)

THE GAM-ANON SUGGESTED STEPS OF RECOVERY*

1. We admitted we were powerless over the problem in our family.
2. Came to believe that a Power greater than ourselves could restore us to a normal way of thinking and living.
3. Made a decision to turn our will and our lives over to the care of this Power of our own understanding.
4. Made a searching and fearless moral inventory of ourselves.
5. Admitted to ourselves and to another human being the exact nature of our wrongs.
6. Were entirely ready to have these defects of character removed.
7. Humbly asked God (of our understanding) to remove our shortcomings.
8. Made a list of all persons we had harmed and became willing to make amends to them all.
9. Made direct amends to such people whenever possible, except when to do so would injure them or others.
10. Continued to take personal inventory and when we were wrong promptly admitted it.
11. Sought, through prayer and meditation, to improve our conscious contact with God, as we understood Him, praying only for knowledge of His will for us, and the power to carry that out.
12. Having made an effort to practice these principles in all our affairs, we tried to carry this message to others.

---

* Reprinted with permission of the Gam-Anon International Service Office, Inc. Adapted from the Twelve Steps of Alcoholics Anonymous with permission of AA World Services, Inc., New York, N.Y. (See editor's note on copyright page.)

Australian National Council on Compulsive Gambling
P.O. Box 114
St. Pauls, N.S.W. 2031
Australia

Canadian Foundation on Compulsive Gambling
505 Consumers Road
Toronto, Ontario M2J4V8
Canada
(416) 499-9800

Gam-Anon International Service Office, Inc.
P.O. Box 157
Whitestone, NY 11357
(718) 352-1671
(718) 746-2571 (fax)
www.gam-anon.org

Gamblers Anonymous
World Service Office
P.O. Box 17173
Los Angeles, CA 90017
(213) 386-8789

National Council on Problem Gambling
208 G Street NE
Washington, D.C. 20002
(202) 547-9204
(800) 522-4700

SELECTED BIBLIOGRAPHY

American Psychiatric Association. *Diagnostic and Statistical Manual of Mental Disorders.* 3d ed. Washington, D.C.: American Psychiatric Association, 1987.

Beattie, M. *Codependent No More: How to Stop Controlling Others and Start Caring for Yourself.* 2d ed. Center City, Minn.: Hazelden, 1992.

Behrmann, M. "On the Road Again." *Newslink, Canadian Foundation on Compulsive Gambling* (spring 2000): 1.

Bergler, E. *The Psychology of Gambling.* New York: International Universities Press, 1958.

Blaszczynski, A. "A Winning Bet: Treatment for Compulsive Gamblers." *Psychology Today* 33 (December 1985): 38–46.

Brown, B. "The Adaptation of the Alcoholics Anonymous Program by Gamblers Anonymous." Paper presented at the Eighth International Conference on Risk and Gambling, London, August 1990.

Brown, R. I. F. "The Contribution of the Study of Gambling to the Study of Other Addictions." Paper presented at the Eighth International Conference on Risk and Gambling, London, August 1990.

———. "The Effectiveness of Gamblers Anonymous." *The Gambling Studies: Proceedings of the Sixth International Conference of Gambling and Risk Taking.* Edited by William Eadington. Reno, Nev.: University of Nevada, 1985.

———. "Models of Gambling and Gambling Addiction as Perpetual Filters." *Journal of Gambling Behavior* 3 (1987): 224–36.

Buckley, J. T. "Teen Gambling: An Epidemic." *USA Today,* 5 April 1995, p. 4D.

Carnes, P. *Out of the Shadows: Understanding Sexual Addiction.* 3d ed. Center City, Minn.: Hazelden, 2001.

Chamberlain, R. E. "Gambling: New Treatment Ideas for an Old Addiction." *Professional Counselor* 3, no. 3 (November–December 1988): 37–39.

Ciarrocchi, J. "Severity of Impairment in Dually Addicted Gamblers." *Journal of Gambling Behavior* 3 (1987): 16–26.

Commission on the Review of the National Policy Toward Gambling. *Gambling in America.* Washington, D.C.: U.S. Government Printing Office, 1976.

Consoli, J. "Teenage Gambling a 'Terrible Problem.'" *Hackensack (N.J.) Record,* 3 March 1994, p. 2.

Custer, R. L. "An Overview of Compulsive Gambling." *Addictive Disorders Update: Alcoholism, Drug Abuse, Gambling.* Edited by P. A. Carone, S. F. Yoles, S. N. Kiefer, and L. Krinsky. New York: Human Sciences Press, 1982.

Custer, R. L., and L. F. Custer. "Characteristics of the Recovering Compulsive Gambler: A Survey of 150 Members of Gamblers Anonymous." Paper presented at the Fourth Annual Conference on Gambling, Reno, Nev., December 1978.

Custer, R. L., and H. Milt. *When Luck Runs Out.* New York: Facts on File, 1985.

Darvas, S. "The Female Pathological Gambler (FPG)." Paper presented at the First National Conference on Gambling Behavior of the National Council on Compulsive Gambling, New York, November 1986.

———. "The Spouse in Treatment." Paper presented at the Fifth National Conference on Gambling and Risk Taking, New York, October 1981.

Dickerson, M. *Compulsive Gamblers.* London: Penguin Books, 1984.

Evans, H. "Luck Won't Be a Lady Tonight." *New York Daily News,* 24 September 2000, p. 32.

Fishman, T. "Dead Men Trading." *Esquire,* February 2000, 45.

Franklin, J. F. "Family Counseling and Therapy for Pathological Gambling." Paper presented at the Fifth National Conference on Gambling and Risk Taking, New York, October 1981.

Galski, T., ed. *Handbook on Pathological Gambling.* Springfield, Ill.: Charles C. Thomas, 1987.

Gamblers Anonymous. *Sharing Recovery through Gamblers Anonymous.* Los Angeles: Gamblers Anonymous Publications, 1984.

Gowan, W. *Early Signs of Compulsive Gambling.* Center City, Minn.: Hazelden, 1988.

Graham, J. R., and B. H. Lowenfeld. "Personality Dimensions of the Pathological Gambler." *Journal of Gambling Behavior* 2 (1986): 58–66.

Grodsky, P. B., and L. S. Dogan. "Does the Client Have a Gambling Problem?" *Journal of Gambling Behavior* 1 (1985): 51–58.

Guart, A. "Cashing in on Underage Bettors." *New York Post,* 9 July 2000, p. 3.

Hand, I. "Compulsive Gamblers in Outpatient Behavior Therapy and in GA Self-help Groups." Paper presented at the Eighth International Conference on Risk and Gambling, London, August 1990.

Heineman, M. "Can I Stop?" *Recovery Now* (August 1988): 9–31.

———. "A Comparison: The Treatment of Wives of Alcoholics with the Treatment of Wives of Pathological Gamblers." *Journal of Gambling Behavior* 3 (1987): 27–40.

———. "Compulsive Gambling: Structured Family Intervention." Paper presented at the Eighth International Conference on Risk and Gambling, London, August 1990.

———. "Getting Sober Wasn't Enough." *Focus on Family* (April 1986): 32–35.

———. "Parents of Male Compulsive Gamblers: Clinical Issues/Treatment Approaches." *Journal of Gambling Behavior* 5 (1989): 321–34.

———. *Sharing Recovery, Overcoming Roadblocks.* Center City, Minn.: Hazelden, 1988.

———. *When Someone You Love Gambles.* Center City, Minn.: Hazelden, 1988.

Holden, C. "Against All Odds." *Psychology Today* 33 (December 1985): 38–44.

Ingram, R. J. "Transactional Script Theory Applies to the Pathological Gambler." *Journal of Gambling Behavior* 1 (1985): 89–96.

Israelsen, B. "Graying Gamers: Elderly Turn to Casinos." *Salt Lake (Utah) Tribune*, 20 June 2000, p. 2.

Jacobs, D. F. "Effects on Children of Parental Excesses in Gambling." Paper presented at the Seventh International Conference on Gambling and Risk Taking, Reno, Nev., August 1987.

———. "A First Look at the Special Vulnerability of Children of Problem Gamblers." Paper presented at the Eighth International Conference on Risk and Gambling, London, August 1990.

———. "A General Theory of Addictions: A New Theoretical Model." *Journal of Gambling Behavior* 2 (1986): 15–31.

Jason, D. R., M. L. Taff, and L. R. Boglioli. "Casino-Related Death in Atlantic City, New Jersey." *American Journal of Forensic Medicine and Pathology* 11, no. 2 (1990): 112–23.

Jenkins, C. "Caught in Gambling's Web." *USA Today*, 17 March 2000, p. 3.

King, A. *Diary of a Powerful Addiction*. Manitoba, Canada: Crown Publishing, 1999.

Lefever, R. "Compulsive Gambling and Addictions—Implications for Treatment." Paper presented at the Eighth International Conference on Risk and Gambling, London, August 1990.

Lesieur, H. R. *The Chase: Career of the Compulsive Gambler*. Cambridge, Mass.: Schenkman Books, 1984.

———. "The Female Gambler." Paper presented at the Seventh International Conference on Gambling and Risk Taking, Reno, Nev., August 1987.

———. *Understanding Compulsive Gambling*. Center City, Minn.: Hazelden, 1984.

Lesieur, H. R., and M. Heineman. "Pathological Gambling among Youthful Multiple Substance Abusers in a Therapeutic Community." *British Journal of Addiction* 83 (1988): 765–71.

Lesieur, H. R., and S. Blume. "The South Oaks Gambling Screen (the SOGS): A New Instrument for the Identification of Pathological Gamblers." *American Journal of Psychiatry* 144 (1987): 1184–88.

Lesieur, H. R., S. B. Blume, and R. M. Zoppan. "Alcoholism, Drug Abuse, and Gambling." *Alcoholism: Clinical and Experimental Research* 10 (1985): 33–38.

Livingston, J. *Compulsive Gamblers: Observations on Action and Abstinence*. New York: Harper Torchbooks, 1974.

Lorenz, V. *Releasing Guilt*. Center City, Minn: Hazelden, 1988.

———. "Some Treatment Approaches for Family Members Who Jeopardize the Compulsive Gambler's Recovery." *Journal of Gambling Behavior* 5 (1989): 113–26.

———. *Standing Up to Fear*. Center City, Minn.: Hazelden, 1988.

Lorenz, V., and D. E. Shuttlesworth. "The Impact of Pathological Gambling on the Spouse of the Gambler." *Journal of Community Psychology* 11 (1983): 67–76.

Lorenz, V. C. "Dysfunctional Family Life among Pathological Gamblers." Paper presented at the Eighty-seventh Annual Convention of the American Psychological Association, New York, September 1979.

Lorenz, V. C., and R. A. Yaffee. "Pathological Gambling: Psychosomatic, Emotional and Marital Difficulties as Reported by the Gambler." *Journal of Gambling Behavior* 2 (1986): 40–49.

———. "Pathological Gambling: Psychosomatic, Emotional and Marital Difficulties as Reported by the Spouse." *Journal of Gambling Behavior* 4 (1986): 13–25.

Lorenz, V. C., and R. L. Politzer. *Final Report, Task Force on Gambling and Addiction*. Baltimore: Department of Health and Mental Hygiene, 1990.

McCormick, R. A., and J. I. Taber. "The Pathological Gambler: Salient Personality Variables." *Handbook on Pathological Gambling*. Edited by T. Galski. Springfield, Ill.: Charles C. Thomas, 1987.

Miller, W. R., ed. *The Addictive Behaviors*. Oxford: Pergamon Press, 1980.

Nakken, C. *The Addictive Personality: Understanding the Addictive Process and Compulsive Behavior*. 2d ed. Center City, Minn.: Hazelden, 1996.

Nora, R. "Profile Survey on Pathological Gamblers." Paper presented at the Sixth National Conference on Gambling and Risk Taking, Atlantic City, N.J., December 1984.

Oxford, J. *Excessive Appetites: A Psychological View of Addictions*. Chichester, England: Wiley and Sons, 1985.

Palermo, D. "Loneliness Can Spark Addiction." *Gulfport-Biloxi (Miss.) Sun Herald*, 30 June 2000, p. 1.

Pokorny, M. R. "Compulsive Gambling and the Family." *British Journal of Medical Psychology* 45 (1972): 355.

Ramirez, L. F., R. A. McCormick, A. M. Russo, and J. I. Taber. "Patterns of Substance Abuse in Pathological Gamblers Undergoing Treatment." *Addictive Behaviors* 8 (1984): 425–28.

Reno, R. A. "Gambling Bug Bites More Teens." *Wilmington (N.C.) Morning Star*, 13 March 1996, p. 5.

Richtel, M. "Place Your Bet: A Vegas Casino, or a Virtual One?" *New York Times*, 13 August 2000, Business section, p. 1.

Romano, J. "Teenage Gambling at Schools and Track." *New York Times*, 10 January 1993, sec. 13, p. 1.

Rosenthal, R. "The Pathological Gambler's System of Self-deception." *Journal of Gambling Behavior* 2 (1986): 108–20.

———. "Withdrawal Symptoms and Compulsive Gambling." Paper presented at the Eighth International Conference on Risk and Gambling, London, August 1990.

Shellenberger, D. "Participating in the Stock Market: Investing, Speculation, or Gambling?" *Massachusetts Council on Compulsive Gambling Newsletter* 12, no. 1: 1.

Shulman, A. "Catching the Wave." *Newslink, Canadian Foundation on Compulsive Gambling* (winter 2000): 1.

Simon, R. "Some Online Investors Can't Seem to Say No to Playing the Market." *Wall Street Journal,* 4 August 2000, p. 1.

Stein, S. "The Role of Support in Recovery from Compulsive Gambling." Paper presented at the Eighth International Conference on Risk and Gambling, London, August 1990.

Steinberg, M. "Compulsive Gambling and the Family—Couples in Recovery." Paper presented at the Eighth International Conference on Risk and Gambling, London, August 1990.

———. "Utilizing the Couple Relationship to Enhance Treatment Outcome for Compulsive Gamblers." Paper presented at the First National Conference on Gambling Behavior, New York, November 1985.

Taber, J. I. "Common Characteristics of Pathological Gamblers and Some Interventions Which Seem to Help." Paper presented at the Fourteenth Annual Convention of Divisions 23 and 26 of the American Psychological Association, White Sulphur Springs, W.Va., February 1983.

Tepperman, J. H. "The Effectiveness of Short-term Group Therapy upon the Pathological Gambler and Wife." Paper presented at the Seventh International Conference on Gambling and Risk Taking, Reno, Nev., August, 1987.

Volberg, R., and H. Steadman. "Refining Prevalence Estimates of Pathological Gambling." Paper presented at the Second Annual Conference on Gambling Behavior of the National Council on Compulsive Gambling, Philadelphia, November 1986.

Volkoper, C. F. "Suicide among Gamblers: A Review of Research." *Proceedings of the American Association of Suicidology, San Francisco* 26 (1993): 152–53.

Wanda, G., and J. Foxman. *Games Compulsive Gamblers, Wives and Families Play.* Downey, Calif.: Gam-Anon, Inc., 1971.

Wexler, A. "Results of a Survey of Compulsive Gamblers." Unpublished mimeo, 1980.

Wexler, S. "A Chart on the Effects of Compulsive Gambling on the Wife." Parlin, N.J.: S. Wexler, 1981.

What Is GA? Center City, Minn.: Hazelden, 1988.

ABOUT THE AUTHOR

For the last twenty years, Mary Heineman has been a practicing clinician specializing in pathological gambling.

She holds a master's degree in psychology and a master's degree in social work; she is a certified social worker and a certified compulsive gambling counselor.

Presently, Ms. Heineman is a national trainer, lecturer, and consultant in the diagnosis and treatment of pathological gambling. She is the author of numerous journal articles in addition to *Sharing Recovery, Overcoming Roadblocks; When Someone You Love Gambles;* and *Losing Your Shirt.*